Ex-soldier, ex-sail
magician, stupid project addict, obsessive
ponderer – John Donoghue has rambled and
digressed from Marsupial Elvis to No Place
– taking a sideways look at life and gathering
a wealth of anecdotes en route. He obviously
has too much time on his hands.

John Donoghue

Shakespeare, My Butt!

[signature] Jan 2011

1st edition 2004 (Central Publishing Services)
2nd edition 2005 (Matador)
3rd edition 2008 (Matador)

Matador
9 De Montfort Mews
Leicester LE1 7FW, UK
Tel: (+44) 116 255 9311 / 9312
Email: books@troubador.co.uk
Web: www.troubador.co.uk/matador

ISBN 978-1906510-596

Mixed Sources
Product group from well-managed
forests and other controlled sources
www.fsc.org Cert no. TT-COC-2082
© 1996 Forest Stewardship Council

Typeset in 11pt Stempel Garamond by Troubador Publishing Ltd, Leicester, UK
Printed by The Cromwell Press Ltd, Trowbridge, Wilts, UK

Matador is an imprint of Troubador Publishing

For Bethan

Acknowledgements

If you think I owe you a debt of gratitude for your help, support, inspiration, supply of biscuits (delete applicable) – then you are probably right.

Thanks to everyone...especially to the Lowest of the Low.

...and if anyone asks to borrow this book, kindly tell them to bugger off and buy their own.

Cheers

John Donoghue
www.marsupialelvis.com

CHAPTER ONE

Marsupial Elvis

Somehow, Sparky and GoGo were still living with me. Susan always seemed to be in too much of a hurry to take them with her and I was seriously thinking of charging them board and rent. To be honest, I think she was just a bit fed up with them. After all, they didn't seem that exciting and had clearly outstayed their welcome at her house. I actually felt a bit sorry for them, just swimming endlessly around their little tank, past their ornamental sunken castle, until someone told me that goldfish only have a six-second memory. I felt sorry no more. What a fantastic life they must have! Every six seconds they were having a new adventure and what could be better than discovering a sunken castle?

"Look GoGo, a sunken castle!"

"Wow Sparky, that's amazing!"

"Look GoGo, a sunken castle!"

"Wow Sparky, that's amazing!"

"Look GoGo, a sunken castle!"

"Wow Sparky, that's amazing!"

Here I was, feeling bored with their apparent lack of amusing antics, whilst they were having the time of their lives. I thought about putting a little deep sea diver man next to the castle, but they would probably 'OD' with excitement and, by the time Sparky had finished telling GoGo about the castle and the diver, he would have forgotten what he had started talking about; it would be unfair.

"Look GoGo, a sunken castle … and what's that … Oh, my God … a deep-sea diver! I wonder if he's dived… No, no, hang on, I've lost the thread … what was I on about again?"

I had also been joined by Hammy the hamster. Hammy was no trouble really and spent most of the day driving about in his small toy car. He was meant to be the classroom pet at Deborah's school, but she had lent him to me in case I grew bored whilst Barney was away.

Oh, and in case I forgot to mention it, Barney was away.

Sorry, it's a bad habit of mine that I really should overcome. I tend to flit back and forth between things like a butterfly, without properly explaining what's what. Don't worry, I'll try not to do it again. No promises though.

* * *

By way of mitigation, it had been an eventful twelve months – a watershed year.

Thanks to a marsupial Elvis, and to the begrudging appreciation of man's best friend, I had revealed the 10 steps that anyone could master to becoming an Alpha male (or Alpha female for that matter). With the Lowest of the Low in tow, I had journeyed around some of the more bizarre named places in Britain taking in the likes of 'No Place', 'Pity Me' and 'Wetwang' en route. Moreover through this I had discovered the secret of my excess, and learnt that thankfully it's never too late to re-start your life over again …to say this is my year zero – a new Monday in my life. (Yes, yes, of course I'll share all this with you as you travel through the book with me – just be patient).

Less significantly, but just as important, I had also found out that it's probably a bad idea to take a laxative and a sleeping tablet on the same night.

* * *

I run spasmodically and, by that, I don't mean I have a bizarre running style but that I go running two to three times a week.

It's a pleasant run, past a large park at the end of my street and then mostly through the woodland by the river's edge and, because the river is tidal, the scenery and wildlife change with the ebb and flow of the tides. At high tide, I have seen the best that nature can offer, from seals swimming upstream following the spawning salmon, through to swans swanning about on the sun sparkling water, and dutiful ducks leading their downy ducklings in line as if off on some summer's outing.

At low tide I have seen the best that ASDA can offer in the form of shopping trolleys half sunk in the slimy brown sludge along with various other flotsam and jetsom including a revolving clothes line that must have had an accident, a crate of empty Brown Ale bottles and a shoe – that must have been some hell of a night out!

There are not many sparrows about though. Apparently they are becoming scarcer. I think pheasants are the new sparrows. I'm not sure what sparrows are supposed to be now. Maybe the old pheasants? Elsewhere, be it high or low tide, herons hide amongst the reeds on the bank, fishermen sit patiently on the water's edge and I swear I've heard the hollow tapping of a woodpecker in the trees.

My running circuit takes me along the river bank (with either the high or low tide views en route), over a small pedestrian bridge, then back the other way (same view – except back to front!) and over a single road bridge back to my house. It's about two and a half miles all said but I round it up to three in a pathetic effort to look impressive. However, if anyone dares to pour scorn on my meagre exercise, I remind them that I ran the last London Marathon, dressed as a banana. (I didn't actually run the marathon at all. In fact I think it would probably kill me but, as long as the banana's identity remains a secret, I will take full advantage of his anonymity).

* * *

By this stage in my life, I had lived on both land and sea, on both sides of the English/Welsh border and eventually on both sides of the aforementioned river. I had served in uniform in the British Army and the Royal Navy, been both a single and happily married man, felt like a small person in the big city, and the nearest I had got to being a big person in a small world was visiting the model village in Bourton-on-the-Water.

But a year ago, I had an ex-wife, lived on my own on the South side of the river, wore a suit to work and had no idea how the year would unfold.

My main source of amusement, apart from the pub, was my hobby – magic. Sadly not the running around the garden naked at night in the company of some fit vestal virgins – with my luck I'd probably step barefoot on a slug anyway. Not even the chopping a woman in half type magic. No, my magic was the close up sort that happens in your hand or in front of your eyes so you can't deny its impossibility and is designed to impress attractive single young ladies. Well, that is if you don't tell them how it's done – otherwise you run the risk of suddenly reverting in their eyes from a mysterious and (hopefully) sexy man to a vision of a slightly sad bloke who's never properly grown up, sitting in his darkened bedroom practicing with a deck of cards while 'normal' people are out enjoying themselves in some trendy wine bar that probably used to be a bank.

Significant others in my life at that stage were Bethan, my ten year old daughter, who manages to guess how all my tricks are done, and my good friend Deborah who comes complete with her seven-year-old Border Collie dog called Tess.

I regarded it as something of an achievement that I had reached my current age, bearing in mind that I had led such a reckless childhood by today's standards. Oh my stars, the dangers I faced when I was small – both physical and mental. It was a world devoid of pushbike helmets, children's TV on all day, friendly Russians and bottled water. (Water ...in a bottle ...that you pay for!!! Why would you need that when there was 'council pop'?) As for mobile phones, we didn't even have a full 'land' phone in the house – we had a 'party line' shared with next door, so that when they were on the phone you couldn't make a call (and just had to sit quietly on the stairs and listen into Mrs Davies conversation instead!)

I'm not quite sure why, but in those days we also answered the phone quoting our own telephone number.

"Hello Cardiff 499456". I'm not too sure why we did this as surely the caller knew the number they had just rung. I'm pretty sure we didn't open the door saying our address too – but I'm not ruling anything out. These were odd times!

There was no such thing as safety caps on medicine bottles in those days either ...but if Health and Safety regulations were lax then, they seem to have gone much too far the other way now.

My sister rang me last week to tell me the news that the Doctor had prescribed her some suppositories. She explained to me that the instructions had read *'insert in rectum'* closely followed by *'keep out of the reach of children'*. A short biology lesson to assist in rectum location covered the first part of the instructions. There was a short pause on the phone while she re-read the second part of the instruction. I assume she was doing this because the next thing I heard was an alarmed voice imploring "What sort of person do they think I am?"

I calmly informed her it was just standard procedure to print it on all tablet bottles and nothing personal was meant by it. I explained to her that it's like when it says on the box that four out of five people suffer from diarrhoea, it doesn't mean that there is one crazy person who actually *enjoys* it – it's just they way they write things on medicines nowadays. She seemed happier at this explanation but I told her that if she was still concerned about keeping things out of the reach of children, just to wear a pair of high heels for a few days to be on the safe side.

Sorry, where was I? Oh yes I remember now – growing up. So instead of high tech gadgetry when I was growing up, we had ads for X-ray specs, the Beano and Dandy, scary supervisors (parkies) in the park whose aim was to seemingly stop you having fun, and dogs wandering the streets leaving little white turds that would silently explode into a cloud of dust if you kicked them. This was a time when twenty five pence was decent pocket money and the only thing 'race issues' meant was who ran the fastest. Hell, we even drank squash out of communal beakers with our friends – and sometimes we didn't even know what side they had used first.

Then, as now, we had the dreaded BCG injection, but I'm sure due to some sort of time zone difference or some such thing, it hurt more in my day than it does now. I can still remember the clarion call 'My BCG, my BCG!' if anyone ventured within the 10 yard exclusion zone surrounding my left arm.

We were also the last generation to grow up not using computers in school and shock, horror – as scary as it may sound to children today, I didn't have a Playstation or Gameboy because they hadn't been invented, so I had to use my imagination (my Luddite tendencies followed me into adult life to the extent that, when someone first told me they had a Palm Pilot, I thought it was some type of bizarre instruction manual for a five-finger shuffle).

Instead, we played football up at Cyncoed Park, went swimming down the Empire pool, and played 'Escape from Colditz' whenever we could. Oh, and we cycled a lot. I had a dynamo on the bike that powered the lights when it got dark, which was good, except when I stopped at a junction, the wheels ceased powering the dynamo, the lights went out and I was plunged into darkness, which was bad. What a rubbish invention. A palm pilot sounds a lot more fun.

I was also frankly shocked when I discovered, years later, that you didn't actually look cool at all riding a Chopper bike whilst wearing your jumper tucked into your trousers. My God, this was a dark time when some people even felt the need to tuck their shirts into their underpants too!

I was never trendy enough to do the tucking or own a Chopper, but even so I was devastated to find out years later that even my ideas of cool were un-cool. Unthinkable as it may be, sometimes we even ran around with sharp things, and despite threats from my Mum and all my friends' Mums, I don't recall anyone's eye ever being poked out (last recorded incident of eye being poked out whilst playing with sharp thing – some guy called Harold in 1066). All these Mums were additionally programmed to chorus "You won't feel the benefit" if we dared enter the house without taking our coats off first. We were also affected by a bizarre medical phenomenon back in those days that meant if you accidentally swallowed your bubble gum, apparently it wrapped itself around your heart.

Yes, life may have been hard for us thirty-somethings when we were children, but the one thing we did have that children nowadays don't seem to possess, was a decent taste in music. After embarrassing my daughter sufficiently by dancing like the wallies on 'Top of the Pops', I retreat into the kitchen and listen to the music I like. One of my favourites is an Australian called Nick Barker.

*   *   *

When I first heard the song 'Thylacine', I thought it was about some dreaded hereditary disease, a new strain of penicillin or distant cousin of the BCG, but when Nick Barker sang, "You're famous; the marsupial Elvis," I knew I was way off. It turns out that a Thylacine was also known as the Tasmanian Tiger, which was a bizarre mix of different animals. Starting from the front, which is as good a place as any to start – it had the head of a large dog, followed by the front part of a wolf and the back half of a tiger, finishing off with a rigid tail. On the undercarriage, it had 'wolfy' front legs, the back legs of a hyena and, to complete this exotic mix, a pouch like a kangaroo. I say, 'was' because they were hunted into extinction in their native Australia, with the last one, named Ben, being kept in captivity until he finally succumbed to old age and, in 1938, joined the ranks of the Dodo.

Since then, in true 'Elvis' tradition, Thylacine sightings have been reported year on year, although to my knowledge, one has never been spotted working in a chip shop in Newcastle; the Marsupial Elvis indeed.

Therefore, when I was asked to choose a venue for my birthday treat, there was no hesitation – it had to be the Zoo. What other animals would I shortly only be able to see in a glass case, stuffed with mattress filling and with marbles for eyes?

Destination: Edinburgh Zoo.

CHAPTER TWO

Run for Your Lives!

Have you ever seen a Bush Dog? I suppose you could best describe it as looking like a Lakeland Terrier and, if you have never seen a Lakeland Terrier, you could best describe it as looking like a Bush Dog.

This Bush Dog, and for ease of typing he will be called Billy, lived at the Zoo, in a big room with a glass wall at the front and a little door at the rear of the room that led to somewhere else; I don't know where. Billy would appear at this door, potter into the room for about four yards and then turn round and potter back, disappearing into this unknown land beyond the door. He repeated this at intervals of about a minute, although he sometimes left a gap of around five minutes as if he was a bit scared of being labelled predictable.

Bethan and I probably spent the majority of our time, and certainly longer than anyone in polite society should, standing and waiting for Billy to appear, complete his four yards, turn round and potter away. We were amused when, once in a blue moon, Billy would come right up to the glass and peer out before hurrying back, but we were even more amused when other zoo visitors would come and look into Billy's room to see what we were looking at. Invariably, they would come when Billy wasn't on parade and, after thirty seconds or so of looking into the empty area, they would wander off, in search of something more exciting.

At this stage, Bethan and I would shout to each other

something along the lines of, "Look, look! He's balancing that ball on his head!" As the unsuspecting onlooker ran back to catch a glimpse of this feat, only to find themselves once more looking into a bare room, we would mutter sadly to each other, "Awwwww, he's just run in."

In case you ever pay a visit to Edinburgh Zoo, with the intention of seeing this 'ball on head' phenomenon and then decide to sue because it never happened when you were there, let me make it clear now that it never occurred when we were present either. And that man and the girl running out of the zoo, and down the steps shouting "Run for your lives, they're loose!" ...that was us too. We are sorry. We didn't mean to create panic. We were just content with fooling innocent members of the public and seeing Billy potter.

* * *

I suppose it was thanks to Billy that, later on in the Zoo's 'pencil and rubber' shop, I felt drawn to a book on dog psychology. It looked fascinating so I bought it to read on the train home.

It appears that all modern dog breeds are descended from the wolf – yes, even the ones that resemble a large rat and those that look as if they need a good iron. Despite the fact that dogs have been domesticated and bred to perform different roles, they still retain seventy five per cent of the wolf pack instincts. These wolf packs can vary in size, from two to twelve wolves, but they all have a leader and a strict hierarchy or pecking order. The leader, or top dog, is known as the Alpha male. Thereafter, the other dogs develop a kind of 'squash ladder' of seniority and regularly challenge each other, vying for a better position and consequently higher status, with the perks that go with it.

The stronger wolf will be the one who forces the other into submission during a confrontation and subsequently takes his place on the ladder until he, in turn, is challenged and so on. Seniority has its perks too. When a kill is made on a hunting expedition, the rest of the pack steps aside enabling the top dog and his mate (the Alpha female) to eat first. After they have had their fill, the other dogs take their turn in order of seniority, through to the lowest of the low. Wolves, it transpires, are also very social animals – playing, hunting and sleeping together, with order of seniority dictating how close you sleep to the top dog at night.

This was all new to me. The closest I had ever come to studying wolves up to that point was watching repeats of 'It's the Wolf'. For the uninitiated, this is a cartoon in which a wolf is in pursuit of a lamb-like creature. "It's the wulaff, it's the wulaff!" the cartoon lamb would shriek in a very high-pitched irritating voice, upon spotting his 'wolfish' stalker. He was so irritating that you started to wish that the wolf *would* catch the little fucker and eat him alive but, alas, it never happened.

Anyway, the point is that it hadn't helped my under-standing of dog psychology at all. In fact, as a piece of scientific research, I think it was flawed on several levels. To be honest, even as a cartoon, it was pretty rubbishy – give me 'Champion the Wonder Horse' and 'The Flashing Blade' any day.

Moreover, the bottom line is that the favourite saying of old women, "Rover is like a furry human. He thinks he's one of the family," doesn't quite hit the nail on the head. Rather, it seems that Rover doesn't think he is one of the family at all, but considers that we are all part of *his* pack.

* * *

As I was out running past the park, I had noticed a variety of dogs and humans who all looked like they may have been from the same pack. There were some smiling humans, taking their dogs for a walk and there also appeared to be some dogs taking their unhappy humans for a walk. I thought dog walks were meant to be fun all round?

Some of the humans threw tennis balls for their dogs to fetch and some of the dogs brought the ball back and dropped it at the human's feet, whilst others had to be chased all over the park in order to retrieve it. What was going on? Surely *all* dogs were pre-programmed to fetch tennis balls – in the same way that all men have an inbuilt Pavlovian response to the click-clack of high heels? We just *have* to turn around to see who is wearing them. We can't help it.

Some of the people in the park spoke in whispers to their dog, who then responded by doing what was asked – much as I would do if I was on a night out and a promotions girl in a PVC cat-suit came over to me and whispered for me to do something – actually make that 'anything'.

Other people were shouting their pet's name repeatedly, growing more incensed with each yell as their dog sniffed something at the other side of the park, apparently oblivious to their owner's frenzied pleas – much as Deborah would ignore me if I was ever brave/stupid enough to tell her that I *had* chatted to a girl in a PVC cat-suit on a night out.

Some owners also seemed to have a bizarre hobby which looked as if it consisted of saving up all of their dog's poo and taking it home in a bag. Me? I've no need for a poop bag. I normally just find that my running shoes have special in-built dog poop magnets that the salesperson obviously didn't think they needed to tell me about when I bought them. I take my helping of dog poop home with me wedged in the intricate patterns on the sole. Incidentally, as an aside, I have also found another marketing opportunity for the people who make cotton buds. Why the hell would I want to take home a whole bag of poo as well? Practice?

The book I had bought at the Zoo explained it all to me (except the poo in bag stuff!). The humans with the well-behaved dogs had established themselves as the top dog and their pets knew where they stood in the pack. Not being top dog wasn't humiliating for the dog either, as a dog is just content to know where it stands. As the human is usually the owner, he or she should take that top dog slot and those people having problems were the ones who were still having their position on the squash ladder challenged. They had yet to resolve who was the top dog in their own family or pack.

Reading up on how a dog's mind operates also opened my eyes as to how I had inadvertently undermined my friend's efforts to allow her dog to know its place. At Deborah's, I found it amusing to encourage Tess to climb up onto the sofa to watch TV. In the wild, it's only the top dog that climbs up high to oversee his domain, so I was inadvertently offering Tess an invitation to be kingpin, and I've also lost count of the number of times I've literally offered a 'squash ladder' confrontation in the form of a game of tug of war with a plastic string of sausages. I could go on, but the saving grace is that it's only with other people's animals that I have messed things up and not my own. I wouldn't make those kinds of mistakes with my own dog.

Oh, by the way, I decided to get a dog.

CHAPTER THREE

The Dog from U.N.C.L.E.

For those of you who have never seen an 'Uncle Kenny' dog, it's a bit like the ones you used to see on wheels, being pushed around by children or senile old Majors. I'm not exactly sure if its official name is an 'Uncle Kenny' dog but, since my great Uncle Kenny bred them, that was the name that stuck. Urban myth has it that he once entered a dog at Crufts, but I think that is just a malicious rumour.

Incidentally, annual trips from Cardiff to Brecon to see Kenny and his dogs in my childhood was the closest I ever came to interacting with dogs unless, of course, you count the time when Matthew Quinn's dog bit me when I was in Form Three.

Since starting this chapter, I have been reliably informed that an 'Uncle Kenny' dog is actually a Welsh Wire Haired Terrier, so this breed appealed to me as being the ideal candidate for my first dog. There was this tenuous link in my past and, if I squinted a bit, I could almost imagine him as a large version of the Bush Dog.

* * *

He was going to be called 'Billy' too, or even 'Billy Two'.

I suppose it was the challenge factor which instigated this. Could I think like a dog and a top dog for that matter? Would I be able to train a dog to be obedient, based on the principles of the wolf pack? It seemed basic enough – forget modern manners

14

and think like a dog. As an Officer in the armed forces, I had been taught to ensure that the soldiers/sailors ate before I did. However, in my new pack, this was going to be turned on its head if I was to remain the top dog. I, as leader, would eat first and only then would Billy be given his food (as an Officer I was also taught 'not to bleed in front of the men' and to always carry a tool for getting stones out of horse's hooves, but these nuggets of wisdom seemed less relevant to the training of the dog).

Manners normally dictated that I opened the door to let someone through but, in the wild, it's the top dog that leads the pack on their journeys. Billy would be junior to me, so I would be conveying the wrong message if I let him go through a doorway before me, up the stairs before me or allow him to choose where we should go on our walk. No Billy straining on the lead, wrenching my arm off, for me. I would be the one who decided where we would venture that day and Billy would trot alongside me.

In my quest for inspiration, I even read several books on what passed as good manners in this green and, with the proper social graces, hopefully pleasant land. Even pumping was covered, although they rather delicately called it 'passing wind'. The following advice was proffered:

In aristocratic circles, the correct thing to do if this happens is to carry on as if nothing has happened and the entire company should carry on as if they had not noticed.

Based on my theory of turning etiquette on its head, I deduced that if my dog farted, he should look sufficiently surprised and I in turn would point and laugh.

I was always told that I had the distasteful habit of sulking if things didn't go the way I wanted them to (school report circa baby class infants – Donoghue is sullen and easily vexed). Now, sulking was to be the order of the day if things didn't go my way. This principle was based on the fact that puppies love attention and, if you take that away, they are devastated and, in future, will seek to avoid the cause of its withdrawal. So, if Billy doesn't bring back the tennis ball in a game of fetch, my theory dictates that I should stop playing and ignore him. It seems that I would also need to master the art of actively ignoring the dog as it is no use ignoring someone unless they know they are being ignored. I would need to make it obvious that I preferred to read the paper, rather than play with a naughty puppy. Playtime wouldn't include tug of war games with strings of sausages either. Opportunities to challenge my position would be avoided, if at all possible.

My sofa also formed part of my strategy, as there would be no encouragement for Billy to oversee his domain from the comfort of my furniture. Firstly, it's my domain and, if anyone is to watch over it, it's going to be me. Secondly, I'm sure that what may now seem like a cute puppy struggling to clamber up, won't appear so appealing when it's a dirty, wet and fully grown dog, fresh in from the muddy garden, leaping onto my armchair, even if there was an everlasting sale down at the sofa showroom. If I want Billy to be the lowest of the low in my pack, I need to keep him as the lowest of the low in the house too and this includes preventing him from jumping up.

Mind you, neither would he be encouraged to do that dog thing on the floor of sitting down, poking his two back legs in the air and then pulling himself around with his two front legs. If I interpret this correctly, the filthy little hound is effectively using the carpet a scratching post for his bum hole. Not nice.

Apparently, if he knows where he stands in the pack, he will be a much happier dog and I knew that I would be a much happier owner!

* * *

I soon discovered that dog ownership takes much more research than I had first thought and this entailed learning about my potential pet's characteristics, as the only one I could recollect was that they seemed very bouncy. As I began to accost strangers, innocently walking their dogs, to enquire about temperament, training and other 'doggy-type' questions, I encountered my first major disappointment. As bouncy as they are, Welsh Wire Haired Terriers do not excel at off lead training; rather, they excel at off lead running away!

This was a devastating blow in my quest for the ideal Billy. I had made a sketchy plan of what I wanted from a dog on my daughter's whiteboard. I needed a running companion, which had to be suitable for off lead training and also be good with children.

Billy had failed selection.

Time to seek an alternative dog. Time to seek an alternative name. Billy would forever be linked with what might have been. New name, new dog and back to the whiteboard!

* * *

When I was eight, instead of having a puppy, my sister Kate arrived and this eight-year age difference is something we have agreed to carry on for the rest of our lives – it makes things so much easier when calculating ages on birthdays and so on. I now get on very well with Kate, who also goes by the nickname of 'BooBoo'. This is worth knowing in case I lapse into lazy colloquialisms later on in the book and it is also worth knowing that the current harmony which now exists between us was not always so.

There were six of us in the Donoghue pack. Apart from my dad and mum, I had two older brothers and a younger sister, the aforementioned Kate. Anyone who has the remotest knowledge of science, mass and volume and all that stuff, will realise that six people into one Ford Cortina shouldn't go. But it did, and often. The car journey from Cardiff to Cwmbran takes about fifteen to twenty minutes nowadays but, in the early Seventies, the geographical make-up of South Wales must have been different because the journey would take ages.

We lived in Cardiff but my Nana and cousins, Jason and David, lived in Cwmbran; not together. Well, Jason and David did, along with Peter, Helen, my Uncle John and Aunty Eileen.

What I mean is that my Nana and my cousins didn't live together in some bizarre hippy commune but, having said that, I think my Uncle John probably secretly wished that he *was* in a hippy commune. He is retired now and should be doing 'old people' stuff, like talking incessantly about his ailments and grumbling about how things are not as good as they were when he was young, but not so with Uncle John. He has grown a ponytail, plays the bongos, roller-skates, goes ceroc dancing and listens to jazz music. Listening to jazz? Now there is a sure sign of madness if ever there was one. His only concession to old age is going on like a grumpy old guy about how much money is wasted having all the signs and literature printed in Welsh as well as English, just to pacify a slack handful of Welsh speakers (or sign writers with a bagful of spare consonants). Cardiff/Caerdydd – so good they named it twice.

Some places in Wales have developed jokey second names. For example Llantrisant, home of the Royal Mint is also known – maybe a bit unkindly – as 'The hole with the mint'. Whilst for other places – like Merthyr – well let's just say that one name is one too many!

The main cause of my unhappiness with my sister was borne out of the compulsory seating arrangement in the Cortina. Mum and Dad sat in the front, while Paul and Neil, my brothers, each sat next to a window on the back seat. Kate sat between them in a baby seat while I was left to sit directly in front of her, crouched up in the foetal position, on the bump between the rear footwells, all set to be catapulted out like a human cannonball, in the event of an emergency stop.

In itself, apart from just being there, it could be reasonably argued that Kate was not responsible for my unfortunate position. What Kate was responsible for though was pummelling my back with her feet, at every opportunity. We once travelled to France for a family holiday and it was only when we reached Calais that anyone thought of removing her shoes. The passing years have eased both my back and any tension between us. Furthermore, the promise of seeing an

'Uncle Kenny' dog had made her reconsider her fifteen-year boycott of the North East of England where, by pure coincidence, I had been living for the last fifteen years. But there was now not going to be any 'Uncle Kenny' dog.

'Plan B' was needed.

CHAPTER FOUR

Plan B

With hindsight, a dog on wheels may have been a better option, being cheaper and marginally easier to train, although, I must concede, not without its problems when going upstairs. I am certain though that, after the initial disappointment, Kate would have been fine.

However, the dog on wheels only remained a fond idea, as non-permanent marker pens were already heading for the whiteboard. 'Plan B' entered its embryonic stage when Deborah insisted that 'Plan B' dog should reflect its owner who, in this case, was me. I assumed she meant that being young and handsome were the qualities we now sought in my potential new pack member. The fact that she may actually have meant 'shallow and vain' was a distinct possibility, which I chose to ignore at that stage.

Dog breeds were now fed through the complex matrix selection process that combined both my wish list of dog qualities and someone else's perception of me. One breed seemed to have both the characteristics I was looking for and, according to Deborah, matched my personality.

Thankfully, I was independently assessed as not being a 'toy dog' person (I guess that ruled out 'wheelie dog' too). A sheepherder or cattle driving dog, it seems, did not reflect the inner me and, despite my security background, I was deemed not to be a guard dog of the Rottweiler or German shepherd variety. Apparently, my military background did not make me eligible for a fighter like a John Bull pug either and, to me, a Shih Tzu was a zoo with no animals and, anyway, is actually another type of dog which I am not. Terriers would be no good for me either – too much running off and I am neither a large game dog nor a non-sporting one.

Apparently, I am a Labrador.

(Note to reader: I'll just wait here for a couple of minutes while you decide what breed of dog you are. Just let me know when you are ready to go on).

❖ ❖ ❖

Ah, interesting choice you've made there!

Anyway, where was I? Oh yes, I remember now. Whether it had been 'Plan A' or 'Plan B', nothing could have prevented the most difficult part of my whole dog-training project. I had to convince my daughter, Bethan, that having a dog was going to be a good thing and, if I failed to win her over to the cause, the whole idea would have gone the way of the pear. So much for me being top dog!

"So, are you still thinking of getting a dog?" she asked on the way to the park. I hadn't realised that Bethan even knew I was thinking about it but I guess she realised that Billy the Bush Dog had made an impression on me.

❖ ❖ ❖

My daughter's mum is a teacher and it is easier if I just call her Susan which, as luck would have it, is actually her name. Susan is a Head Teacher no less and I met her when we were at high school together – Lady Mary High School to be exact. (When we were both pupils I hasten to add – if she had been Head Teacher then, it would have been just wrong. Every schoolboys dream maybe, but just wrong all the same). Her family had moved down from the North East and her father worked for a pop drink conglomerate that had a factory in Cardiff. Despite this, they were Catholic. When I was at Naval College years later, I needed a partner for the Summer Ball. I had asked Christina Stone, who used to sit in front of me in History, but she couldn't go and suggested Susan instead. I rang Susan and asked her if she wanted to come as my guest and, when she asked me where it was, I told her that the Captain held his balls in the College grounds.

Britannia Royal Naval College in Dartmouth is where all Royal Naval Officers complete their initial training and it is a magnificent venue for a ball, with its fine, proud buildings, packed to the gunnels with history and overlooking the Dart River estuary. During the day, there would be rowing contests, with the Captain's wife presenting medals to the winners and shyly kissing the Cox of the winning crew.

Later, in the evening, Officers, resplendent in their best mess uniforms, would dance the night away with beautiful girls in ball gowns.

Susan arrived by train for the ball and I thought I would impress her by picking her up from the station in my friend's two-seater sports car. He drove as I had yet to pass my test and, although I'm sure I looked quite dashing as I met her at the station, appeared slightly less so when we realised that there were now three of us to fit into the car. I made the journey back, laid out along the parcel shelf.

There is probably a law against that nowadays – or there should be anyway – something/anything should be put in place to prevent stupid blokes like me from having the opportunity of going out with attractive, intelligent women in the first place.

But I digress, again! It's a habit that I have picked up. Still it's free, legal, fun to do and, unlike some other habits, won't affect your eyesight.

* * *

I guess Bethan has inherited her love of teaching from Susan and, with every visit she comes prepared to conduct a lesson. At first, these lessons were 'off the cuff' but now she arrives, equipped with copious typed notes. She even downloads teachers' guides from the Internet to see if her schoolteacher is following the lesson plan in the correct way. In her bedroom, which I have now converted into her own classroom, I sit attentively, whilst being taught by Miss Donoghue.

Interestingly, I think I have learnt more from these lessons than I did at school and, if anything, I had assumed that English comprehension would have become easier in the twenty first century. I remember when I was back in Lady Mary High School, having to write long descriptive pieces about this or that character and I always gave them a Roman nose, as that seemed a great expressive feature and one that might even impress Miss Tucker.

With the advent of PCs and Word documents, I thought the need for all that narrative would have disappeared and it would suffice to say, "Times New Roman, you know the type?" Apparently not. I had also adopted the maxim of 'If in doubt, insert a semi-colon', as no one really knows when they should be used anyway and the reader would then accept my apparent superior knowledge of the English language. Bethan knew though and my reign of haphazardly using punctuation marks ended. To add insult to injury, either because I was too busy annoying Donna Herford and Katherine Kavanagh, who used to sit in front of me in class at Lady Mary, or I was out taking a pee at the time, they appear to have invented a whole new stack of English grammar rules in my absence.

In my new 'school', the whole curriculum is covered in different lessons and I even receive an end of year report. Bethan has also put me on the 'Further Literacy Scheme for English', so I must be doing well (or so I thought until Deborah told me that this was the syllabus for 'children who need more support'). Despite that, I even gave her a box of sweets and a badly spelt 'thank you' card at the end of term, in the hope that I would be able to survive the six weeks of summer holidays without getting shouted at in class.

* * *

Consequently, when Bethan called a conference to discuss the idea of me owning a dog, I knew this was serious. This wasn't just going to be a fun chat; this was the real thing. It was going to be a make or break situation, with Deborah and I making our case to the chairperson (Bethan) who would then probe our arguments and ultimately give the deciding vote on whether 'Plan B' dog would make it off the drawing board.

We both set about preparing our rationale for me having a dog. In all fairness, Bethan is much more sensible than me and wanted to know if I had really thought about the consequences of training and looking after a demanding animal or whether I was just doing this on a whim. She had witnessed the trouble I brought upon myself with her mum, when I returned from the fair with Bethan clutching a goldfish in a bag.

Even though she is not that keen on dogs herself, we were given a fair hearing and the conference was impressively conducted – in fact, better than most conferences I have attended in a professional capacity. Luckily, I had recently completed a substantial amount of research on dogs – reading books on their psychology, together with standard training procedures. On the basis that copying from one source was plagiarism, but blatantly copying from many was 'research', I had a file full of 'researched techniques' for training 'Plan B' dog. I had also 'road tested' the techniques on Tess, Deborah's seven year old collie. The answer, by the way, is, "Yes, you can teach an old dog new tricks". After the cases were presented and the cross-examination was over, I waited tensely for the verdict.

I was as tense as someone in England trying to pay for goods with a Scottish ten pound note. If you have ever tried that, you'll know how tense I mean!

'Plan B' dog was meant to complement my time with Bethan, not to be something that detracted from her enjoyment of her visits so, if she didn't support the scheme, it would have to be forgotten. Bethan returned to the room. Thumbs up!

CHAPTER FIVE

Naming Baby

I phoned my dad to tell him the good news.

"Hello Dad, it's me."

"Hello Boy. How's um, how's err…?"

"Bethan?"

"How's Bethan?"

"She's fine Dad. I'll put her on in a sec. I'm going to get a dog!"

"Bloody hell boy, why do you want to do that? *We* never had a dog."

"I know we never had a dog but I thought it would be good company. I was thinking of getting an 'Uncle Kenny' dog."

"He's bloody dead boy!"

"I know Uncle Kenny is dead Dad. Anyway I'm going to get a Labrador now."

"What do you want to get a big slobbery thing like that for?"

"It's not big and slobbery Dad, it's a Labrador. I thought he could come running with me."

"He'll bloody run off Boy."

"I'll train him not to."

"They're as thick as two short planks."

"No they're not. Blind people have them …" and so on.

He seemed pleased for me.

* * *

'Plan B' dog needed a name. 'Cerberus' was the original devil dog and Greek legend has it that he was huge – bigger than a horse, with three heads. He guarded the underworld and allowed the dead in, but not out again and, in itself, that is no bad thing otherwise we would be overrun with ghosts. The ancient Egyptians called Sirius the 'dog star' and it is visible for most of the summer. The Egyptians actually believed that Sirius was responsible for the summer heat, hence the phrase 'The dog days of summer' to describe those hot balmy summer days. 'Sparky' was the name of the Labrador in Kurt Vonnegut's 'Breakfast of Champions' (very good book – very bad film). Sparky was unable to wag his tail because of an automobile accident and had no way of showing other dogs how friendly he was so he had to fight all the time. 'Scooby Doo' (proper name 'Scoobert Doo') belonged to Shaggy and helped to solve mysteries as they toured around in a camper van with a serious bloke, a geeky girl and a really smart looking girl. 'Frank' on the other hand is the black Labrador up the road. 'Melanie', 'George', 'Maxine', 'Titch' – the point is that there's an infinite number of names you can call your mangy hound or snappy bitch. Anything goes.

Choosing a name is one thing but then you are stuck with it for the rest of your pooch's life. You have to shout it out in the park too and so, what might have been acceptable for Guy Gibson of 'Dambusters' fame to call his dog, may not be so suitable today! Look it up – I'm not going to tell you in this book and risk being sacked from work! Finding the right name for anything is important.

* * *

Durham has a fantastic history. It sits on the banks of the River Wear – the same one that flows past my house, on its journey to the sea. Durham is also where the Prince Bishops lived. The Normans, worried that the Northern Princes might become too powerful and threaten the King, made the Bishops of Durham into Princes and their magnificent Norman Castle dominates the skyline. The Cathedral, built in 1093, has been voted the nation's favourite building and contains the tomb of The Venerable Bede, who instigated the idea that dates should be calculated from the time of the birth of Jesus.

Thomas Wolsey, the famous Minister of King Henry VIII, who came close to becoming Pope, made his fortune from being Bishop of Durham (although he never even visited the place). The University, founded in 1832, is regarded as next in line after Oxford and Cambridge and its graduates have 'Dunelm' (the Latin name for the city) printed on their degrees. Durham even had its own Dick Whittington, Sir John Duck, who arrived in 1655 as a poor man and ended up a rich and famous mayor. He lived on Silver Street, which is so called because that's where silver coins were made in the Middle Ages.

For the Millennium celebrations, a new state of the art theatre and performing arts complex were built to enhance this ancient City. With so much history to draw from and so many links with prominent people from days of yore, what did the good councillors of Durham call the new magnet for the arts; this contemporary focal point?

'The Gala'! It makes it sound like a bingo hall but, once again, I digress.

* * *

The debate for a suitable name for 'Plan B' dog raged on in the car, on the way back from a visit to Durham town. Some people advocate calling their dog the first thing that comes into their head when they see their new pup, but I thought I would take out some insurance against any lack of inspiration at the crucial time. I read that in America, there were three children christened 'Latrine' last year plus one unfortunate girl called 'Chlamydia'. At least there was no one called 'Rubella' which had made the list the previous year. Goodness knows what had inspired *their* parents.

In France, the government used to promulgate an official list of names that you had to choose from. Maybe it wasn't such a bad idea after all, except I guess it kind of depends on how big the list is. The famous boxer and grill salesman George Foreman must have had a tiny list (or imagination), because he named *all* his five sons George.

My friend in junior school was named Richard by his parents. All very well except his surname was Holder. Didn't they think ahead to what his name would be shortened to? The poor guy sounds like he could be one of those optional extras in a luxury car...or a hi-tech upgrade to a Palm Pilot!

Meanwhile, 'Plan B' dog names had been tossed about like a kitten in a tumble dryer and, just like the kitten, we were all getting a bit sick of it now. Bethan suggested "Arnie".

"Barney?" came a voice from the back seat, which was probably Deborah's.

"Yes, Barney!" replied Bethan.

So it came to pass. 'Plan B' dog was thereafter officially referred to as Barney.

* * *

Just as finding the source of the Limpopo River was difficult, so was finding the source of a 'Barney'. He had to be a black Labrador as Deborah had insisted that they didn't seem to age as much as Golden or Chocolate 'Labs'. Observations in the high street had also caused me to believe that you have a much higher chance of going blind if you have a golden one. And while I'm on the subject, why don't those people with guide dogs give themselves just a little bit more of a chance of seeing by not wearing such thick dark glasses? And those signs in Braille? Obviously a good idea – but how are they supposed to find them in the first place. I saw a 'Do not touch the hot plate' sign in Braille. Enough said. Mind you, it's a general bloke thing anyway. If someone tells you something is "really hot", you always feel a need to see what their version of 'hot' is compared to yours. We always seem to think that we have a superior resilience to high temperatures that means we... *Christthat'stakenmyfeckin'skinoff!*

He also *had* to be a 'he'. Firstly, the name Barney lent itself to a 'he' (although I do remember, as a child, having a cat called Susie which, it was later discovered, was actually a boy cat. However, having the wrong name can actually be character building as Johnny Cash tells us in the song, 'A boy called Sue' or maybe it is just embarrassing).

Secondly, it was decided that Barney should be a 'he' as both Bethan and I sniggered like school children whenever Deborah mentioned the word 'bitch', although I suppose Bethan did have a kind of excuse, as she *was* still a school child. Anyway, regardless of the reason, Barney was to be a boy.

❖ ❖ ❖

Puppies sold in pet shops only seem to exist in comedy sketch shows nowadays and puppy farms are frowned upon. I accepted this boycott of puppy farms although the concept still intrigued me. What did the puppies grow on these farms and how had they adapted the farm implements to fit their tiny paws?

It seems that the ideal time for a puppy to be taken from its mother and re-housed is when it is eight weeks old but, all in all, finding a reputable breeder with an eight-week-old black boy Labrador is no cakewalk. Suddenly, bingo! An Internet search resulted in finding Black Labrador pups for sale, at great expense, down in rural Oxfordshire.

A phone call established that one of the litter still remained – a black boy Labrador puppy and, according to his owner, a handsome one at that. Young and handsome – this must have been what Deborah had meant. There was a downside, however – he would not be able to count as well as his brothers. During the birth, in an effort to free him from the birth sac, his mother had nipped one of his toes off. At least he was unique. This was going to be Barney.

Deposit dispatched, all I had to do now was wait until the appointed time.

CHAPTER SIX

A Short List of Long Demands

When I venture down to the restaurant in various hotels, I sometimes have a thin red horizontal line across my forehead, which is caused by the pressure of the elasticated rim of a shower cap. I sometimes sit watching telly in my 'home from home', wearing the free shower cap, just to feel as if I am getting my money's worth from the establishment. I also bring the shower caps home, in their unopened packets, along with the tiny plastic bottle of shower gel and the disproportionately large one of shampoo and conditioner. You would need a lot of hair to get through all that shampoo in one go, or maybe they are just being prepared in case you bring a pet chimp along. I do all this on what my daughter would call 'sleepovers' and the organisation I work for would describe as 'non taxable expenses'.

Since my work, on occasions, takes me all over the UK, I realised that Barney would need to go on sleepovers too but, instead of accompanying me to a hotel and sitting in some stale, impersonal room, sporting a strangely outdated plastic cap, he would stay with friends who had 'volunteered' to look after him for the night.

* * *

As Barney's arrival was some weeks away, I decided to make the best use of this time and, after much soul searching, I resolved to adopt the heavy burden of Moses to the dog world and put together some guidelines on how dogs should behave. These would be known as 'The Ten Commandments of Dog'. I had toyed with the idea of using the traditional style of command-ments:

"Thou shalt not sniff butt."

"Thou shalt not hump leg."

"Thou shalt not lick your own butt and then go and lick your owner's face as if you are pleased to see him."

I even thought that the 'butt' word, instead of the 'arse' word, might make it more universally acceptable but I realised I was onto a loser. I was a realist and realised it was futile to direct orders that wouldn't be obeyed. I also realised that I had to make it seem appealing to my chosen audience.

I rather thought Abraham had spoilt the whole impact of signing up with some other religions too, by condoning that 'thing' about having to chop off the end of your 'wotsit'. Sweet Jesus! To be quite honest, I don't think it could have helped recruitment one bit and that was for the supposedly Chosen Race! God created us with a design fault that we needed to correct ourselves? Surely some mistake? Just correcting this 'minor oversight' would be fraught with its own dangers – one slip of knife and you'd probably end up getting the sack. I know I'm a 'Cavalier' Catholic and that we decided to opt out of that one anyway, but I'm only trying to help!

I would do the job properly too and, instead of just a one liner for each Commandment, I would elaborate a bit. That one about coveting your neighbour's ass always seemed a little vague. Don't beat around the bush; just spit it out. Are you serious about the 'donkey' thing or are you alluding to something else? You were specific enough about the 'willy' thing – why go round the houses with this one?

Not wishing to be sued for copyright or anything, I thought I would make my commandments 'top down'. Instead, top dog would be in charge of implementing the commands since this seemed safer than allowing the lowest of the low to interpret what he or she chooses to understand by each decree. Also, to avoid any talk of plagiarism, the Commandments would be written 'bottom up'. That is, it would look as if it was the lowest of the low's idea all along and I would use lots of exclamation marks too, to make it look even more urgent. Genius or what?

If every dog adopted the Commandments, dogs would be interchangeable and so, arranging for Barney to be looked after for a sleepover, would be easy. I even had a personalised introduction, which I thought was a nice touch and I also left number nine flexible so that it could be amended to fit the relevant breed. Barney would be my vehicle in the dog world to spread the word.

❖ ❖ ❖

"Hello, I'm Barney. Thanks for looking after me. To get the most fun out of me, it would be best if I behave like a good dog. To behave like a good dog, I need to know where I stand in the 'pack', (that's you lot by the way). Where I stand is – *you* are Top Dog, not me. If I think I'm Top Dog, I'll start to do what *I* want to do, not what you want me to. If you follow the Ten Commandments, both you and I will have a much better time together.

One: Playtime
Don't play rough with me, as it will only make me think that it's OK to nip or bite. Tug of war games are like a challenge to be Top Dog to me, so leave it out Boss! I like 'fetch the ball' and games like that. If I don't give the ball back when you say 'Leave', don't wrestle it off me – just ignore me. I'll soon learn to let it go.

Two: How Do I Learn?
I love attention – any attention. Good or bad attention!! I'll keep on doing what gets me attention. So, if I keep on barking to be let

in and you come out and tell me off for barking (bad attention), then let me in. I'll think, *"Hey, barking gets attention ... I like that!! And it gets me let in!!!"* And, guess what I'll do next time I'm outside when I want to get in?? Instead, ignore me and only let me in when I'm a good dog. I may jump up too. It may be cute now, but it won't be much fun when I'm a big dog! If I jump up when you come home, just turn your back and ignore me. Only turn around and praise me when I've settled down. I'll think, *"Jumping up doesn't get me attention ... but if I'm settled, I get attention"* and guess what I'll do next time you come home? I'll do what gets me attention. Praise me when I'm good and I'll keep doing what earns me praise. Get the message Boss?

Three: School Time

I've learnt/am learning/will learn some words in Dog School to make me a good dog so I can please the Top Dog.

SIT ... to sit
DOWN ... to lie down
COME ... to come back to you
STAY ... to stay put
HEEL ... to walk nicely with you when I am out
GET BUSY ... to have a wee or poop
FETCH ... to fetch something
LEAVE ... to let go of something
NO ... what to say if I'm naughty
BED TIME ... When it's bed time!

I'm not that bright, so just use the words above and *no* extra ones. "Good Barney, lie down for me," or "Go to bed you fool" just confuses me!! Word overload!! Just say, "Down" or "Bed time".

Four: Shouting

Don't shout at me. I have good hearing. It's just like talking to a Frenchman; you don't need to shout to make him understand – you just need to speak in words he understands. See 'School Time'!

Five: Telling Me Off

I don't mean to be naughty but sometimes I am. Unless you catch me in the act of doing something, it's no good telling me off, as I'll have forgotten what I'm being told off for! I'll think I'm being told off just for being there! If you *do* catch me doing something I shouldn't, just say, "No", and, if need be, pull me off the furniture or correct what I'm doing. Not, "Naughty Barney", "Bad Barney" or "Why you little ...". Just say, "No" please. I am eager to please, so I'll be disappointed to know I've upset Top Dog. No need to smack my snout either Boss. Just be consistent or I'll get confused again!

Six: The Lowest of the Low

I'm a dog!! I don't need to sit on the settee, or lie on a comfy bed. I have fur and pads. If I'm let up on the sofa, I'll think I'm Top Dog. Climbing on things or getting up high makes me think I'm Top Dog, overseeing my domain. Say, "No" and get me down. Keep me low and I'll behave better.

Seven: Dinner Time

The Top Dog always eats first. Please don't give me my food until after you have finished your meal. And don't feed me bits from your table or you'll never get rid of me!! While I'm on the subject, why share your chocolate bars and snacks with me? I wouldn't share my dinner with you.

Eight: Walkies!

I love 'em!! Top Dog says I must walk on the left of you and that my front paws should be level with your left leg. If I get too excited and start jumping up and stuff, tell me, "No", and then stop and ignore me until I calm down. If I pull on the lead or start getting ahead, tell me, "No", and gently pull me back into line. Try walking really slowly and praising me when I'm good. You'll enjoy going for walks in future if I'm a well-behaved dog so it's worth keeping me in line. Oh, and Top Dog always goes through doorways first! (That's *you* remember!) I'll learn day by day. Promise Boss!

Nine: I'm a Retriever

So I'll retrieve stuff! If you find me with your slippers or best toy, don't chase me to get it back. I'll just think it's a game (and remember I like attention). It's better to tell me to, "Fetch" and then "Leave". At least you'll get it back ... and remember I don't mean to be naughty ... I didn't know it was important!! Keep it away from me in future.

Ten: Have Fun!

Have fun with me. That's what I'm here for!

I enjoy myself better if I know where I stand ... and *you* will have a better time if I know where I stand too. I'm a dog!! But *you* are Top Dog!!"

Adogs.

CHAPTER SEVEN

The Abominable Showman

I must have been pretty simple as a child. From Mrs O'Leary in Baby Class Infants, through to Mr Cunliffe in Standard 4, not forgetting Mrs Cligett, Mrs Mottram and Mr Keane en route – all must either be shaking their heads in disappointment or turning in their graves. Delete where applicable.

It's not that they weren't good teachers, because they were, but rather because they failed to rid me of some very basic misconceptions that I harboured during my formative years. They have even changed the name of my Primary School, from 'Our Lady, Queen of the Universe' to 'Christ the King' in an effort to disassociate themselves from me. The misconceptions are thus:

Geography: If you go down the street where I lived in the suburbs of Cardiff, past the sweet shop, through the woods and past the field that is now a housing estate, you will come to a pipe that goes across the river. It's big enough to walk on and the supporting structure acts as handrails. We used to call it the Pipe Bridge. My mistake was that I was convinced that England was over the other side of that bridge and, naturally, in England they all wore bowler hats and carried umbrellas. I was very disappointed when I eventually found out that it was, in fact, Llanrhymney on the other side – just another bit of Cardiff and also, as it happens, home to my brother's friend, Gary.

Gary was instrumental in me winning a goldfish at the fair, in that he leant over and put the ping-pong ball in the jam jar when the lady wasn't looking. In those days, we had it hard – no guaranteed prizes every time! I named the fish 'Gary', funnily enough, in honour of Gary. He (the fish that is) lived for a record breaking fifteen years, in stark contrast to the four hour life span of most fairground fish that make the journey home, swimming in their little plastic bag. I am not sure what the life span of the human Gary is and it's always seemed to me not the sort of thing that one should make guesses about. I wish I hadn't brought the subject up now.

I'm sure it was Gary who shocked a pleasant American family who had 'adopted' him on his trip to the States years later with his apparent revelations of the dope smoking habits of the British. They had invited him round for Sunday dinner and he sat, open mouthed, at the impressive range of meats displayed on the table. "Isn't this like Sunday dinner back home Gary?" they enquired politely. "No" replied Gary. "Back in Britain we just share a joint."

Anyway, it wasn't just the Pipe Bridge that held such mystery for me. When we drove to Cwmbran, we always turned off to visit my Nana before we reached a tunnel, built into the hillside. My mind boggled at what might lie beyond and, in later years, I did go through the tunnel. On the other side, there is a factory with a big sign that reads something like, "Every time a monkey leaves here, it's a wrench." They make monkey wrenches.

The other area of ignorance lay in my understanding of religion.

In my simple mind, things seemed pretty black and white. I guessed, as Catholics, we were the white and Protestants were the black. Not literally, you understand, just metaphorically. At that age, I was only aware of these two religions – you were either a Catholic or you weren't. And if you weren't a Catholic, I assumed you must therefore be a Protestant. It was nothing bad – it was just that, because I was a Catholic, I believed the things we did were the 'right' things to do. To go camping, as we did, was obviously the right thing to do whereas caravanning was therefore inherently wrong. Consequently, I logically assumed that Protestants adopted this practice. We had squash, which meant that the more glamorous drink of fizzy pop must logically be Protestant.

It was like French – everything could be classified 'Le' or 'La' except, unlike French, there was no 'cop out' with the wishy washy 'Les'. You could name anything and I could classify it as either Catholic or Protestant. And I mean *anything*. Not just the obvious things like cats (Catholic) and dogs (Protestant), but you name it and I could give it a religion (only of the two I was aware existed anyway). If we use apples as an example: Golden Delicious apples (Catholic) and Granny Smith's (Protestant). Generally, it was a good guide to classification that, if something was exciting, fun or exotic, it was probably a good guess that it was Protestant. You could probably argue that a Granny Smith apple or a dog are not that exciting, fun or exotic but, if I didn't have them, that was enough to make me think they *must* be more exciting, fun or exotic than whatever I had.

BBC – Catholic, ITV – Protestant; 'Blue Peter' and 'Swap Shop' – Catholic, 'Magpie' and 'Tiswas' – Protestant.

My dad worked for the Electricity Board, so logically Electricity was Catholic, therefore Gas was Protestant. Tea without sugar was Catholic, tea with sugar was Protestant. Crunchy peanut butter was Catholic – so smooth peanut better was Protestant.

I could go on, so I will.

Feeling guilty (Catholic), having a great time playing Buckeroo (Protestant); wearing everlasting nylon shirts to school (Catholic), not wearing everlasting nylon shirts to school (Protestant); vanilla ice cream (Catholic), tutti-frutti ice-cream (Protestant); lace up shoes (Catholic), slip-ons (Protestant). There was also a tantalising rumour that Protestants had things like Wagon Wheels (a biscuit ...the size of your head?!) and Kit-Kats in their biscuit barrels, instead of plain Rich Tea.

The concept of someone not wearing nylon watching

'Tiswas' on a colour telly in a caravan whilst playing Buckeroo, feeding their dog a Granny Smith, whilst simultaneously drinking coloured pop and eating a penguin dipped in tutti-frutti ice-cream, just blew my mind! All in all, 'Proddy's' seemed to have a better time than we did.

I am pleased to say that I am now cured and I neither expect Barney to be wearing a bowler hat nor to watch ITV.

❖ ❖ ❖

My friend Deborah is a teacher. She once told me that the best two things about teaching were July and August ...oh, and hearing that asbestos cladding had been found in the school roof – two extra weeks off – Yoohoo! She teaches in a pretty rough part of Darlington – the part that would probably be described in any Lonely Planet guide as 'a shithole'. An ASBO is probably the only qualification the kids from there would get.

As a special treat, last year I performed a magic show for her class and I was called 'The Fang' for the big event. The Fang is a character from a song, who came down to Earth from Mars, thought he was John Donoghue for a week and went home again, smiling. It was therefore deemed appropriate that this should be my name. Every day, during the month leading up to the show, various posters were displayed, such as 'Fifty million Fang fans can't all be wrong', 'The Fang: Taking Fun Seriously', or 'Coming soon – The Abominable Showman'.

After the show, everyone was given a special certificate plus a poster of The Fang. He looked young and handsome, or was it shallow and vain? Anyway, they were all very excited.

Deborah was excited now. It was two days to 'Barney' day but I was feeling more wary than excited. I have always tried not to get too excited for fear of being disappointed.

One Christmas, when I was about twelve or thirteen, Paul, Neil, Kate and myself all trooped downstairs to find piles of presents waiting for each of us. My pile of presents was next to Paul's and, between them, was a black Panasonic tape recorder.

It looked too good to be for me so I didn't want to claim it, because I knew that, if I assumed it was mine and then found out that it was really for Paul, I would have been both extremely disappointed and embarrassed (even more embarrassing than realising you've put your wheelie bin out on the wrong day).

When Paul had moved his pile to the relative safety of the settee, the black Panasonic tape recorder remained on the floor. When my dad asked me if I liked my new tape player, I was so ecstatic that I still can't find the right words to describe the feeling. I felt like someone had given me the moon on a stick.

I subsequently spent many happy hours in my room, taping my records or the top twenty, direct from the wireless. In those days, it involved playing the record or radio very loudly and placing the tape recorder next to the speaker. There was also the constant risk of noise from visitors to the room and many recordings carry the sound of my mum calling me down for tea.

My mum died a few years ago and it's at times like that when you realise those little things that were annoying then, mean everything to you now.

* * *

Today was 'Barney' day minus one. Preparations were being made but, as Bethan continually reminds me, long car journeys can be boring.

Try this to liven things up a bit. Next time you are driving and need to sneeze, at the same time as you actually let rip, sneakily pull the front windscreen wash lever, just as the contents of your sneeze would supposedly hit the windscreen so that there will be a torrent of water hitting the screen. For best effect, as the wipers wipe your 'sneeze' off the glass, don't even look over to your passenger – just act as if nothing has happened. You may allow yourself a sly glance out of the corner of your eye to see the reaction it provokes. Mucho merriment.

Don't despair if you happen to be travelling by aeroplane on your holidays and there is no windscreen/sneeze opportunity.

Instead just get a spare oxygen mask, wait until the person next to you has dropped off to sleep, slip on the mask, then nudge them awake and prepare for the belly laugh of the century as you watch their amusing little antics as they flail about, totally consumed by panic.

Alternatively if you are not in a sneezy mood, try quickly double flashing your headlights as the car in front of you passes a speed camera. The driver will just see flashes in his mirror and be convinced he was flashed by the device. Actually come to think of it, that's not very nice at all ...but somehow strangely fun.

It was going to be a long return journey to Oxford and the 'dog' books I had read all emphasised that it could prove to be a traumatic experience for the puppy, being taken from its mother and driven to its new home. They suggest that classical music should be played in the vehicle to relax the dog but, having searched through my CD collection, the closest I had to anything remotely classical was 'Cosi Fan Tutti Frutti' by 'Squeeze'. Barney would have to enter his life in the North East with a different soundtrack. Two CDs by 'Overnight Jones', the best of 'Weddings Parties Anything' and something by Ron Hawkins would have to do in place of Mozart and Puccini. Deborah and I set off to Cheltenham – tomorrow was Barney day.

※ ※ ※

The village we were headed for in the Oxford countryside was about an hour's drive from Cheltenham. I wasn't even sure if this dog existed as, since the initial chat with his owner and sending the deposit, communication had been minimal to say the least. I hadn't exactly been lying in bed at night like the agnostic, dyslexic insomniac, wondering if there really was a dog, but I did have my doubts. Deborah was confident though.

Our directions took us up a long gravel drive into a court-yard surrounded by a large farmhouse and various outbuildings and Jonathan, the owner, was there to greet us. As it is only good manners, we greeted Barney's mum first – a fine looking chocolate coloured Labrador. Chocolate? Surely some sort of horrible mistake had occurred. I thought Barney was supposed to be black!

Apparently, Barney and the rest of the litter were in one of the outbuildings and, as the door was opened, they all looked up expectantly and started jumping around in a mini frenzy. One of this mad bunch was picked up and deposited in the courtyard. He was as black as coal – the type of coal that was extra black. Apparently, you can have chocolate, golden and black Labs mixed up in one litter. This was to be my new best friend; this was Barney.

As he scampered around, Jonathan explained about his toe again. It was almost impossible to tell that he was one toe short on his left paw and it didn't seem to make the slightest difference to him anyway.

As the 'scamperee' scampered backwards and forwards, he was given to me to hold. It was as though I was a new dad who didn't know how to hold his baby properly. I dropped him on his head onto the gravel and was secretly grateful when it was suggested that we should go inside to complete the paperwork.

Barney's pedigree name is 'Hartscrest Baghdad'. Jonathan had been watching the war in Iraq when the puppies were born and, as a result, Barney's brothers and sisters had pedigree names like 'Hartscrest Basra' and 'Hartscrest Euphrates'. I was just thankful that he wasn't 'Hartscrest Weapons of Mass Destruction' or we might never find him if he ran off. Hartscrest Baghdad or Barney as he was now to be known, could trace his family back further than I could and came from very good stock, with many generations of low hip scores and high eye scores. I know – it didn't mean much to me either – but, if you just happen to be a Labrador, these are the things you would wish you had too. Someone had described this breed as being 'an eating machine on legs' and we were taken through his current feeding habits.

With the final settlement having been made and, after a promise to send photos at Christmas, we were ready to make the journey home.

Barney had been living away from his mother in the outhouse, with his brothers and sisters for a while now, so it would not be such a wrench leaving her. This was no monkey. The cat box I had borrowed for the trip was deemed unnecessary so Barney began the long journey back, sitting on Deborah's lap.

I was quite prepared to do the sneeze/windscreen trick if he appeared bored.

Barney was the perfect traveller, sitting on the passenger's lap for the entire journey. Even my choice of music was given the paws up as it obviously soothed the savage beast in him.

We had decided that it might be more reassuring for him to share his first night away from the rest of the litter with another dog. Deborah's dog, Tess, was the unwitting victim.

We had agreed that the dogs should meet on neutral territory or, at least, in Deborah's front garden. When we arrived, Barney bounded up the path as Tess padded out of her house onto the grass. Little did she know how her sedate life would be turned on its head by the arrival of this jet-black 'thing' and a rolling, barking, nipping struggle ensued whilst Tess asserted her dominance over Barney.

Barney retaliated as soon as he bounded into the house by seeking out Tess' bed in the conservatory and laying a fresh turd on it. The bed had to be ritually destroyed later as Tess would have no more to do with it after that sorry event. As if to add insult to injury, during the night, Barney climbed into the big bucket that contained Tess' food and ate his way out of it. When we came down in the morning, Barney resembled a barrel with legs.

A pool of wee and another turd on the conservatory floor completed the picture.

CHAPTER EIGHT

That Thin Wild Mercury

You don't have to be particularly bad to be punished; you just have to get caught. It's worthwhile bearing this in mind as, at various times as a young sailor, I had been confined to the ship, locked up in cells shore side or given extra duties. In turn, on the rare occasions when I did something worthy, I was praised. I preferred the praise to the punishments and I therefore decided that my technique for training Barney would be based on praise.

If Barney did something good, like obeying an instruction, he would be praised. As an eating machine on legs, he was highly motivated by food too, so he would receive a food treat sometimes as well. Conversely, if Barney did something bad, like jumping up or biting, the praise would be taken away from him. He would be ignored. There are some excellent books on dog training and I had compared my ideas to theirs. I seemed to be on the right track.

There is a tale about two Police Officers who went to the house of an elderly lady to take a statement from her. She made them both a cup of tea and ushered them into the front room where they all sat discussing the purpose of their call. As they talked, the door was nudged open and a German shepherd dog pottered into the middle of the room. The dog looked around and then proceeded to squat down, and with his back legs all a quiver, he proceeded to deposit a fresh steaming turd on the lounge room carpet. The Police Officers exchanged sideways glances but didn't say anything. After all, it was the woman's house and everyone has different standards – it wasn't up to them to admonish the hound. They looked over at house owner, but she just acted as if nothing had happened. Instead she just avoided looking at the dirty beast and his doings, picked up her tea cup, took a sip and continued to politely chat to the officers. Meanwhile, the dog, having done his dirty deed, pottered back out of the room.

After twenty minutes the Officers were ready to leave but by this time curiosity had got too much for them. As they thanked the lady for the tea, one of then asked why she hadn't said anything when her dog had come into the room and pooped on the floor.

"*My* dog?" replied the old woman. "I thought he was *your* dog!"

It transpired that the dirty dog belonged to neither. He was just a random dog who happened to be passing and as luck would have it, wanted a poo at the same time. I guess the front room was just a warm place to do it!

Whilst the Officers had stayed silent respecting the rights of the woman to act as she wanted in her own house, she had in turn assumed that it was their Police dog who had come in, done his business and then presumably went back out to wait in the car, and she had just been too polite to say anything. That's what happens when you assume too much!

I suppose the only trouble with the dog manuals is that too many of them seemed to make assumptions as well – assumptions about the knowledge I supposedly already possessed. I was a first-time dog owner, with no previous experience and assumptions were no good to me. It may be obvious to everyone else, but I wanted to know things such as when you should start training your pup. When can you reasonably expect pup to master this or that objective? When can you move on to more advanced stuff? Am I playing with him enough? How long does the nipping stage last? Will he *ever* stop peeing in his bed? The dogs in the books only seemed to need one reprimand before mastering anything. However, I had the feeling it might be slightly different with Barney.

I compared my technique to a couple of management books too and, whilst they seemed to agree with the notion of receiving what you reward, they also warned against the dangers of inadvertently condoning inappropriate behaviour.

In 'The Greatest Management Principle in the World' by Michael LeBoeuf, there is a fable:

> "*A weekend fisherman looked over the side of his boat and saw a snake with a frog in its mouth. Feeling sorry for the frog, he reached down, gently removed it from the snake's mouth and let it go free. But now he felt sorry for the hungry snake. Having no food, he took out a flask of bourbon and poured a few drops into the snake's mouth. The snake swam away happy, the frog was happy, and the fisherman was happy for having performed such good deeds. He thought all was well until a few minutes passed and he heard something knock against the side of his boat. The fisherman looked down and, with stunned disbelief, saw the snake was back – this time with two frogs!*"

Aha, too much warm fuzzy niceness wasn't going to do the trick and, as compassionate as I am, I realised I might need back up.

The ultimate weapon in my arsenal would be a water spray. I had seen on TV how good they were at persuading rioters in various European Capitals to reconsider their 'scampish' activities and instead return home for a nice cup of tea. A plant spray bottle, filled with water, would be called into play when ignoring was not an option. If he was barking at three in the morning, I didn't think my neighbours would support my passive appeasement stance. The water spray would be called into action so I bought two plant sprayers from the garden centre.

A couple of weeks later, a Sainsbury's store near Durham sold a super soaker ...

❊ ❊ ❊

Meanwhile, Bethan had experienced her own 'Road to Damascus' moment. From being none too sure about the concept of Barney, she was now more than eager to spend my money on his creature comforts. Trips to the pet shop resulted in a multitude of toys and, in the main, these were made of materials that weren't to be found elsewhere in the house. The principle behind this is that a puppy doesn't know the difference between his stuff and your stuff. If you teach him that it's OK to chew a toy made from the same material as your jumper, for example, don't be surprised if your jumper is the next item to be chewed. Most toys we bought were made of rubber and I *don't* have any rubber clothes – honest! Having said that, I must admit that a soft squeaky toy Dalmatian in a stripy jumper, chosen by Bethan, did make it through this selection process.

She also designed and input the details into the clever machine that engraved his identity disc. Collars and leads soon followed. A soft pillow bed with funny puppy motifs was *her* choice, along with a large ceramic water bowl, which we reckoned couldn't be upturned, even by an enthusiastic pup.

I'm not sure if they were meant to be stealth bowls, but a couple of metallic food bowls were purchased that had a rubber ring around the bottom of them to muffle that 'metal on concrete' sound as pup shuffled it along with his nose, whilst eating his food. Surely this 'nose in bowl' issue was some kind of design fault in dogs (as is the tail in air when happy, forcing you to look at its arsehole). Regardless, we bought one bowl for home use and one for his sleepover kit.

Trips to various garden centres failed to produce a kennel. We knew what we wanted – a traditional one like you find in cartoons, with a pitched roof. Nothing fancy – not one with central heating and curtains like 'Gorgeous George' the pampered Boxer dog up the street has. No, a simple kennel would be fine. If it was good enough for the dog out of 'Tom and Jerry', it would be good enough for Barney. An ad in the window of the corner shop eventually saved the day and an overly large kennel was ordered based on some wrong measurements provided by my good self. Despite looking as if it was meant for a baby elephant, I kept it on the basis that Barney could have sleepovers with his new found chums in it when I was away, and secondly, I would never ever get troubled by any Jehovah Witnesses again as after one look at the construction, they would assume I had the beast from Hell living in my back yard. (They would end up having their own domestic Damascus experience – a Domestos experience? – anyway that's what I'd probably need to clean up the mess they left!) Bethan made up another disc, to hang on the front of his new house. He needed to know where he stood in the pack and this would remind him. It read, 'The Lowest of the Low'.

At great expense, a new gate was erected across the back yard and I *mean* at great expense! It wasn't electric and it didn't open with a clever remote control device but, after seeing how much I paid to have it erected, you could be forgiven for thinking it had all those features and more.

Finally, a space was needed inside the kitchen area for him to sleep at night, which meant that Jerry had to go. Jerry was a large mechanical giraffe – the sort you inserted ten pence into and had a ride on and, in this case, it was an old type ten pence piece. A former girlfriend had given it to me. Her father had a stately home and Jerry had adorned the teashop. She had kindly restored him for me and I had given him to Bethan one Christmas.

In the centre of the market place in Durham City is a statue of Charles William Vane Stewart, the third Marquis of Londonderry, seated on his war horse. A great cavalryman, in 1808, he led the Hussar Brigade and was adjutant general to the Duke of Wellington who, in turn, had nicknamed this flashing blade, 'The Bold Sabre'. If you ever have a quiz down at your local pub, you might like to know that, if a statue of a soldier on a horse has both legs in the air, the rider died in battle. If the horse has one leg in the air, the soldier died as a result of his wounds received in battle and finally, if the horse has all four legs on the ground, the person died of natural causes. The third Marquis of Londonderry's horse has just one hoof raised.

Anyway, where was I? Oh yes.

During World War II, apparently one of my ex girlfriend's relatives had suggested that the statue should be melted down to make shells and bullets. Londonderry may not have survived the Napoleonic War totally unscathed, but he seemed to have made it through the Second World War unmolested and he still stands, proudly looking down on the comings and goings in the market place. Jerry, being a comical sort of happy prancing giraffe had all four hooves off the ground as he merrily bounced along, supported as he was by some sort of 'shaky back and forth' type mechanism under his belly. I had no idea about the significance of this particular hoof arrangement, particularly for giraffes, but I suppose you could hazard a guess that it meant he was yesterday's toy and, as such, wouldn't survive the arrival of my new and exciting playmate. Jerry was unceremoniously ridden off into the shed.

❖ ❖ ❖

Bethan came over especially early one Saturday to take Barney to have his first set of injections. I had tried to take some photos of him but he was so jet black he just came out as a black blob. I thought he looked like he was made from black mercury and, when I rang and told my brother this, he feigned confusion.

"Is he a liquid metal?" he asked and pointed out that mercury wasn't black anyway, for that matter. He was sounding like that 'comic book' guy from the Simpsons.

Bethan and the thin, wild 'mercury' played in the front garden. At the start of the day, she had been very wary of him and would jump upon his approach but, by the end of the day, she had already taught him to sit and we were treated to a lesson entitled, "How to train your dog", with Bethan using Barney as a practical prop.

His quarantine wasn't wasted and, over the next couple of weeks, until he was ready for his final set of jabs, he grew used to wearing his collar, walking on the lead, responding to his name and still more sitting.

Most of the books I had read advocated getting up several times during the night to let the puppy out for a pee. As much as I loved my new best friend, I didn't love him *that* much. He was tethered on a short lead to an area in the corner of the kitchen/dining room where he slept on his little pillow bed.

This little pillow bed often adorned the roof of the kennel in the early days, as it dried in the sunshine, and I think the fact that knowing the postman knew he had wet his bed embarrassed him into learning to control his bladder pretty quickly.

The second set of injections completed, Barney was ready for the outside world.

CHAPTER NINE

Doggy Style

I had been too late to fight fascists in the Southern Seas but there had still been time to take up arms against the Communists in the East. The Falklands War may have been over but the Cold War was still as chilly as ever.

During this tense stand off, both sides spent a great amount of money, time and effort, gathering information about each other. I had been a sailor in the Royal Navy and spent some of this time getting chilly on such a mission, gathering information.

I guess our assignment at the time was deemed 'secret' as we weren't even allowed to tell our families where we were going. (If you happen to work for the Ministry of Defence, and the mission hasn't yet been de-classified, please skip the next few paragraphs). There were no letters sent back and forth and no phone calls. Instead, we were allowed to send a number of words to our loved ones, each month, via the 'Comms' room. We would give our twenty-word message to the Communications Officer who would then have it checked to ensure that we were not giving out any useful information that might be intercepted. This was then transmitted to a member of the Women's Royal Naval Service (Wren) in Whitehall or some such place (at that time, women didn't go to sea). From there, the message was relayed on to our wives or girlfriends (or both).

I deduced it was a Wren on the other end as one of the sailors, after being away from his young lady for four or five months, was taken to task for writing something that the

Lieutenant said was unsuitable for a young girl to have to pass on. The next week, the rating had obviously mended his ways and had thought deeply about his relationship and decided to commit to this young lady and use the money he had earned in the pursuit of romance as he promised her a pearl necklace on his return. Message approved – message sent.

I always assumed that the messages came out the other end on a long thin ribbon of paper but, only ever being on the transmitting end, I never knew. You would have to ask Susan.

Luckily, I never suffered from sea sickness, unlike the hero of Trafalgar, Admiral Lord Nelson, who suffered from acute sea sickness all his life. It can't make for a happy voyage if you don't like the rolling and pitching of the ocean, as a friend and 'almost' sailor once told me. His ambitions to join the Senior Service were put on the back burner after he took the ferry from Holland to Harwich and discovered that this particular type of aquatic illness comes in two stages. He described vividly how initially, you feel so nauseous, sweaty and queasy that you are genuinely scared you might die. Secondly, you feel even more nauseous, sweaty and queasy that you are genuinely scared you might *not* die.

He didn't actually die, but didn't need nature telling him twice and joined the Infantry instead. He told me he was much happier marching about on dry land and that I should try it sometime. I told him I might one day.

Overall, HMS Brilliant was a happy ship – unlike HMS Norfolk. The anti-submarine frigate had been headed for Hamburg, but for some reason, the crew weren't granted shore leave on their arrival. Whilst the official ship's motto might be 'Serving, I preserve', after their planned fun down the Reeperbahn was curtailed, the sailors gave her the new unofficial maxim 'No Singing, No Dancing, Norfolk'.

Where *we* were actually heading for were the Russian waters beyond the Arctic Circle and I was a Sub Lieutenant on board HMS Brilliant. On the 12th March 1985, at latitude 67 degrees 30 North and longitude 13 degrees East, we crossed the

Circle and into the land of the Midnight Sun.

Here, the Captain stopped the ship and many of the guys climbed from the quarterdeck into the water and quickly out again, just to be able to say that they had swum in the Arctic Circle. Not exactly shore leave, but the next best thing! We stopped the ship fairly regularly in the Mediterranean for such activities but, on this occasion, the sailors didn't seem to want to linger in the water for too long. We were all awarded certificates, signed apparently by Neptune, declaring us to be loyal and trusted 'Bluenoses'. All icebergs, whales, narwhals, sea lions and other creatures of the frigid north were ordered to show us due deference and respect, under pain of his royal displeasure. So there!

We were to proceed into the Russian territorial waters and observe their naval exercises, reporting back on their warships. The stakes were quite high in that we were told that if the Cold War ever got hot, as front line troops our life expectancy was about the same length of time as it took to boil an egg. I don't think they were talking Ostrich eggs. The British Army Journal in February 1949 offered the following helpful advice – *'The best defence against the atom bomb is not to be there when it goes off'.* Really? Is it really??

Anyway, we were there so we best used our preparation time by building additional structures on the deck out of old fenders and boxes in Blue Peter style, resembling extra radar and weapon systems, to confuse the enemy. In turn, I am sure they did exactly the same.

We then spent months in defence watches, noting down every detail we could about the Soviet vessels and probably spending far too much time detailing the additional structures that seemed to have sprung up overnight on their decks.

Innocent as it may seem, they didn't like us doing this and would use larger vessels to shield their exercise activity from us. Then things started to heat up a bit when we sustained damage after being rammed. The force of the impact sent me falling through a hatch and I ended up cracking my head open. As I lay there bleeding the deck a deep vermilion, I officially became a casualty of the Cold War.

However, the whole secret affair was exposed when a Soviet plane overshot the landing area on its ship and ditched in the sea. We were first to the rescue and took the pilot back onto our vessel before handing him back over to his countrymen. This was too good an opportunity to practise discretion and, suddenly, we were all over the papers at home.

'Our boys in the arctic save Russian pilot'.

I had become one of 'Our Boys'. Normally in the papers we are reported as 'drunken squaddies/sailors' but something like this happens and we suddenly become 'our boys'. Most bizarre.

Anyway, Mission Accomplished for this boy; time to put a candle in the window ... there's a traveller coming home.

Apart from these moments of high drama, the tour was quite uneventful and you might even say boring. As you laid in your scratcher with the safety belt on so you wouldn't get thrown out of bed as the ship tossed and pitched in the stormy seas, there was plenty of time to ponder on stuff that you wouldn't normally ponder on unless you really *did* have too much time on your hands. Did you know that, if you assume Rudolf is at the front, there are 40,320 ways to rearrange the other eight reindeer? And what were these reindeer games the other reindeers wouldn't let him play? I had arranged a couple of 'spot the difference' competitions but had to abandon this pastime in the end after an outcry when it was found out I was sometimes posting up two identical pictures for a laugh. So, what was the perfect antidote to boredom – a beard growing contest!

I returned home with a full set. This didn't prove to be a big hit with Susan and I was encouraged to remove it. To be honest, I think it was also a slight fire risk and, if anyone else has ever removed a similar amount of hair in one go (Whitney?), I'm sure they will readily agree that it doesn't half feel cold when all that insulation has been shaved off.

My next experiment with my 'look' was to follow many years later.

✻ ✻ ✻

Resplendent in Army combats, with the regulation whistle chain linking into my left breast pocket, MP (Military Police) armband, red beret, weapon and moustache, I thought I was Clark Gable with a sub machine gun. A teaspoon, as it happens, had replaced the whistle, as I believed I would more likely be required to stir a brew rather than whistle for help. We were on exercise in Wales and I had arranged to meet my best mate Tim.

Tim and I first met when we were in the Royal Anglians and he has remained my best friend ever since. He was now the recce platoon commander and, since I was with the Military Police, we hadn't seen each other for a while before reaching Sennybridge.

I wasn't sure if we had agreed to meet at the Police Station or the Mess and neither was Tim, which resulted in me walking from the Police station to the Mess and Tim walking from the Mess to the Police Station.

At first, he walked straight past me, as he didn't recognise me at all. Maybe he really thought I *was* Clark Gable!

Actually, my period of believing I was 'Ladies' choice' was very short lived when Tim later explained that he had just thought that I looked like, "Any other bastard Military Police Corporal," and had, therefore, thought it best to keep well away, on the other side of the road.

I retained the moustache for a while, but it didn't seem to hold the same attraction for me after that. In the end, efforts to keep both sides even, constant uneven trimmings and hasty re-trimmings, left me with something resembling a Hitler-type affair so I decided to call it a day with this particular experiment and revert to the world of the clean-shaven.

My current look is unshaven, with tired eyes, sticky up hair and a tennis ball in one pocket as I get up at 'whip crack sparrow' to take Barney out for his morning constitutional. As luck would have it, apart from the tennis ball, I think this look *is* the latest fashion too.

❖ ❖ ❖

I must admit, as much as I hadn't wanted the Communists to triumph, I wasn't particularly bothered if dogs suddenly took over the world, as I had been pretty decent to Barney and I was sure that he would see me right. However, I had not bargained for his complete ambivalence to the things I did for him.

The path along the riverbank varies in distance from the water below. Sometimes, it is almost level with the river when the tide is in and at other places, it is twenty feet or so above it. On one of his very first walks, Barney was hopping about in one of his mad half-hour sessions, jumping like a spring lamb, until he made one leap too many and jumped off the path, down the near vertical bank and straight into the water.

Despite the fact that I had recently taken out full insurance on him, I leapt into action. I had no idea whether he could swim or not and the current can be quite strong in certain parts. The only place that I could scramble down was ten yards or so upstream and, as luck would have it, Barney was doggy paddling in that direction too. Grabbing the sodden dog, I wrenched him out of the water, thrust him under my left arm and struggled up the bank, cutting my hands on the brambles, whilst encrusting myself in a foul smelling concoction of dirty river water and thick mud in the process.

On reaching the top, he just pottered off and went to sniff something new – no thanks or grateful glance at his saviour. Nothing! The sodding sodden dog.

The times I had cleaned up his stinking turds because he didn't seem to have the time; the numerous occasions I had bought him toys and the meals that I lovingly prepared every day seemed to count for nothing. Unlike Scooby Doo, he hadn't even solved any mysteries yet. I was beginning to feel that maybe I had bought a dud.

CHAPTER TEN

Trouble Over Bridgewater

Whitby is where Dracula came ashore when, disguised as a dog, he jumped ship and ran up the 199 steps to the old Anglo Saxon church of St. Mary – as a black dog so it happens! This was also to be the location for *my* black dog's first big day out.

Situated on the Yorkshire coastline, Whitby's skyline is dominated by the ruins of St. Hilda's Abbey, high on the East Cliff. Spreading below is a maze of alleyways and narrow streets, running down to the busy quayside. Captain Cook once lived there and it was, at one time, the main whaling port for the North East of England. Today, it's a combination of a quaint old fishing village and tacky holiday resort.

Don't get me wrong – I'm not knocking tacky holiday resorts. Bethan and I have spent many a happy hour on the two pence waterfall machines. We start by raiding my retirement fund (a big bowl of one and two pence pieces under the sink) and then proceed to feed all the coins into the machine's slot, including all the winnings, until there is nothing left. I've never been quite sure what we achieve but we seem to have fun doing it. In fact, whoever owns a two pence waterfall machine is onto a winner as, in all my years, I've never heard anybody say, "We're eight pence up – let's call it quits while we're ahead!"

Don't ask me how it was done but somehow Deborah had taught Barney to walk to heel. The first walk in the outside world started with about three yards' worth of sparks flying from Barney's bum as he sat down, refusing to co-operate and had to be dragged along the street. But, thereafter, he knew the game was up and walked perfectly.

So it was that Bethan, Deborah, Barney and I arrived in the town for the first of many socialisation trips. Apparently, it's important for a puppy to be exposed to as many things as possible in the early days, to prevent him developing a negative reaction when he comes across something unfamiliar in later life.

He was like a little hoover, eating all the dropped bits of ice cream cones and sweets as he was led through the thronging streets, which made us wonder if we should have called him 'Dyson' instead. He was patted and fussed over by the whole world and his wife and even got to have a good sniff at the doorway of a kipper-smoking shed (where kippers are smoked before onward progression to the breakfast table, as opposed to some bizarre kind of club where kippers can relax and have a fag). He also learnt what it was like to feel the sand between uneven numbered toes and to climb too many steps in one go. He slept all the way home.

This expedition was followed by days at Beamish Country Park, Durham town, the Waldridge Fells and just about anywhere else where he could encounter new experiences.

❖ ❖ ❖

One big advantage Barney did have was that he allowed me to meet a whole load of new people. Everybody wanted to meet this cute thing.

I had read about a system some years back for remembering names – all you had to do was associate the person you wanted to remember with some characteristic of theirs. Next time you wanted to recall their name, you just conjured this image in your mind and their name would come to you in a flash. The trouble with this was that I found I just stuck with the idea and, in the end, it was easier to remember people by the nicknames I had invented for them, rather than persevere with the next step.

On holiday in Tunisia with Deborah, we didn't know

anyone's name. Everyone was just given a nickname based on some characteristic, something they had done or, as in one case, because I had dreamt it. We had 'tortoise girl'; 'the couple on the outside'; 'the beanies'; 'Debso's stunt double' and 'the 2nd richest couple in Durham', to name but a few. One particularly attractive twenty-something girl was christened 'Flip flops and lip gloss' because she told us she was a body parts model, and both her feet and mouth had been used in adverts. During a trip to the desert, unsurprisingly our guide took a particular fancy to 'Flip flops and lip gloss', chatting her up and promising he could get her work as a hand model at his friend's jewellery shop, but I really think he just wanted to get her legs a part.

At dinner in the desert, the 2nd richest couple regaled us with the tale of their trip to the 'medina' or market place a few days earlier. It was actually the wife who began the story, which was obviously causing her husband much embarrassment as he was shaking his hands and making 'keep quiet if you know what's good for you' type gestures behind our backs, but to no avail. Well to no avail to her, but as for me, on seeing this, I pulled my chair in closer and listened even more intently.

Apparently, whilst in the medina, they had been approached by an Arab who enquired whether they wanted a 'special' personal tour behind the scenes at a Mosque. He then led them through the narrow streets to a side door and, as they entered, they were advised to take their shoes off and advised that it would be polite to give the 'shoe attendant', (who looked uncannily like the Arab's mother) some coins.

They were then led into a room, which looked very much like someone's front room, but with a table at the end. As they looked around someone's front room with a table at the end, another Mosque assistant then informed them that it was customary for visitors to lay some money on the table (bizarre as it may sound, this assistant also bore an uncanny resemblance to the Arab). As the 2nd richest husband produced his 20 dinar note, he was told that it was custom, before laying it on the table, to "kiss your money". Despite the fact that he felt like he was on some Tunisian version of 'You've been framed', he duly complied by kissing his money goodbye.

He told us he felt that he had been conned – the victim of the world's politest mugging – and I believe he was right. To be fooled was one thing, but to be told to kiss your money goodbye and to actually *do so* was too embarrassing for words, he confided in us.

"This will be *our* little secret?" he implored. Yes, it would be – our little secret, all the other people on the bus' little secret and now your little secret.

Overall I enjoyed Tunisia ...the friendly people, the scenery and fascinating places. El Jem just looks like any other small town in the middle of the desert, yet it is the home of a magnificently preserved amphitheatre that could seat 60,000 spectators (and where much of the movie Gladiator was filmed). The next day we were in the Troglodyte village of Mamata – which was featured in the film Star Wars as Luke Skywalker's home. The Troglodytes live in caves that they dig vertically into the ground – you can actually stand on the edge and look down into them. From Mediterranean coast, through ancient cities, sun baked deserts and rugged mountains – Tunisia is a fantastic place to visit. Except for one big disappointment – sparrows. Don't get me wrong, I like sparrows. We are losing our sparrows in Britain – I miss them – but I was expecting to see something just a little more exotic when I got to foreign climes. Tunisia however was full of little familiar brown sparrows. I just felt like they were all taking their holiday the same time as me and that we should all feel a bit embarrassed that we had booked the same holiday resort. What happened to flocks of wild budgies and brightly coloured parrots. Personally Deborah likes a cockatoo and I love any exotic bird. But sparrows? I'm sure I even recognised a few of them. It seems however that some of our little feathered friends couldn't afford the fare for the flight home as when I got back to Britain, there seemed to be even less sparrows about than when I had left.

Back home, the names continued. The woman who knew everyone's business in the street was 'Badfinger' because she had once come to me for advice when she had cut hers. Bill, who had lived next door to me, was a Marine during the Second World War and, when he died, Terry moved in. But for me, Terry would always be 'Bill's replacement'. A lot of detailed analysis and mature thought goes into each name you understand; for example the skinny woman up the road is called 'Skinny woman', the weird kid down the street is 'Weird kid' and a woman I know who uses too much mascara is 'Panda'. The fat guy up the road is 'Spiderman' because he looks like he couldn't get out of the bath on his own while the old woman three doors down is 'The Olympic Flame' because she never goes out, and so on, ad nauseum.

Apparently, even *I* was not immune from this treatment, as I was subsequently informed by Tim that, when I first appeared at the barracks, I was known as 'That Welsh Bloke'. The benefit of being Welsh in somewhere as English as Cambridge meant that my nickname was based on my nationality as opposed to some embarrassing characteristic. At school in Wales, where everybody at school was Welsh (except Susan), I was known as 'Donkey'.

I also shared a generic nickname, of course. As a Military Policeman, the other soldiers knew me, along with my fellow MP's, as a Monkey. I never really figured out why we were called this, as it was us who put *them* behind bars.

Despite having lived in the same street for seven years, people at the park end had always seemed a bit of a mystery to me. This group of shadowy figures actually turned out to be very pleasant individuals who would stop and chat, passing the time of day with the ingrate and myself as we went on our daily meanderings.

Barney had solved his first mystery!

* * *

There are many books available on how to train your dog and a few excellent ones on dog psychology. There are also some very good books on how to raise your baby, with all the relevant technical information included. What I couldn't really find was a book on how to be a good dad and how I could really develop the bond with my daughter, so I eventually decided to take matters into my own hands. I still remember a treasure hunt that I went on as a child and how much I had enjoyed it. I therefore resolved to arrange a treasure hunt for Bethan.

It was at a time when Bethan was studying the Egyptian period at school, so I decided that the hunt would have a similar theme. Drawing a map of the local area, I worked out good locations to hide each of the clues. The next task was to actually devise rhyming clues. As it was an Egyptian affair, the clues were then converted into hieroglyphics and carefully written onto parchment paper. Finally, to make it seem more authentic, the paper was soaked in tea for several hours to age it and then torn around the edges. Decoding books had been prepared for her and her friend and, on the morning of the hunt, I ran and drove to the different points, placing everything in position.

A picnic lunch of food that would have a Pharaoh-type theme (chocolate marshmallows as sphinx dung, etc.) was prepared and the scene was set. After the weeks it had taken to plan the event, it was all over in about four to five hours but I felt that every second I had spent on it had been worth it. Bethan and her friend loved it too.

The point is that, if you want something to work well, it's worth putting in the effort.

Similarly, I knew that if I wanted to own an obedient dog, I would need to put in the effort with Barney. However, realising that he probably wouldn't really appreciate a treasure hunt, I enrolled my new best friend for a series of puppy socialisation classes at the local dog centre.

Sitting in a hot stuffy arena at nine on a Sunday morning was not my idea of the ideal way to spend the last day of the weekend, but I was standing by my principles and Barney, in turn, was standing by me. Bethan, Deborah and I had already spent a considerable amount of time training our pupil so I hoped that he was already going to be ahead of most of the class.

I had learnt at an early stage in the forces not to volunteer for anything and, with that philosophy in mind, we quietly sat back while Barney just excelled at whatever activity was called for at the appropriate time. We hadn't set ourselves up as something special so that the others would love to see us trip and fall off our pedestal. Instead, we were just one of the team who seemed to pick things up quickly. When the trainer asked the owners how they would like their pooches to walk and one girl replied, "Like Barney!" I knew we had cracked it. At least, superficially anyway. However, his prowess in the exercise ring concealed a deep, dark secret. The image of Barney as the perfect pup was as misleading as a whited sepulchre.

* * *

I have a varied taste in music, which is imperative with a ten-year-old daughter. I suppose I first became interested in music generally during my last few years at school and records by 'Elvis Costello' and 'The Jam' initiated my collection. Forty five revolutions a minute. I seemed to have missed out on the 'New Romantics', and a whole swathe of the Eighties in general, because I was away at sea (I also seem to have missed out when they explained how sudoko works and how much fun it's supposed to be). When I returned, I picked up with 'The Style Council', 'Madness', 'Billy Bragg' and 'The Men They Couldn't Hang'.

To Bethan, who is used to CDs, the concept of plate sized vinyl records seems very strange. The quality on them was nowhere near as good as CDs and it was sometimes a revelation to discover what people were actually singing.

It seems that Whitney Houston was 'saving all her love for you', rather than 'shaving off her muff for you'. I preferred my version. In 'La Isla Bonita', Madonna was saying that 'last night, she dreamt of 'San Pedro', not 'Some Dago', and the 'trendy vicar' that Neil Diamond sung about in the Seventies never existed either – there never was a 'Reverend Blue Jeans'. I also went along with what I thought Kim Carnes was saying, but I always wondered why, in the 'Bette Davies Eye' song, she was saying, 'All the boys thinks she's a spaz,' when I thought they were supposed to like her. Apparently, I now learn that they thought she was a spy (and while I'm on the subject, Sam or Dave from 'Sam and Dave' wasn't telling you he was some bizarre kind of superhero called 'arsehole man', but rather was eager to inform you that he was 'a soul man').

I still have my collection in a big box under the stairs, although the apparatus to play them on has long since departed. Today, my CD rack is filled with the likes of 'The Lowest of the Low', 'Weddings Parties Anything', 'Overnight Jones' and 'Me First and the Gimme Gimmes'. I've had to keep up to date with the top ten though, via Bethan's car play list and, before that, in every Army truck, there would always be one squaddie who had brought along a ghetto blaster tuned into Radio One.

I put up with it but I do prefer songs that tell a story. I know that sounds old fashioned but I like to hear the lyrics. However, for some inexplicable reason, when it comes down to it, I seem to like songs with lists in them best of all. And, if you are talking about list songs, the greatest must be the one hit wonder, 'You're moving out today' by Carol Bayer Sager. If you can't remember it, it's the one that goes:

"Pack up your rubber duck, I'd like to wish you luck.
Your funny cigarettes, your sixty one cassettes," etc.

There are lots of "la la la la la las" in it too because she is so happy that he is moving out. I know how she feels – sometimes I would happily start singing if Barney were to pack his bag with his little food bowl and collection of toys and wander off into the sunset.

Generally, he is a great companion but, now and again, he

turns into a canine version of a Nazi storm trooper. Maybe Carol could make a ditty out of some of the items he has destroyed, either of his own volition or egged on, and often assisted, by Tess.

He no longer has a bed after eating his own (twice), together with Tess' replacement bed. I also had to buy a new telephone after he bit off the connection end and Deborah has had to say, 'Goodbye' to some candle holders and several ornaments. My astro turf doormat has now been trimmed to resemble a map of Australia, whilst the aglets on shoelaces (the plastic bit at the end of the lace for 'pub quiz' reference) hold a strange fascination for him.

Deborah's garden has been almost denuded of plants and replaced with deep holes. Large sections of the yard wall have had the paint scraped off them and my dining chairs have suffered bite marks on the lower reaches. Various escape attempts have resulted in my beloved new fence looking as if it has been attacked by a very large and very hungry wood eating monster. Postcards stuck onto the fridge along with the fridge magnets that held them there have also been unceremoniously eaten and shat out by that so-called 'Man's best friend', including a postcard of the Pope (straight to Hell Barney – do not pass Go – do not collect £200 worth of dog biscuits!). Gone is my 'useful stirring stick' that is required to be kept (by law I think) by all males over 21 to prove they are a proper bloke. I even think he has changed the station on my radio. A hole was chewed in a brand new fleece, two hours after being bought and my notebook, containing all my ideas and things that should be invented, is now papier-mâché (how about a freezing spray so that soft turds can be frozen and more easily collected and bagged?). I left a trail of water through the house as I filled a watering can and took it into the garden, only to realise too late that Barney had earlier chewed a big hole in the bottom of it.

Deborah has had plugs chewed off two lamps (she was most upset that they weren't switched on at the time!) and, to top it all, having checked the small print of my insurance, I don't think I'm covered for, 'Act of dog'. All in all, Carol could write a bloody 'list' musical about him as he potters from room to room destroying things.

> *"Pack up your rubber bone, I hope you never phone,*
> *So no more walks at eight, I'll stay in bed till late,*
> *La la la la la la, la la la la la la …"*

CHAPTER ELEVEN

Soldier 'X'

Barney was not well. I returned from work one day to be greeted by an horrendous sight.

The vilest turd imaginable adorned my yard and it was so disgusting that even the flies refused to settle on it. Barney lay half in and half out of his kennel, with his head in his paws, looking pathetic. His sad eyes looked at me the way they do best – sadly. However, I had not completed my Special Investigations course with the RMP (Royal Military Police) for nothing and I deduced that Barney was somehow the culprit in this sorry scene. He was in no condition to be interrogated though and I guessed that, in his state, the only way he could have communicated to me was by farting and I doubted that he could even do that safely.

When I'm feeling ill, I want all the sympathy that I so richly deserve as I plunder one of my hypochondriac supply kits, packed with various pills and medication. As I potter about rattling, I am also open to offers of comics and cake-like things.

Yet, Barney wasn't able to ring me at work and tell me he was feeling a bit under the weather. He probably had pains where his butterflies should have been, but he had been left alone, to suffer in silence. I felt guilty.

The warning signs had been there on his morning walk. After depositing his first poop of the day, he had sprinted off as if he wanted nothing more to do with it. He had half resembled a giraffe as he completed this exercise, stretching his neck so that his sniffing apparatus was as far away as it could possibly be from the stink-making mechanism. I had searched in vain for the deposit with my bright blue poop bag as he pretended nothing had happened.

I didn't know what I could do to ease his suffering so I rang Deborah. Deborah said it would pass, so I filled his bowl with fresh water, gave him a pat on the head and went in to watch telly.

Just to reassure anyone who is concerned, Barney was fine the next day; hopping around like a mad thing as if nothing had happened.

I am under the impression that there are supposed to be about seven or so dog years for every human year so, the fact that he was fully recovered the next day, would be like a human taking the week off to recuperate – the canine malingerer!

❖ ❖ ❖

That day, I read a report about Ben the Thylacine. They were thinking of cloning him with some of the DNA he had so conveniently left behind. I have never had any strong views either way on cloning but that seemed like a good idea. I missed Ben.

I once knew a girl called Joanne who laughed at all my jokes. I missed her too. She should definitely be cloned as well – a few times. She was a girl in a million, which is great really because that means that there are at least another twenty six or so like her pottering about just in England and Wales alone.

I was also fully aware that people became attached to their pets. On walks with Barney, strangers would often stop us and, as they petted Barney, or tried to avoid his wee as my puppy became over excited, they would say something like, "We had a Labrador once." I knew that a sad tale was about to follow and it would entail a story about a faithful companion who had gone to that big park in the sky, where dogs sniffed each other's bums to their hearts content. I was at a loss what to say to them and wondered if I was supposed to say, "Here have this one then." I felt like it sometimes, but more out of being sick of Barney than in any act of compassion. Cloning a pet was something I hadn't needed to ponder on before.

As for cloning Barney, it all depended on which day of the week I was asked. I was going through a love/hate relationship with Barney at the time and I wondered how he would have felt if he had known this.

In turn, I wondered what Barney thought too sometimes. I wasn't sure, but I had a hunch. It was probably something along the lines of, *"Sleep, food, turd, food, play, sleep, food, run about like a mad thing, turd, food, sleep."*

❋ ❋ ❋

I, on the other hand, was thinking about hosiery. We were at the camping shop searching for a length of hose for the camping gaz cooker. I asked the assistant if they stocked such a thing and he replied that they sold it by the metre. As I feigned ignorance of where the meter was, to nobody's amusement, Deborah noticed something outrageous.

The focus of her fascination was a wildly extravagant claim being made about a tent that could be erected in *twenty* seconds. If this was the case, it was indeed miraculous. The last outrageous claim I had come across was at a furniture store called, 'The Sofa King'. They had claimed that their prices were, 'Sofa King Low'. As a Catholic, of course, I had been on camping holidays numerous times and, due to the British weather, on more than one occasion, I have even had to take part in digging a mini moat around the tent. During one particularly torrential downpour, my dad had to use the axe to excavate a channel through the middle of the tent to let the water flow out the other side whilst choruses of, "Don't touch the sides! Don't touch the sides!" abounded. Curse those Protestants in their cosy caravans!

The rain was part and parcel of 'doing the right thing' but

the one aspect of these holidays that I really didn't enjoy was erecting and taking down the tent. I was also normally assigned blowing up airbed duties. I have never taken any illicit drug, but I guess they must produce that same spaced out feeling that blowing continually into a rubber inflatable bed creates. Hell, there were even self-inflating airbeds in this camp shop!

Stopwatch in hand, the female assistant was challenged to produce a three-berth tent in the requisite time. In its dormant state, the tent looked a bit like a collapsed spider but the assistant grabbed the spider's body, pulled him upwards and his disjointed legs just snapped into place.

Twenty-seven seconds – what a con! Still, I was in a forgiving mood. Sold – one spider tent. This would be just the thing to impress Paul.

* * *

You may recall that I have two brothers, Paul and Neil. They sat in the back seat next to the windows but time has moved on. Paul has his own car now and I believe he sits in the front.

He has had a varied life, having been a labourer and almost becoming a Doctor. He has also performed experiments on people (more in a 'how can we cure Alzheimer's?' sort of way rather than a 'Joseph Mengels' approach; or something like that – I forget now). A year or so was spent as a science teacher in the roughest comprehensive in Wales and he has also sold drugs (again, more in the line of 'how can we cure Alzheimer's?' as opposed to supplying Crack and Speed to his former pupils).

His current incarnation is that of police officer in the South Wales Constabulary or 'Heddlu' as about 0.2% of the population of Wales would prefer to call it. I am not certain if that percentage is correct but, apparently, 87.3% of all statistics are made up anyway. I'll have to check with my Uncle John. Like the phantom banana, Paul has actually completed the London Marathon too.

His family are the living embodiment of the Simpsons and,

what is more, we had planned to go camping with them in the summer.

I could just picture it now. A few practice drills and the technique would be mastered. Within twenty seconds of arriving at the campsite, Deborah and I would be sitting outside our tent, drinking beer, while Homer, Marge and the crew struggled with their pile of poles and canvas.

Paul had started off by saying that we should meet halfway, having somehow calculated this as being the Birmingham orbital ring road, although he had said that there wasn't a lot for the kids to do there. Consequently, his rather flexible notion of halfway was extended, with me going all the way down to South Wales.

Did I mention that Barney would be coming too?

※ ※ ※

Meanwhile, Barney had gone deaf! My obedient pup wasn't obeying my commands anymore. Maybe I had been playing the music too loud after all. It must have driven him potty too because he seemed to prefer eating horse dung in the park to playing 'fetch' with me. Most scary of all, he was even developing immunity to his corrective water treatment.

If he were a country right now, he would be planning to invade Poland. He was even committing the heinous crime of 'hanging about' while I was eating. I could see someone else's hand in this, or was it a paw? I suspected Tess' influence.

Whilst she was normally a perfectly well behaved bitch (pause for sniggers to subside), she did have a few habits I'd rather she didn't pass on to my pup. The hanging round the table was one. Tess also seemed to have a barking problem and, if Debs went near her lead, Tess would be spinning around yelping, until she got the walk she expected. The barking was the same when anyone rang the doorbell. I suspected that I knew the cause and I suspected that Deborah knew that I knew.

If this were a film and not a book, we would now hear

funny, shimmery type music and the screen would go all wobbly. As we emerged on the other side, Deborah would have a different hairstyle and be wearing hot pants or something similar. The whole scene would be dazzling, as if it had been sun bleached and Tess would be a puppy.

Jingle, jangle, jingle, jangle. Deborah would be shaking the collar and lead. "Walkies! Who wants to go on a little walkies? Tessie wants to go on a walkies," and so on, ad nauseam. Deborah would only desist when Tess was wound up into a little frenzy.

Presently, Deborah would be sitting on a sofa as the doorbell goes. It is probably one that plays a tune, just to help reinforce the fact that this was a long time ago. "Who's that, Tessie? Who's at the door? See who it is, good Tessie." Good Tessie, at this stage, would be barking and scrabbling at the door. More shimmery music and wobbly screen and we are back to the present day.

I hear no comment from Deborah. She knows I am right.

I preferred Barney's relative muteness. I was determined not to let him tell me what we should do together but other factors were at work. Barney was becoming an adolescent and my seven year to one year theory was coming back to haunt me. I had a rebel dog on my hands. He might look like a cute version of Sweep, with his big ears flapping in the wind as he darted about with his squeaky toy, but this was no ordinary Sweep ...this was the arrival of Che Sweep!

* * *

When we are out on our walks, if another dog is walking towards us or if we are approaching a tasty looking dump of horse manure, I usually put Barney on the lead until we pass them/it. After we pass, I let him off the lead again and it never seems to occur to Barney to turn round and go back to visit his new playmate/snack. Instead, he just happily dwells on what is ahead of him.

It is just this type of behaviour that has prevented dogs from taking over the world. At five months, Barney can walk, run, fetch and forage for food, whereas the baby up the street can barely sit up on his own at that age. Instead of exploiting this natural advantage, the dog just potters on, looking for more stuff to sniff – stuff that's in front of him. Meanwhile, baby grows up, gets a dog of his very own, who in turn grows up and just potters on, looking for stuff to sniff – stuff that's in front of him. So much for evolution! It would be cruel to mock Barney's IQ level too much though, as I have known a few people in my time who would make him look like a genius.

* * *

We were in Amsterdam. We seemed to have spent that whole summer either on exercise or docked in Amsterdam or Hamburg. I was on HMS Newcastle, a Destroyer, and our next tour of duty was due to be the 'Armilla patrol', keeping the Gulf open during the Iraq/Iran war.

A friend of mine, meanwhile, had spent the whole after-noon writing a letter and telling all his adventures to a female friend, who he said had an 'amazing body'. I didn't ask if it was the 'Roll up, Roll up' type of amazing or a 'perfect ten' sort of amazing. They say love is blind, but in his case I would hazard a guess that it's probably just a bit short sighted. Anyway, as we proceeded ashore for some more adventures, he stopped under-neath a big sign which seemed to read something like, 'Jesus is my friend', whereupon he posted his cherished correspondence into a large red metal dustbin. In hindsight, he admitted that the 'post box' had looked a bit dirty and seemed to have a rather large mouth on it. I don't think Jesus was his friend after all.

The next contender was a soldier in my platoon who, in a bid to keep his breath fresh and healthy, gargled with mouth-wash daily, which was good. However, not fully knowing the mechanics of the process, he then spat the contents back into the bottle. By the end of a few weeks, it was swimming with sediment and unidentifiable 'bits'. Of course, this was not so good, although we did all admit that it was very cost effective.

Finally, a fellow officer on my promotions board was telling me of his first, and nearly last, military experience.

Arriving late for his pre-Army liaison exercise, he was thrown a sleeping bag and told to get his head down. The rest of the unit had already set up camp in a clearing in the woods and were sleeping in the darkness. The standard issue sleeping bags, at the time, had a zip up the middle and toggles dotted along each edge. This was so that the bag could be folded into the middle and toggled up, before being rolled up and stored in the pocket attached to the pillow end. In the dark, Soldier 'X' unrolled the green sleeping device, felt around for the toggles and untied them. The sleeping bag was now in position to take his tired body but, in his weary state, he had overlooked the zip.

He subsequently told me that he rationalised this in his mind thus, *"There can't be a zip as this is the army and the sound of a zip might alert the enemy – hence the silent toggles."* He then lay on the bag and attempted to do up the toggles around him. He could just about tie the ones around his feet, the ones round his thighs were tight and he could only manage the chest ones if he breathed in and continued to do so in short pant-like actions. He said he had the worst night of his life, trussed up like a hungry caterpillar, panting in shallow spurts for fear of popping open the attachments, and freezing cold as the large oblong gaps between the straining toggles were no defence against the chill night air.

In fact stupidity has got to such epidemic proportions that the government have even started to tax it now. The stupider you are, the more tax you pay. Except instead of calling it a 'stupid tax' they called it 'The National Lottery'.

❊ ❊ ❊

Bethan was busy shining the torch around on the kitchen floor while Barney was intent on chasing the mysterious blob of light that seemed to be moving erratically around the same area.

"Dance monkey, dance!" I shouted from the sidelines.

I had already taught Barney how to shake hands and the thought of getting him to dance on command appealed.

Bethan is the real dancer of the family and her shelves are straining under the weight of awards and trophies. She has appeared in shows and pantomimes and seems to have a real talent but, to be honest, she seems to excel in anything she tries.

I, on the other hand, have only ever won one trophy. It wasn't even a trophy really – it was a football medal. I had led my team to victory in an RMP inter-unit football match. My magnificent tackle was the talk of the ladies in the Mess afterwards, but I was most proud of my fantastic winning goal. I gave my medal to Bethan but, when I asked her about it recently, she said it was probably in one of her drawers somewhere. Maybe. Perhaps.

Barney danced on. The sight of animals performing human-type acts has always amused me.

In Tenerife, I even saw a parrot riding a pushbike – a small, parrot-sized pushbike I hasten to add. It happened in a zoo – if it had occurred in the wild, it would have been just a bit too bizarre. In Tunisia, I watched guinea pigs sitting, eating at the table and, in Poland, observed a chicken playing a guitar. I once read that, in Germany, a guy had trained his black Labrador to make a Nazi salute on command but that's just naughty.

Whilst at the zoo, I was approached by a Spanish couple who asked me to take their photo. I had been waiting for an opportunity like this for years. As they gave me their camera and posed together, I made a big show of squaring them up in the viewfinder. Then, at the last moment, I pretended to make a run for it with their camera, before stopping and taking the picture. The look on their faces was a picture, so to speak – a mixture of panic, relief and giggling, all rolled into one. It was the same type of smile you have when you see someone catch their pocket on a door knob – you know you shouldn't find it funny, but you can't help it. I wish I could have been there when they had it developed. They laughed, I laughed and the parrot cycled on.

❖ ❖ ❖

Dancing aside, Barney is developing into quite an agreeable little companion. They say that small things please small minds and I think they must be right. I like routine and I had started one with him. In the morning, when I come downstairs, I pretend to act shocked to see a small dog, sitting, wagging its tail in the corner of the kitchen. In turn, Barney humours me and pretends to act equally surprised and excited to see me.

At other times, his little mind must think that I'm cold, as he will just turn up, unannounced, with a single sock or a used pair of underpants from my washing basket, in a bid to keep me warm. Charming!

He even seems to know that he has affected my finances, having to pay for all his accoutrements and those breakages at Deborah's house. Since his arrival, many is the time that Elizabeth Fry has looked up at me with those sad eyes and that lonely expression on her face as she sits, without a soul for company, in the emptiness of my wallet.

Therefore, he understands that I can only afford one tennis ball and so very kindly goes and gets it and brings it back for me, if I have been careless enough to throw it away when we have been in the park.

At other times, he just comes up and sits, leaning against me, or curls up in a ball at my feet. If he is just lying asleep on the floor, I even feel guilty if I wake him as I get up to fetch something. He'll look at me as if to say, "What is it? Do you want me to come with you?" Despite the fact that I tell him it's OK and he can stay resting, he will raise his weary little body and trot after me. Sometimes, I bet he just lies there thinking, "*I'm the luckiest dog in the world,*" or probably more likely "*food, turd, sleep*".

❖ ❖ ❖

Knowing what I now know about dogs, I feel very ashamed of

myself when I think of the time I was at my Aunty Esther's house.

My Aunty Esther is actually my mum's step mum, but that proved too much of a mouthful so she is Aunty Esther or AE to some. No one is quite sure how old she is and no one seems brave enough to ask.

She was explaining how my brother Paul had run the Marathon in aid of 'Hearing dogs for the deaf'. My confusion may have been inadvertently misinterpreted as ridicule, as I began my monologue.

It went along the lines of, "So the owner is sitting reading and the phone rings. The dog then jumps up, runs over to his owner and starts nudging him with his nose and running back and forth between him and the phone. '*Aha*', thinks the owner, '*Bonzo is telling me the phone is ringing*'. Owner picks up the 'phone. 'Hello, hello … anyone there? Hello … There's no one there you stupid mutt!' Deaf man then replaces the receiver and proceeds to kick dog up the arse for disturbing his read for nothing." And so on.

She waited until after I had finished my tirade, following which an uncomfortable silence had descended upon the room. She then uttered a single word. Having *since* looked it up in the dictionary for clarification, I now know that she thought I was an unpleasant and/or stupid person/also an unpleasant term for female genitals.

Poor Aunty Esther. I never realised she suffered from Tourettes.

CHAPTER TWELVE

It Must Be Someone's Birthday

When I was young, I harboured an ambition to become a Priest or, more precisely, our local Priest harboured an ambition for me to become a Priest. Even then, Father Dunn seemed like he was an old guy. He spoke like a Dalek and, later on, became Cannon Dunn. Maybe they wanted to fire him. I didn't know what his first name was and neither did I expect that I should know. In those days, it was, 'Father Surname', not 'Father First name'. Anyway, Father Dunn approached my dad to see if I wanted to join up.

I thought long and hard about it. It seemed a good position and I would have a captive congregation every Sunday who would *have* to laugh at my jokes. When I was a boy, visiting Priests would give Mass every now and again and one or two would tell a joke during the sermon. They were rubbish but they still managed to produce a polite laugh from the congregation.

I suspected that, having to look after the sick of the parish, would soon make me sick of the parish, but the joke thing still had me hanging on. When the Father visited our house, it was a special event and he would normally decline the sedate cup of tea in favour of something a little stronger and he was visiting houses all day long! For someone like me, who wasn't going to set the academic world on fire, it might be a good option. It seemed that the only real talent needed was to look sympathetic and occasionally chant something in Latin, in a 'sing songy' voice, which sounded rather like, "I can play dominoes better than you can."

Brother Paul, in the family sense rather than the 'monk-type' sense, once bought a car from a Priest. The Father had explained that there were a number of different lights on the dashboard and he wasn't exactly sure what they all did. He told Paul that the green light came on when the headlights were on and, now and again, a blue light would appear next to it. He wasn't exactly sure what that was for but, when it was on, people in other cars tended to become more friendly and flash him with their lights as if to say, "Hello."

Having to work at the weekend wasn't what I really wanted in a job either but it seemed to be par for the course for a member of the clergy.

What ultimately put me off was that I had no interest at all in golf. It seemed that, every Wednesday, all the Priests would gather together and play eighteen holes. I remember one visiting Priest explaining during the sermon that Father 'X' had died whilst taking a putt on the 14th green, on the previous Wednesday. He said it caused the rest of the Priests much distress, as they had to carry him round as they played the final five holes. There was a shuffle of feet in the congregation and someone coughed. I don't think they were too sure how to take that. Maybe this was what they meant by, 'A bridge too far'.

I decided that a career in the Priesthood wasn't for me just yet; maybe later. For now, I would go for the life of sin, conveniently followed by a deathbed repentance. With the Priesthood option temporarily out of the window, I needed to look for another career.

Unlike Bethan, who has a variety of different hobbies and interests, at her age I was just content to ride around on my bike with my mate 'Hicksey' or play football up in Cyncoed Park. Around about the time we had to choose our options at school, I realised that I didn't really have a clue what I wanted to do.

Then my dad took me to see the Military Tattoo, held in Cardiff Castle. I remember vividly to this day that there was the most fantastic re-enactment of 'The Defence of Rorke's Drift', one of the most glorious episodes in British Military history.

In a small Swedish mission station, in deepest Zululand, in January 1879, around one hundred soldiers from the 24th Regiment of Foot, The South Wales Borderers, held out against nearly four and a half thousand Zulu warriors. The rifles used were the single-shot Henry Martini type.

Twenty thousand rounds of ammunition were fired and rifle barrels became so hot that fingers and palms were scorched and the soldiers had to use rags to hold them. They had been firing continuously, changing shoulders when they became too bruised and sore from the recoil. Fierce hand-to-hand combat ensued and, whilst bayonets were effective, they often snapped off in the struggle. The soldiers' clothes were ripped and stained with blood. Many could hardly speak due to the choking smoke and the heat but, against all odds, the garrison held out. Eleven Victoria Crosses, the highest award for gallantry, were won that day – the most ever to be awarded in any single action. The Castle echoed with the sound of gunfire. This was fantastic.

Elsewhere, Sailors challenged Soldiers in field gun trials; marching bands filled the air with their music and motorcycles raced around the arena performing death-defying stunts. I also noticed that the girls seemed to look in awe at the men in their uniforms – a Venus Flytrap.

I had found my vocation. I would serve my Queen and Country, conscripted by the thought of adventure and women, rather than any ideology. Here was something to live for rather than something to die for, and something to be proud of, whichever way you looked at it.

✳ ✳ ✳

We have a chequered military history in our family. Great Uncle Bert had won the Military Medal during the Great War, while during World War II Great Uncle Josh had been in the Royal Navy protecting the convoys (and sunk) and Great Uncle Arthur had been a bomber pilot in the RAF (and shot down). My Great Uncle Jeff had served in the North Africa campaign and trained as a sniper but due to having the hiccups too much had been transferred to a mortar platoon. I guess hiccups and being a sniper don't go that well together. According to legend, it was Great Uncle Jeff who had brought a monkey back from the war.

"He'll have to sleep in the out-house" said my Great Aunt Vera.

"He can't – he's used to the warm – he'll have to sleep in the bedroom with us" replied Jeff.

"What about the smell?"

"Well I've put up with it for 20 years, the monkey will just have to get used to it too."

I cannot confirm if this is a true story or not, and neither can my fact checking service – i.e. Kate. However, I do remember the old adage *"never let the truth stand in the way of a good story."*

Actually I think it was great uncle Jeff who had also told me that Rommel was called the Desert Fox because he used to sneak behind the British lines and upturn all the dustbins.

Anyway, back to soldiering. My dad had been a Private in the REME (Royal Electrical and Mechanical Engineers) during National Service. Paul had expressed a desire to join up several years before but had been vigorously talked out of it by my parents, however they must have had a change of heart as they seemed to encourage me all the way on my chosen path.

If the South Wales Borderers still existed as an entity, I am sure I would have joined them but, by then, they had amalgamated with the 41st Regiment of Foot to become 'The Royal Regiment of Wales'. So, instead, I applied to join the Senior Service – the Royal Navy. Seeing the world appealed and I looked pretty good in blue. I could always try green later.

I went through various interviews, familiarisation visits

and weeks away at different Naval bases, before I found myself at the Admiralty Interview Board. This consisted of several days of intensive command exercises, psychological questioning and board interviews. We were observed at every stage of the process, to ensure we were the right calibre to join the service.

I was accepted for a short Career Commission (six years) and they asked me to join straight away. I didn't even need to complete my A-level studies. I had just started the Sixth Form, however, and my parents persuaded me to stay on to complete them so that I would have something to fall back on. I agreed and my start date to commence my Officer training at Dartmouth was put back until autumn 1982. In the meantime, school took a back seat as I prepared myself.

Every morning, I did a ten-mile run, followed either by rowing around Roath Park Lake or swimming, down at the Empire Pool. I also worked in the greengrocers down the road to earn some money for other activities. Byron owned the shop and was ably hindered by his Father, old Mr Lewis. My dad always likes to tell the story of an unfortunate incident that occurred at the Greengrocers.

One day, a giant of a bloke sauntered into the shop.

"I want half a lettuce."

"We don't sell half lettuces," John replied.

"My wife sent me out for half a lettuce, so I want half a lettuce."

"I told you, we only sell whole lettuces."

"You're not understanding me. I want half a lettuce and I want it now!" John told him he was going into the storeroom to see the Boss.

"Byron," said John, "There's a big, ugly, thick idiot who wants half a lettuce."

Byron motioned for John to look behind him and there was the big, ugly, thick idiot, standing right behind him.

"… and, luckily enough," John continued quickly, pointing

to our new friend, "This gentleman would like the other half."

But I digress.

I once met one of my teachers in there on a school day afternoon when I was supposed to be in the class he was meant to be teaching. We both agreed that it was maybe best to keep this between ourselves.

The money I had earned at Byron's paid for me to take the bus up to North Wales, to go on a rock-climbing course but, after discovering the local beer, my money ran out and I had to hitch hike back again.

Eventually, Peggy, the Deputy Head called me in to complain that I was missing out on too much school. She only really seemed bothered about me missing my Religious Education lessons. Sister Alphonse, one of the teaching nuns, had shared Father Dunn's aspirations and was disappointed in me. I didn't feel very religious myself but maybe they saw something good, deep inside me. Very deep and very well hidden.

* * *

Indeed, years later, after I had joined up, there were occasional multi-denominational church services held onboard ship. It was the type of service that was meant to be attended voluntarily but you were tasked extra duties to fill your spare time if you didn't go.

The Padre would always begin his sermon with something like, "In a way, Jesus was a sailor ..." and would go on to explain how, just as we were keeping the demon of communism at bay, so Jesus was holding the demon of sin at bay.

I would also attend such services when I later joined the Royal Anglians. As we stood in a semi circle in a clearing in the woods, with the smell of damp webbing in the morning breeze, the Padre would begin his sermon; this time with something along the lines of, "In a way, Jesus was an Infantry soldier ..." He would then go on to explain how Jesus led his Christian soldiers in some adventure or other against sin.

As a Military Policeman, I also attended services to hear, "In a way, Jesus was a Royal Military Policeman ..." And so on.

I never realised I had so much in common with Jesus after all.

* * *

What I didn't have in common with Jesus though was the fact that, due to the lucky coincidence of him being born on Christmas day, everybody remembered *His* Birthday. Alas, not everyone remembered mine.

I suppose He had the drawback of receiving only one lot of presents – mind you, pretty good ones at that – although I'm not sure if they were supposed to be for Christmas or His birthday. The gold was fantastic, and I'm sure I'd like the Frankenstein mask, but I'm not really sure what I'd do with the Myrrh.

Bethan's birthday is in early January and, after all the excitement of Christmas, I didn't want her to be overlooked like me. Something had to be done.

The idea was hatched of producing a calendar with all the family's birthdays displayed and, to make it a bit more interesting, it would have pictures on each month, indicating some unusual or funny place sign from the North East.

I live close to Washington, the original Washington that is, where George's relatives came from. The districts of Philadelphia and Columbia fall within its boundaries and the villages of Quebec and Toronto are only just up the road too. I thought that one of these could provide a good photo opportunity but, in the end, it was decided to settle on the Big Apple. New York is a small village near North Shields – more like a small gooseberry really, but it would do as one of our 'months'.

Bethan had already explained to me how she had seen a funny sign on the way back from an outing to the seaside, some time back. Someone had amended the sign for Shilbottle with a horizontal piece of black masking tape, to make, 'Shitbottle'. We liked that. That was funny in our books and, in a pathetic effort to try and be original, we decided to pay a visit, equipped with a vertical piece of black masking tape, to the village of Snitter. Barney could pose next to the amended sign for added effect.

Also, it seems that many of the places in the North East owe their names to the Norman French language. Bearpark is sadly not a place where bears go to play, but rather a corruption of the original French name, 'Beau Repaire', meaning beautiful retreat – how times have changed. It sounded as if it would fit in as an 'October/November' sort of month.

Maybe we should have learnt something from the Americas and just kept the original French name. Baton Rouge sounds a fantastic place, full of romance and mystery but, if it was over here, we would have probably renamed it 'Red Stick' by now.

On the map, close to Hadrian's Wall, we found Once Brewed. I was confident that we would also find a Twice Brewed, hiding there somewhere. No one seems to have any idea what was brewed there but they would do for us. Dirt Pot was not far away but it was now in competition with Crackpot, near Richmond, in an effort to make it onto every self respecting Donoghue's kitchen wall.

Not that far from Hadrian's Wall is a place called 'Wallish Walls' – not far from 'Stony Heap'. I'd like to think that they were maybe both called just 'Wall' long ago. One was a town full of show-offs and the other was populated by shy insecure introverts. The show-offs would be bragging about how good their village was ... "we've not got just walls ...we're Wallish Walls!"

The humble folk in the other village would then just say "Aw fuck it, we're just a Stony Heap compared to them" – and the names would stick. I bet that's how a lot of places got their names originally ...well maybe not *exactly* like that, but you get the idea.

Actually at one time the north of England was inhabited by ancient Britons whose language closely resembled modern day

Welsh. Later the north was invaded by Germanic speaking Anglo-Saxons who referred to the native Britons as Welsh, meaning foreigner. Many ancient Britons fled west to escape the Anglo-Saxons and their place of refuge became the country we know today as Wales. Some Welsh though made a stand and their presence is remembered in place names containing the elements Wel or Wal.

Foggy Furze seemed to derive from the old Norse and described a piece of ploughed land where coarse grass grew and Deaf Hill was probably the place where that guy lived who thought up the 'hearing dogs' idea. Both were possibilities.

My favourite so far was 'No Place'. It can be found, or not as the case may be, on the road out of Durham, towards Stanley. It appears that the hamlet was located on the border of two parishes and neither parish wanted to accept responsibility for it. I guess either there were a boat load of sinners there, or more probably, they weren't that generous with their collection. Either way, it became No Place. A sign pointing to No Place would make a good 'September'.

'Deborah and John only' visits were also planned to Great Cock Up, Low Bell End, Wide Open and Wetwang.

CHAPTER THIRTEEN

The Shooting

Pity Me was the location for the first photo shoot. It seems very aptly named, situated between the Arndale shopping centre and the outskirts of Durham City, with the council rubbish site just over the road. They are currently building some flats on a piece of wasteland next to the big roundabout there and a big sign tells me, 'This will be the place to be seen'. Yes, if you are on the way to the tip with a piss stained mattress maybe, but otherwise I suggest not.

Some say the name Pity Me derives from 'Petit Mere', meaning small lake, but I prefer the more fanciful suggestion.

Saint Cuthbert is one of the most venerated of English saints. It was Cuthbert who converted Lindisfarne from Celtic Christianity to Roman Christianity and, after his death, the Lindisfarne Gospels were written in his honour. In 875, his body was removed from Holy Island, following Viking raids, and eventually laid to rest on a site in a loop of the River Wear. The magnificent Durham Cathedral was built on the site and his tomb can still be seen there. It is said that the wandering monks, tasked with taking his remains to Durham, dropped St. Cuthbert's coffin on the way. Cuthbert is then supposed to have pleaded with them to take more care and take pity on him. I know, I know, but he was supposed to be a miracle-working saint wasn't he?

I would be likely to have more pity on anyone actually living there at the current time. The sign looks more like an omen than a helpful roadside location indicator.

Bethan and I posed under the large 'Pity Me' sign and looked sad and miserable as befits such a notice. Barney just sat there and managed a sort of grimace.

As Deborah finished taking the photo, I noticed a scary old bloke with a patch over one eye, looking out of a window at us. Bethan had already made it safely back to the car by then and, when I told her of the image I'd observed, she made a detour to clock the 'thing' herself. We all then hurried away, too frightened to look back.

* * *

In military investigation, there is a term for those occasions when a particular action or reaction could reasonably be expected to happen in response to an occurrence – but did not. We call it a 'non barking dog'.

The term comes from the case of 'Silver Blaze' in Conan Doyle's 'Memoirs of Sherlock Holmes'. Silver Blaze is a prize race horse being protected by a stable boy and guard dogs. The night passes quietly, however the next morning the stable boy comes round from a drugged sleep. Silver Blaze is missing.

Inspector Gregory: "Is there any point you wish to bring to my attention?"
Holmes: "To the curious incident of the dog in the night time."
Inspector Gregory: "The dog did nothing in the night time."
Holmes: "That was the curious incident."

That is, it would reasonably be expected for the dogs to bark – but they didn't, suggesting that the thief was well known to them. Hence a 'non barking dog'.

The locals response to Pity Me was a non barking dog in my opinion. They had just walked past the sign as if nothing was up (or looked scary and a bit put out that we had rudely imposed on their non barking doggery). I guess in the case of places, a barking or non barking reaction depends on familiarity with the place.

I couldn't just ask people if there was anywhere with a bizarre name locally – they wouldn't know! It just wouldn't register as bizarre to them. I looked over at Barney for any suggestions. He was scratching his head with his leg. Cheers Barney, you're a great help.

* * *

The rest of the calendar would need to be put on hold for the time being as I was being abandoned. Bethan was off for a week or so, on her residential summer school. In previous years, she had attended dance and swimming schools but, this year, it was music. I think, at age ten, I was still cycling around with Hicksey, well, except for that one summer that I devoted to the humiliation of ants.

There always seemed to be regular convoys of ants marching to and fro in the backyard of our house in Carisbrooke Way when I was a boy – and that's when I hatched my cunning plan. I built a small enclosure a yard or so away from a regular route with plasticine (Plasticine Catholic – Playdoh Protestant). I then ordered a platoon of Airfix First World War French infantry to guard it. Apart from the assorted riflemen in different poses patrolling the perimeter, there was also an officer wearing a kepi, a soldier using his entrenching tool (finishing off the barricades), a military cyclist, bugler, observer with telescope, flag-bearer and a signaller with pigeon. Finally, but most importantly for my fiendish scheme, there was a soldier carrying a sack of supplies who I made sure was clearly visible for several days making his way back and forth to the plasticine fort under military escort. Aha, the trap was complete. I then placed a spoonful of sugar inside the enclosure – but not just any spoonful of sugar – a spoonful of sugar liberally mixed with a few grains of salt!

The next step of the plan was to sit and wait. Any self

respecting soldier knows that if an advance is going well, it's probably because you are marching into an ambush. These ants though seemed too cocky to ponder on basic military theorem. Instead I was confident that they would be so curious as to what the French soldier was carrying into the barricade that they couldn't help but to send out a reconnaissance party to discover what lay within. My cunning trap was complete!

My soldiers meanwhile had strict instructions to pretend to miss the ant recce and the inevitable column of carrying ants that would soon follow, intent on stealing the stock of sugar from the battle hardened veterans.

Hopefully, after scaling the wall (possibly under cover of darkness) each ant would grab a white crystal from the pile within and scurry off back to the ant HQ. There they would present their takings to the Queen ant (possibly seated on a small chair fashioned out of Playdoh – we don't actually know for sure). And that is when my plan would be complete. One ant would present his grain of salt instead of sweet, sweet sugar and then would get a right bollocking from the Queen. The ant would be humiliated. Objective achieved.

In hindsight, I'm not very proud of what I did. No one likes to be shamed. I should know ...it was dustbin day last Friday and guess when I put my bin out. However, I am older and wiser now and realise that it would never happen like that anyway – my plan would never have actually reached fruition. There would probably be a quality control ant sorting out the salt from the sugar at the front door.

In the absence of ant humiliation classes, Bethan had departed on a course to improve her clarinet playing.

Deborah, meanwhile, had departed on her annual trip to Turkey. She had friends there and harboured thoughts of going to live and work over there, teaching English. Every now and again she would try and goad me into showing my hand by saying that she wasn't coming back. I would not be goaded though and continued to keep my cards close to my chest. There are far too many sparrows there to for my liking anyway.

After Bethan and Deborah's departure, I was too scared to check behind the sofa in case I might find a stick with a red spotted handkerchief on the end, containing Barney's toys. Just to be safe, I double locked the door that night and put the bolt across. His little paws would have trouble with that if he *was* planning to escape.

Jesus wept when He felt abandoned but I thought it would be more productive to arrange a campsite for when Deborah returned.

Bethan was due to fly out for a fortnight in Jamaica, shortly after returning from music school whilst I, on the other hand, was going camping with my brother Paul, in Wales.

Paul had called the previous week and told me his theory about camping. He reckoned that the cheaper and more austere the campsite, the nicer the people were who used it. In turn, the more expensive and the more amenities a campsite had, indicated that it was frequented by less pleasant people. Therefore, I was frankly a little taken aback to take a call from him saying that he had found the ideal site. It cost quite a bit he said, but it did have nightly entertainment and a heated swimming pool. The halfway point had also now migrated to a hundred miles beyond Cardiff.

As he was chatting on the phone to me, I could hear Ceri, his daughter, shouting to him that the kettle had boiled dry on the gas ring and was making a funny smell. Aha, so there is a God.

❊ ❊ ❊

Meanwhile, I was up to my old tricks. The Fang's presence had been requested at Chloe's party. Chloe is the daughter of my mate Tim and she had asked if something magical could happen at her fifth birthday party.

Becoming five is a bit of a milestone in anyone's life – especially when you are only four.

My brother Paul had a friend called Toffo, and one day

Toffo's younger brother saw my dad outside our house.

Toffo's brother: "I'm five today!"

Dad: "Five today! That's a splendid age! Just wait here"

Dad then went into the house and got some sweets and chocolates that were obviously originally meant for us and went back outside and gave them all to Toffo's brother.

Dad: "Five today! Oh my word – what an achievement! Well done – here are some sweets as a special present"

Toffo's brother: "I was five yesterday too – and a week ago – I've been five for three months now"

Dad: "Why you little......"

I'm not sure, but it's not beyond the bounds of possibility that Toffo's brother might now work for the Government.

I digress – but nevertheless, five remains a watershed year in any small person's life, so I said I'd see what I could do.

I don't usually perform magic for children as the card and mentalist stuff I do is more intended for an adult audience (aka attractive women). So, in truth, it wasn't really my old tricks I was up to, as I had to source a whole new routine of visual effects for Chloe and her friends. However, I couldn't fail to see a friend's responsibility and so paid a visit to the magic shop in my bid to become 'Party Fang'.

Whether to impress those elusive attractive women or just to entertain children, as long as the magician isn't patronising, magic should just be fun ('patronising' of course, means 'to talk down to people').

In the event, Party Fang had a good time, Chloe had a good time and the other kiddies had a good time; it went well. Children make a good audience. Their minds are still open to new ideas and they enjoy being entertained and I enjoy entertaining.

Many adults also retain their child-like sense of wonderment. They realise that being receptive and flexible in their thinking is a good quality to have. They are the sort of people who enjoy life and see the funny side of everything. They don't mind being silly and laughing at themselves. I like those sort of people – so does Barney.

Some adults though (and when I say adults I actually mean grumpy losers) think they are far too sensible to enjoy magic and they mistake *childlike* for *childish* and I think they are missing out on a lot. Instead, they act like snobbish food critics who, if asked to taste anything different or unusual, 'poo poo' it straight away. This process with Barney normally takes three to four hours.

Have a try of this:

Think of any number between 1 and 10
Multiply it by 9
If the answer is 2 digits, add the 2 numbers together
Subtract 5 from your answer
Convert the number into a letter 1=A, 2=B, 3=C etc
Think of a country that starts with the letter you have
Think of the 2nd letter of that country
Now pick an animal that begins with that letter
Now think of the colour of that animal

There, now that didn't make you feel used and abused did it? It is only a bit of fun. You are thinking of an animal not a bird I hope too. Who except a grumpy old twerp would get themselves all bothered about that? By the way, were you thinking of a grey elephant from Denmark? Well it works out about 80% of the time anyway.

If it doesn't try asking for them to think of any number between one and three. I find they usually go for two.

Anyway, the 'poo poo'er' himself hadn't actually come with me as I thought it might have been too much for him or too much for the kiddies; I'm not sure which.

※ ※ ※

Barney hadn't come running with me yet either. I wanted his

little bones and joints to develop properly first and, on that basis, I never quite appreciate people's enthusiasm for running the Marathon. For goodness sake, the first guy who ever did it dropped down dead at the end!

It was 490 BC and the wars between the Persians and Greeks raged. The Persians had landed a large army on the plains of Marathon, near Athens. The Athenians then sent out a smaller force in a surprise attack against the Persians. Despite being outnumbered four to one, the Athenians were victorious and almost six and a half thousand Persians lay dead whilst less than two hundred Athenians perished. The surviving Persians then fled to the sea and south to Athens where they hoped to attack the city before the Greek Army could re-assemble there.

Phidippides, one of the Athenian soldiers, was then tasked to run the twenty six miles back to the City to deliver news of the victory and also warn of the approaching Persian ships. He followed orders, delivered his message and then dropped down dead from exhaustion.

And that's why the concept of a modern day marathon confuses me. *"Let's find something that could kill us, and see who can do it the fastest?"*

The Greeks won by the way, but I digress.

Barney still surprised himself every time he farted for goodness sake. Running could wait. Instead, Barney and I walked around the circuit most evenings, which we both enjoyed doing. I did, however, have to keep him on his lead when we passed the fishermen dotted around the pond as he began to take a liking to running off and eating their bait – anything from bread to mouthfuls of maggots.

I had lost a couple of pets in unusual circumstances when I was a child and I didn't want a tragedy to befall Barney before I had my money's worth out of him.

In case the stories below appear too shocking, disturbing or frankly unbelievable, let me assure you that I have verified all the facts with my sister Kate, prior to publication.

❊ ❊ ❊

When I was very small I had a large rabbit. The 'very small' and 'large' aspects must be borne in mind here, as I have pictures of me riding on his back. It was an old black and white photo but not so old that we had to hold the pose for a minute or so until the plate developed. That *would* have been difficult. Urban myth has it that once, when we went on holiday, he was sold to the butcher. In their defence, my parents said that they had asked the butcher to look after him while we were away. (Who, in their right mind, asks a butcher to look after a rabbit?) They said he bred rabbits but I suspect that the only thing he bred were rabbit pies. Needless to say, the bunny never returned.

I was older now, and this time in possession of two pet tortoises. In those days, you could go to the indoor market in Cardiff City centre and there would be boxes full of tortoises, all clambering over each other. Those were also the days when pet shops actually did sell puppies!

Toby and Eggbut were my tortoises' names and, apart from pottering about eating lettuce, they would sometimes double up as World War II tanks with various armaments that I constructed from my dad's old pipe cleaners, cigar tubes and matchboxes and would stick with plasticine to their shells. Now and again, my 'Action Man' assisted by copious amounts of rubber bands, would sit astride Toby or Eggbut and trundle around the garden looking for Japanese snipers or maybe even a hiccupping Great Uncle Jeff. It seems that snipers liked to hide amongst the dandelion patch as this is where the tank usually made for. Being found so easily I guess was enough to bring a tear to any Jap's eye but luckily for the wily sniper I avoided picking through the aforementioned weeds to find him for fear of wee-ing the bed. How was I to know that as I had the Action Man action pilot that came in a pair of orange overalls, he probably looked less like a tank commander and more like a sad escapee from Guantanamo Bay ...sitting on a tortoise.

On that basis, rather unsurprisingly, Toby and Eggbut

would occasionally make a dash for freedom. I'd always check upstairs for them, but, more than likely, they had made a run for it through the hedge at the back of the garden and up the school fields to the rear, towards Cyncoed Park. Every now and again, they would be hunted down and caught by friendly people in the street who would then return the naughty pair. Unfortunately, they enjoyed this escapade once too often.

I was in the kitchen one day, when I heard a knock on the front door. My mum answered it and I could hear her talking to two girls. "Never seen them in my life before – you had better hang onto them yourselves girls." And so it was, in that brief statement, Toby and Eggbut ceased to be mine and instead became somebody else's playthings.

Is it any wonder that I have turned out the way I have?

I was determined that Barney would not go the same way as Toby, Eggbut and the massive un-named bunny.

CHAPTER FOURTEEN

Fear and Loathing
in the Gower

Neil, my other brother, who used to sit in the back by a window, now lives in Kew with his family.

The brains in the family made their evolutionary beginnings with Paul, peaked with Neil and went rapidly downhill after that so that poor old Kate was left with virtually nothing. In a bid to comfort her, Paul once told Kate that *everyone* has talents – it was just that she concealed her light under a bushel. Sadly, he ruined this philosophy by claiming, "It's a bloody big bushel though!"

Neil is an international lawyer and is what I would classify as being very rich. I reckon that, if he had a tow bar on his car and he needed a cover for it, he would just buy a brand new tennis ball for the job! No expense spared! He worked in Hong Kong for over a decade and even brought back his servant when he returned to the UK. She is a Filipino lady who goes by the frankly un-Filipino name of 'Tina'.

Despite the fact that he could probably pay somebody to walk for him, Neil likes to go walking himself. He went walking in the Himalayas once, with a goat for company, but I think they fell out with each other about halfway through the trip. To teach him a lesson, Neil ate him. Mental note to self, "*Don't fall out with Neil.*"

Despite their high IQs, when they were about twelve or

thirteen, Neil and Paul crushed up some poisonous berries from the garden, mixed them with water and tried to sell the concoction to strangers in the street outside the house. It doesn't seem the kind of activity that a policeman and lawyer should really be engaged in. Well, at least not a policeman anyway.

Neil hasn't been to visit me since I moved up here but he promised that he would come that summer. I did feel a little isolated up in the North East and was keen for people to come to see Bethan.

My dad hadn't been up to see Bethan either since my mum had died.

It seems I wasn't the only one to have been confused about geography. Despite making numerous trips to London, visiting Edinburgh, catching the ferry over to Ireland, driving to the South of France, holidays in Sri Lanka and weekend excursions to Florence, Dad seemed to believe that the journey to Durham was just *too* far. Maybe he thought it was downhill on the map from North to South and that a ten year old girl should sit in a stuffy car for seven or eight hours each way, to make the pilgrimage to see him instead.

I told my dad this and, by sheer coincidence, a few days later he called to say that he was coming up in late August and would be bringing his new friend, Ann. I am not sure what her middle name actually is, but I'm pretty sure it's not 'tact'. When my Nana was ill in hospital, my sister Kate went up to visit her, along with my dad who, for some reason unknown to me, is also known as Keith. Dad and Ann had gone to visit her the day before. The story goes that Ann had scurried into the ward ahead of him.

"Your mother looks totally different Keith. I think she must be dying." A mixture of shock and panic swept over my dad before the Nurse calmly walked over to him and informed them that the reason my Nana didn't look herself that day was probably because she wasn't herself. It was another old woman in the bed and my Nana had been moved to a different ward a few days previously. They hurried off to her new location. No one appears to have recorded the thoughts of the old woman lying in the bed, accused of pretending to be Nana. Well, what would *you* do if someone rushed up to your hospital bed, gave you a snap diagnosis and then scurried out again?

Note to reader: If I'm ever in hospital, no cheering up visits from Ann please.

❄ ❄ ❄

The black sheep son did actually return to Cardiff once in a blue moon. When there are two full moons in the month, the second one is known as the 'blue moon' and it happens about once a year.

So I usually return to the City where I had grown up once and sometimes even twice a year but, when I do, it is normally just for the weekend. I have done this most years, ever since I left home to join the armed forces. I'm not exactly sure how welcome I am, as the first thing people seem to ask me when I arrive, is when am I going back!

As often happens, when you meet someone far from home who comes from the same area as you, they try to establish some sort of common interest. In the transient world we now seem to live in, people appear to enjoy developing these bonds, however tenuous they may be.

Whilst the Americans I have met always seem to have known someone called 'Taffy Jones' who came from Wales and ask if I know him, exiled fellow Welshmen seem to be more specific.

Do I know this pub or that pub in Cardiff? Have I ever been to the part of town they come from? Do I know this or that person?

Unfortunately, if it has not been on my running route, in Roath Park or the Empire pool, on the Pipe Bridge or within the five mile radius of my house, where Hicksey and I used to cycle, I have no idea what they are on about. As I give disappointing, "No" answers to my potential new friend, I can see their faces drop. I'm sure some even think I am putting on a slight Welsh accent as some bizarre sort of fashion statement. I'm also certain that some even think I am a fake and maybe just pretending to come from Wales to cover up the fact that I have spent the first half of my life in a mental asylum or being brought up by chimps in the wild.

When I do return to Cardiff, I seem to enter some sort of time warp. The day I left to join up has been frozen in some sort of space continuum. Somewhere, in a far off Galaxy, two aliens stare in disbelief at their monitor screens. Not just because they can't understand why Miss Universe is always won by an Earthling, but rather at the scene that is unfolding millions of light years away in a quiet suburb in South Wales.

A 39-year-old man, who has a responsible job, is father to a 10-year-old daughter and who has served Her Majesty during several minor conflicts, suddenly now undergoes a metamorphosis as he pulls up outside a house in Carisbrooke Way. In a 'Quantum Leap' type scenario, even his own father apparently still sees him as a teenager and can only communicate on the level of intelligent parent and stupid boy. In another, unrelated development, the father is only able to respond to this 'teenager' in the opposite dimension. The aliens note down on their 'wahwah recorders' (a recording system whereby thoughts are visualised and then stored in image format onto a floating transparent sphere) that this apparently seems to mean that, whatever the overgrown teenager says, is automatically misinterpreted and responded to in a contradictory manner by the adult.

The strength of the time warp loop varies but its influence does not seem to extend beyond Carisbrooke Way. Elsewhere, tortoises are no longer sold in cardboard boxes; the Empire pool has gone the same way as the actual Empire; the Pipe Bridge no longer leads to England and Miss Tucker no longer teaches English at Lady Mary High School.

* * *

The panic and excitement at the dog training school was over. The initial report of a kangaroo sighting in the field had been investigated and it transpired that it was one of the large Weimaraner dogs having a poop.

There were two Weimaraner puppies in Barney's socialisation class – tall leggy sporting dogs, bred to spend the entire day running in the fields looking for fowl to retrieve. They are competitive, attentive and very energetic.

There were also a pair of Red Setters and, as a breed, they too have high energy levels and are supposed to run about, pointing, flushing and retrieving fowl all day. Someone had slipped up though and hadn't given these two their job description, as they just seemed to lope around and lie down at every opportunity.

A small, bearded rat type thing made infrequent visits to the centre whilst Barney's final classmate was a small part-Labrador/part-something else cross, named Tess, who immediately rolled onto her back as soon as the three-toed one approached.

I have heard that in nearby Chester-le-Street, they were breeding a cross between a Labrador and a Standard Poodle which, apparently, has the same good nature as a 'Lab' but with the benefit of not losing its hair. I think it was called a 'Labrapoo' or maybe even a 'Poudador'. This seemed like a good idea as, just from the hairs I had picked up off the carpet over the last few weeks, I could have made myself a half scale Barney. There were no reports of a Shih Tzu/Poodle cross and I guess nobody would want a dog called a 'Shitpoo'.

As much as I wanted to be top dog in my own pack, I gently encouraged Barney to become top dog in his playgroup, with promises of games of fetch if he did well. Owner egos would be made or broken, depending on whether their pets took a dominant or submissive stance. I think Tess' mum accepted from the outset that her pooch was always going to be the lowest of the low. As it is confusing having two 'Tess' dogs in this book, small cross breed Tess will hereafter be known as 'Tess Two'.

So it was that Tess Two's mum metaphorically rolled over onto her back in submission as did her nubile twenty something daughter who attended the class with her. I suppose we communicated like the parents in any playgroup, as we only seemed to know each other through our charges.

Harvey, Weimaraner No. 1, was Barney's biggest competitor for the top dog slot. Harvey's dad wanted that coveted spot for his boy but Harvey's mum and Deborah were far too sensible to become involved. Red and Alfie, the Red Setters, didn't seem to care *who* was top dog as long as they could have a lie down. Milly, Weimaraner No. 2, had, along with her mum, missed a couple of classes and was a late entry. Nobody seemed to notice the rat like thing and Tess Two continued to lie on her back.

Whilst Barney had the upper hand in the early classes, Harvey's confidence improved as the weeks passed. It seemed a dead heat for the top dog slot as the last class ended so I quickly put the word out that Barney was up for a rematch any time.

Barney was awarded a certificate and rosette as he finished the final class which meant that, at the age of twenty weeks, he had already drawn level with me on the prize stakes. He seemed pretty proud of his awards and I think he would have liked to display them above his sleeping area. If he had a bed, it's likely I would have granted his wish but, since he had eaten it, I refused. It's not that I was jealous of him at all – I was just worried that people might think he was some kind of show-off.

His education wasn't over though and I decided to continue taking that thin, wild mercury thing to obedience classes as he still had a couple of habits that I wished to iron out. He didn't always come back when I called for him and there was still a tendency to jump up when he greeted people. He would bounce up and down, chase his tail in mini circles and shake his little body before taking a leap up at this long lost, new best friend. Whilst his tiny brain was coping with all this, it forgot to tell him that he shouldn't wee all over the place. The combination of jumping up at people whilst wee-ing was in danger of making Barney a social outcast.

✿ ✿ ✿

There had already been a strange sort of start to the day. As I was walking along the river, two thirty something women were jogging towards me on the path. "Isn't he handsome?" one of them commented quite openly to the other, more as a statement than a question. "He's gorgeous," the other added.

I'm sure I was meant to hear their remarks and a mixture of emotions flooded over me. I was, of course, flattered but more than a little embarrassed and I also felt slightly sorry for Barney whom, in all this, they had clearly chosen to ignore. They missed out too, mind you, as normally, if an attractive woman shows any interest in him, he runs over, and licks her face and pants. (There, that's a good example: If only I had paid attention in school and really knew how to use a semi colon properly, I could have stopped that from sounding half as smutty as it did).

Despite feeling sympathetic towards my dog and his hurt feelings, I still made him wait for his breakfast when we returned home. As a matter of course, Barney would be made to sit for a minute in front of his dinner bowl before he was allowed to eat. On the command, he would wolf it down as if he expected me to change my mind at any moment and take the bowl away. He even sucks his belly in to create a vacuum to shovel the food in faster. Good things come to those who wait.

Being a much more sedate dog, Tess tends to pick at her food throughout the day so Barney has realised that there is usually plenty of dry mix in her dish. When we visit Deborah, Tess is normally pottering outside in the conservatory so Barney goes to wait patiently by the door as if he's hoping to go and play with his mate. However, as soon as the door is opened enough, he darts through, straight past a startled Tess and into her food bowl. As I run after him, Barney's tactic is to make his nose dive-bomb into the bowl. He knows that the mix will explode everywhere and, even after I have snatched Tess' bowl away from him, he can leisurely hoover up the debris. Sometimes good things only come to those who wait – if they are fast enough.

Deborah might then say something like, "What goes around

comes around." I have no idea what she is on about and the expression, "It will happen when you least expect it to," always puzzled me too. *What* would happen? The answer it seems is, 'it' and I was about fourteen at the time when I found out what 'it' was.

❖ ❖ ❖

I had gone for a day out at the beach, along with my friend Michael Leeson and his parents whom I addressed as Mr and Mrs Leeson. Bethan seems to know all her friends' parents by their first names but, at that age, I didn't even know that my friends' parents *had* first names.

Mr Leeson, the hero of the piece, was, I guess, about fifty at the time. He was a lecturer at the University and appeared very studious. He was gangly and very quiet and I can't really remember having ever spoken more than a few words to him.

After a day of playing on the sand, Michael and I had climbed the footpath up from the beach to the car park and stood next to the car, waiting for Mr and Mrs Leeson to show. I could just make out the top of Mr Leeson's head bobbing up and down as he started to come into view but then his weary little face appeared and finally the full, mild mannered academic was revealed.

Suddenly, out of nowhere, he seemed to be possessed by the devil. His eyes widened and he threw aside the blanket and straw basket he was carrying. He started to take great strides with his long, gangly legs – strides as long as he was tall. He started shouting obscenities as he covered the ground at a lightening pace and, without slowing, a long gangly arm scooped up a large stone from the floor and, in one fluid movement, it was thrown with considerable force and bounced off the back of a grey Hillman Imp driving out of the car park. The back of the car snaked on the ground and the wheels started to spin as the driver desperately tried to accelerate away at great speed. I could see two children with panic-stricken faces cowering in the back, looking like they were shouting at their daddy to get moving. One looked like he was crying. It was pandemonium in there.

Mr Leeson didn't end his pursuit until the car was well and truly out of sight and he had chased it a good hundred yards or so up the country lane leading away from the car park. We knew he had reached the end of his chase when the screech of tyres faded and we heard a final outburst of expletives echoing in the calm, warm evening air.

By this time, a slightly bemused Mrs Leeson had joined us while Michael and I just stood open mouthed, nervously awaiting the return of the madman. It was only when Mr Leeson saw all three of us standing by the side of his grey Hillman Imp that the horrible truth dawned on him. Michael and I *hadn't* been kidnapped and then forcibly driven off in his own car after all. His car was still parked where he left it and we were standing next to it, unharmed.

Goodness knows what the driver of the innocent car thought as he saw a swearing madman bearing down on him, throwing missiles. His heart must have been beating as if there was a hummingbird trapped inside and the mayhem in the car must have been all consuming, as the frightened children, fearing for their very lives, jumped about weeping and shouting for their daddy to save them. What must have gone through their minds as the rock bounced off the vehicle? Nothing was said. We all got in the car and drove home in silence.

I made a mental note, *"Never buy a grey Hillman Imp."*

CHAPTER FIFTEEN

The Lambton Worm

Just as the milkman was making his rounds and dropping off an extra pint to those who had left a note out for him, Barney and I were out on our morning walk. It was a beautiful morning and the tide was coming in, so the river was actually flowing upstream. The two swans were taking their eight cygnets out for a spot of training on the water and the three-toed one actually stopped jumping about for a while to stare at them. I told him it was rude to do that and so, instead, he tried to surreptitiously scale the embankment on the other side of the path.

I have been climbing many times, having attended a course in North Wales, done quite a bit in the forces and even gone to lessons again a few years back. It was something I felt I should enjoy but I never really did. Bethan, on the other hand, seemed to love it. When we had gone to the Durham County Show, she resembled a little monkey, clambering up the climbing wall.

We had come back from that same County Show with an exceedingly expensive sixty pence stuffed toy panda. It had turned into one of Bethan's 'must have' weekends. To be fair, they don't happen that often but, now and again, there is a 'must have' item that, in simple terms, she must have that weekend. Recent 'must haves' include a set of red hair bobbles and a red T-shirt. Not just any red hair bobbles and red T-shirt you understand – these are specific ones that she has pictured in her head and that I must find by trial and error. It's not that I *mind*; it's just that I would prefer a better stab at success by having a decent description up front. Comments like, "That's too red," or "Those bobbles are too big," still echo in my ears.

It's guaranteed though that, every time we wander into Woolworth's, the day suddenly transforms into a 'must have pencil case and/or folder' day. Actually, I have long suspected that Woolworth's is an agency of the Chinese Government on the basis that they now appear to have relinquished their aspiration of world domination through communism but, instead, are working towards their objective by their merciless supply of useless plastic objects.

The 'must have' at the Durham Show was a large grey teddy bear. Fifteen pounds later, we persuaded Bethan to call it quits with the pathetic small panda we had managed to win. Close, but no bear (in fact the term 'close, but no cigar' comes from the time that cigars were given out as prizes as carnivals – ... just as well we didn't win ... Susan would have gone ape-shit with me if I brought Bethan back with a handful of smokes!). Anyway I'm sure it was the most loved panda in the world until she got home, when it was then tossed aside to become just another stuffed toy in the veritable mountain of them, living at the end of her bed. I bet he didn't even warrant a name. But she was happy.

* * *

The sunshine of the previous days had given way to a light drizzle as we set off on our morning walk the next day. As we went into the woods, Barney was overcome by a sniffing frenzy. It was like watching a speeded up film as he darted about in little figures of eight, his nose hovering a matter of millimetres above the ground. He would bury his head in the foliage on the side of the path, venture high up the embankment and then run down to take up precarious positions overhanging the near vertical river bank, all in his quest for 'sniffery'. His tail which, under normal circumstances, was in a continual state of wag, was now doing a near perfect impression of car windscreen wipers in a rainstorm. I was worried it might come flying off at any moment.

The 'wag' issue had already led to a number of spillages but, thankfully, in Deborah's house, not mine. There was quite a bit of energy in that tail which only seemed to be dissipated, once it had swiped a full wine glass or coffee cup. This led to the modern day phenomenon of 'centreing' whereby all potential energy dissipaters, such as wine glasses and cups, were housed in the centre of the coffee table rather than the risky exposed edges.

The sniffing had become all consuming in Barney's little mind that morning and he had even forgotten that the main purpose of his dad getting up and wandering out in his sticky up hair state was for the wild four legged one to have his dawn poo. I returned home with a still fully loaded dog.

* * *

The next day was the Saturday of my abandonment and, as the sun was beaming again, I decided to take Barney on a full circuit walk that morning.

I don't want to appear to be dwelling on the subject, but it seemed to form a big part of Barney's life and obviously meant a lot to him and, for the sake of medical research, I will therefore continue. In brief, it seemed as if Barney was making up for lost time and this morning's walk was in stark contrast to the 'no-poop' sniffing escapade.

He appeared to be testing out a new theory in his tiny mind. His thought process seemed to be that, if he deposited two poops on his normal twenty-minute morning walk, he should do two poops *every* twenty minutes. A stroll round the circuit took about an hour and I feared he might turn himself inside out in his valiant effort to keep up his quota.

My initial stab at one human year being equal to seven dog years was apparently wrong. As dogs mature much faster than us, it seemed more like fifteen dog years for each human year for the first two years and, thereafter, five dog years for each of ours. On this basis, what I initially thought was a surfeit of poops on this journey was actually, in dog years, only one poop every two and a half days, which didn't seem so excessive after all. What it did mean though was that I was running out of poop bags to clear up his mess. I managed to kick a couple into the river but, in the end, had to resort to opening previously tied up bags to make room for more of Barney's bodily rejects.

I have often moaned about the litter that seems to be left in the countryside but, try as I might, couldn't find any bins and the council didn't seem to be helping themselves here. We even went off route to try and find somewhere to dump the dumps.

I became quite confused as I reached a row of lovely cottages, just plonked along a path parallel to our normal walk when, as we approached them, the path just seemed to disappear.

It seems that some people, who are lucky enough to live in beautiful locations, want to keep them all to themselves. If a right of way passes close by, they will try and put you off the scent by making it look as if you are trespassing on their land if you follow the route. The nicer people in society, who wouldn't dream of disturbing anyone else's privacy, would be deterred in case they did just that, and retreat to seek an alternative route. Meanwhile, the lucky people living in the houses are rubbing their hands together because they have managed to keep all that natural beauty to themselves.

The 'Nazi' and I have never claimed to be members of polite society and so blundered on through. However, even we began to doubt ourselves as we walked across what seemed to be a gravelled drive, adorned with ornaments and flower displays. Eventually, we found the right of way route arrow and the continuing path at the other end of the row of houses, hidden behind a couple of tubs of geraniums.

The cottage owners were obviously seething inside that an 'intruder' had managed to share their fantastic views of the woods leading down to the river. I didn't have the heart to tell them that several bags of turds lay in the bottom of one of their ornamental pots too.

❖ ❖ ❖

There are three pubs over the river from me and behind the middle one is Worm Hill. Barney and I were going to scramble up Worm Hill and perhaps visit one of the pubs on the way back.

Legend has it that, in the Middle Ages, the Lambton Worm wrapped himself around the hill, thus giving it that name. From this base, he would then venture out and terrorise the local neighbourhood. However, as much as I tried to picture a scary worm, even a very long one, I just couldn't make myself frightened. We had dragons in Wales which, I suppose, could be frightening, but a worm was not doing it for me.

The story goes that a young member of the Lambton family was fishing one Sunday but all he caught was a small wiggling worm. Disgusted with his catch, he threw it in a well. Years later, after he had departed to fight in the Crusades, the worm emerged from the well as a huge and ferocious beast. It was like a dragon but without legs or wings. Now that was more like it! We then have the terrorising bit.

When Lambton returned from the Holy Land, he vowed to kill the beast and, as luck would have it, a witch was on hand to offer advice on how to slaughter the worm. He was to wear a suit of armour with spikes on but, as with all good witch advice, there was a twist, and this one was that he had to kill the first living thing he saw after the worm was slain.

Lambton lured the worm into the River Wear outside my house and, as the worm tried to wrap himself around our hero, it was cut to pieces on the armour and Lambton finally chopped the beast's head off. He had planned to have his favourite hound greet him on his return so he could slay that but, in the excitement, our hero's dad was the first to greet him. Needless to say, Lambton reneged on his promise to the witch and the family were cursed in the process, enduring years of untimely deaths for generations.

As I regaled the tale to Barney on top of Worm Hill, I left

out some of the detail. He didn't need to know about the favourite hound bit and, not wishing to frighten him, I also told him that the story had happened near Newcastle and that, afterwards, Lambton suggested that the worm's body be used as a massive sausage to feed the poor.

I finished with the Dickensian quote, "It was the Beast of Tyne. It was the Wurst of Tyne." As Barney looked up at me with a blank expression, a tumble-weed blew across the field in front of me and I swear I could hear a single church bell sounding somewhere off in the distance.

CHAPTER SIXTEEN

Doctor Shit

Snails, oysters and all that sort of food from shells, I must admit, are not my cup of tea. I was a young sailor in New Orleans at Mardi Gras time when I was given my first oyster to try. The music blared, the drink flowed, the shellfish beckoned and I was in the mood for a little romance. The atmosphere couldn't have been more fantastic. The oyster made it half way down my throat before it decided that it preferred the fresh air, did a 'U-turn' and popped back up again, all over the girl in the bikini style cowgirl outfit sitting next to me. She turned to me and very calmly and matter of factly informed me what she thought of me.

"You are an idiot."

The rest of the girls looked at me as if I was thick and I returned to the ship alone.

That was my first and only attempt at food with that type of texture.

It must have been a bit of a hit and miss affair I suppose, working out which molluscs and shellfish were good to eat and which weren't and I guess that, whoever worked out that snails are good to eat, must have also tried slugs some time. (And who was the first guy to say "See that animal munching grass over there? Let's name it a cow. Now let's go and pull those dangly things underneath it and drink what comes out" or even "See that bird over there?…let's call it a chicken and eat the first thing that comes out of its bum").

Frogs' legs are another thing that I have never had a desire to try, but young Barney has. As we made our way through the woods after a heavy summer rainstorm, the mist was rising from the forest floor and I spied a large frog making his way across the path. Not having learnt from previous pointing/eating experiences, I drew Barney's attention to the amphibian. Maybe I thought he would just look and go, "Ooooh," like me but, instead, he tried to fit it all into his mouth. He immediately jumped back, spitting the frog out, and then proceeded to run around sounding like a cat trying to cough up a furball. I had once read an article about the dangers of licking a Horny Toad, but had assumed it was just some sort of adult version of the popular 'kissing a frog' fairy tale. This was just an unpleasant tasting frog though and Barney would live to lick another day. In fact, the next day he ate a snail.

Apparently, many snails were consumed during the Napoleonic Wars and each soldier in the French Army had to carry canned snails as emergency rations. I guess they had to carry them; otherwise they would be too slow to keep up with the marching army. Each soldier was allotted one thousand snails per week.

War in that era was much different than it is today. In battles, only three or four shots per hundred ever hit anybody. The first shot would be most accurate as the weapons were clean and there was time to load them correctly. Thereafter, accuracy diminished as the barrels became fouled and soldiers hurried to reload them in the heat of battle. A good soldier could probably fire about four rounds a minute. In the Battle of Vitoria, it is estimated that over three and a half million musket balls were fired, causing about eight thousand causalities – that works out at merely one hit per four hundred and fifty shots. I guess, after all that fighting, it might be quite nice to sit back and crack open the odd snail or two. In many ways, Napoleon was ahead of his time.

As well as being an excellent General, he was responsible for some dramatic reforms and their influence spread much further than the boundaries of France. He instigated the French Civil code or *Code Napoleon.* Under this, there were no privileges of birth and all men were equal under the law. It is still the basis of law in many countries to this day.

Whilst Paris was the sophisticated hub of reform, the North East of England was a bleak place, inhabited by suspicious hunchbacks and deformed bigots; well, at least in Hartlepool it was. As the fortunes of the different sides in the Napoleonic Wars ebbed and flowed, a French ship was once wrecked in a storm off the coast of this fishing town. The sole survivor washed up on the sands was Claude, the ship's mascot, a little monkey decked out in naval gear for amusement. The townsfolk seized Claude and he stood trial on the beach, accused of being a French spy. His little gibberings were taken as being French. Aha! A confession. Claude was found guilty and hanged until he was dead. The end.

Well, not quite the end. After years of humiliation, being known as the place where they hanged the monkey, the good people of Hartlepool eventually made amends for their folly and, in 2002, elected a monkey as mayor of the City. And sadly enough, it's a true story.

* * *

The truth about my four-legged friend was clarified one fateful morning. Any doubts I may have harboured that Barney was not a Pedigree Labrador were finally ousted when a black clad figure burst through the toilet door as I sat there, snatched the toilet roll and ran straight off. He must have silently crept up the stairs before putting his pilfering into action. Only the fact that the roll was picked up in his mouth gave away the fact that it was indeed him. I had to improvise.

I had to improvise when I was at my RMP selection weekend as well. I had forgotten to take my towel and, after my shower, I had to dry myself on the bedroom curtains (much to the shock of a female Major outside). I was a bit worried when I found she was on the selection panel, but I still got the transfer I wanted, so she must have seen something that impressed her that day anyway. But I digress.

If Kate had been at my house, things would have been different. We don't seem to have been a bright bunch in Carisbrooke Way all those years ago and checking the toilet roll holder never seemed to have crossed our minds. Every now and again a foghorn, sounding, "Toilet Roll!" would emanate from an unfortunate 'sitter' who hadn't taken into account the 'supply verses demand' intricacies of such paper. It had to be loud enough to alert Kate wherever she was in the house and, as the toilet was at the front of the house, it also probably alerted half the street to our plight. Each call was approximately six seconds long and it would continue to be repeated until Kate had completed her duty and fetched a roll, either upstairs or downstairs, depending where the summons came from. In later years, the downstairs toilet was banned from such use. Stink and continued shouts of, "Toilet roll!" were not deemed the best way to greet a visitor.

Another of Kate's jobs in those days was being the remote control for the television. Actual remote controls had yet to be invented, so we made do with Kate. She would sit on the floor and, on command, like a trained monkey, she would leap into action and change the channel to see what was on the other side. There were only the three channels, one of which was 'Protestant' which meant that it normally had the best stuff on anyway.

She was almost made redundant after 'Blue Peter' demonstrated how to make a remote control. It was basically a stick with a rubber end on it that you could jab at the buttons. She was reinstated when this was deemed too dangerous after the telly was almost poked off the stand.

Kate is the original idiot savant and, as such, does still have her uses post invention of the modern day 'safety' remote controls. Despite going through life with little or no common sense, she does have an uncanny ability to remember details. I have now employed her as my fact-checking service, which is handy on two counts; namely accuracy of information and, if anything libellous is contained in the pages of this book, she can officially take the blame instead of me.

Whilst checking these facts, we reminisced about the time when the whole family had gone to France, when she was only an eighteen-month-old baby. As our mum lay on the beach sleeping in the sun, the rest of us played Boules, the French version of bowls. As we played, we noticed that one of the Boules was missing. Paul glanced back to see Kate standing with her feet either side of Mum's head, holding the metal Boule, ready to drop it onto her face. Everyone moved swiftly and a murder in the South of France was narrowly avoided.

We both agreed that we would leave that out of the book in case it made Kate look bad.

* * *

I asked Bethan a couple of years ago if she wanted me to give her pocket money. She seemed surprised and replied that she didn't need any money because, if she wanted something, she knew that she could just ask me and I'd buy it for her. Her logic was pretty sound.

Just before she went to music school, however, she asked if she could do some jobs to earn some money to buy sweets and things while she was away. I asked if she would brush out Barney's kennel, but she said she was wearing her best clothes so I jokingly suggested that she could take over the poop scoop duties for the day, but she informed me that her mum had told her she wasn't allowed to do that. I nearly suggested that she should clean the car but I recalled the time that she had inadvertently cleaned her mum's car with a brillo pad and thought better of it. She offered to do some housework for me but it seemed a shame to waste a hot day inside so, in the end, I paid her for getting me an ice-lolly from the freezer.

Bethan seems a lot more sensible than I was at her age and I was sure she wouldn't spend all the money in one go. When we changed from old money to decimal coins, I was presented with a commemorative pack of the new coinage. The first thing I did was to prise the coins free from the display and spend them at the sweet shop. No Aztec bars, Bazooka Joes or Spangles for me that day. Instead, I bought several bags of marshmallows because they seemed to be bigger and considerably more foam-like than most other sweets clambering for my attention that special day. I proceeded to eat these substitutes for my legacy until I felt sick. You can stuff a lot of marshmallows in too before you feel sick, probably enough to package up a good sized television.

I was always a bit frightened of going on holiday after that in case they changed the currency again, when I was away, and no one let me know. I thought I would look a fool, going into the sweet shop, only to have everyone laughing at me as I handed over 'old' useless money.

Of course, I had the normal children's nightmares too, like suddenly realising I was sitting in school just in my pyjamas, or even less. How I made the bus journey without noticing this fact was conveniently overlooked. The nightmare of calling a teacher "Mum" also became reality on more than one occasion and, while the teacher smiled benignly, the rest of the class would be laughing their socks off. The only thing that would be even more embarrassing would be if I were sitting, resplendent in my 'PJ's', *as* I called her "Mum".

When my oldest brother Paul went off to Medical School for the first time, Kate secretly packed Bruno, his childhood teddy bear, into his case. Of course, his room-mate saw Bruno emerge, blinking in the light as the case was opened and, within days, everyone knew that Paul had brought his teddy with him for comfort. I'm sure it was the shame he felt that contributed to him leaving Medical School before he could qualify; either that or the fact that he was none too bright.

When Paul returned three years later looking dejected, everyone was sympathetic. "At least you tried son," my dad said as he opened the letter Paul had brought home with him. I don't think my brother had meant to show Dad his final report. The atmosphere changed somewhat as Dad read out the tutor's final words. "You have strutted your funky stuff once too often." As Kate, Neil and I all hurried upstairs, I could hear the words echoing throughout the house. "Bloody hell boy, Doctor? Doctor? Doctor Shit more like!"

❖ ❖ ❖

I have never been good at waking up and, although all the signs were there that Bethan was growing up into a small adult, I suppose I really just wanted to press the snooze button and put it off a bit.

The reason I've stayed in the North East is because I wanted to be near Bethan and she only lives a few hundred yards away from me now. I wish I had been as bright and confident as she is when I was ten. Some of the best times in my life have been on our weekends together. All I have to do is think of her and I smile. It's the simple things like wandering down to the park with her dressed in her Scooby Doo outfit, or going for picnics in the lazy summer countryside. We would stay out until late, allowing the long shadows we cast as the sun set behind us, to guide us home. I could swear that days as beautiful as that had been created just for Bethan and me. Nobody can make me feel as happy as she can. I love her very much and I suppose that was making the current situation feel worse.

I guess she was just growing up. She didn't want to hold my hand when we were out because it was supposedly embarrassing and she was also becoming moody. *Very* moody. *Extremely* moody. At other times, she wasn't sure if she could come over as her friend might visit her instead and, anyway, even if she did come over, she didn't want to drive anywhere far in the car and so on. It was that sort of moody.

She didn't even want to play schools anymore – I was gutted because, not only did it seem like the end of an era, but I was on the verge of moving up into the next reading class too!

She was also turning into something of a 'blackcatter'. Nothing seemed good enough, to the extent that if I said I had a black cat, she would have had one that was blacker. The situation was fluctuating and, in the moments when she forgot that she was supposed to act all temperamental, she held my hand again and we laughed and joked at the same old stupid stuff. When she is like that she is the most fantastic company.

I knew it was a phase she was going through, but that didn't make it any easier. I was finding it very difficult to cope with and I couldn't even talk to my mum about it; she'd have helped me. I was feeling very awkward. I know Bethan was probably feeling even more awkward but that was cold comfort. In fact, it made me feel worse. I just wanted it to be like the old times again.

I felt pretty awkward with Deborah sometimes too. Her husband had died and, from things she said about him, he sounded like a really nice guy. I felt like I was second best.

There was a lot of awkwardness going around; in fact I've never seen so many 'awkwards' in one chapter. It is meant to be the most miss-spelt word in the English language, so that might explain away that fact.

The whole situation made me feel sad – sadder than when I was a child and I turned on the telly to watch the Cowboy film, only to hear those dreaded words, "Except for viewers in Wales, who will have their own programme." *Much* sadder, and that's saying something. Maybe even as sad as Florence Ballard.

It was touch and go if I was even as sad as someone Kate had known at school. I can't even name the poor guy, it's that sort of sad, let's just call him 'John Smith'. It was his 18th birthday, and his parents had arranged a table full of the finest finger buffet food and bought every type of drink under the sun for him to mix cocktails for his chums, and generally have a fantastic time celebrating his coming of age. They had even arranged to go out for the night to leave him to party the night away, away from the prying eyes of the adults. That's the good bit – but this is the bad bit – no one came. Not a soul, nobody, nil personages, not anyone, zero, zilch. His parents arrived back in the early hours to find him sitting like a despondent Kermit on the stairs. If that is not one of the saddest stories you've heard, I'd like to hear a sadder one! (well, I wouldn't actually). If it had been me, I would have stolen a few ornaments, spilt some wine on the floor, force fed myself half the food, made the cat sick behind the sofa, peed on the bathroom floor and maybe left a couple of condoms around the house just to at least *pretend* that some sort of wild party had just occurred.

(And if I *was* the poor guy who had suffered this 'I've got no mates in the entire world and people will stand and point at me and say "there's that sad bloke" till the end of time' humiliation, I would make it my solemn duty to hunt down the bastard who leaked the story and shove the entire finger buffet where the sun don't shine ...but I digress).

Of course John Smith wasn't his real name, it's actually Russell Jones.

Oh shit!

One of the supposedly helpful things people say is that the darkest hour is the one before dawn. It may be, but the darkest hour is also the one where it is most dark! When I was in a difficult or unpleasant situation in the Forces, I would get through it by mentally preparing myself. Whether it was interrogation, sitting in a cold wet trench, or on a particularly boring tour of duty, I would tell myself to get on with it because it would be over in a few hours or a week or six months, whatever the relevant timescale was. The trouble here was that I had no idea how long this would last. I suppose I would only get to know where this was going when I arrived.

A year before, Bethan and I had sat together in a coffee shop in Durham. Bethan, as usual, had ordered the largest piece of chocolate cake that money could buy and we had belly laughed at something or other as we often did.

I now sat there alone and, as I looked out of the window in my pensive mood, I felt that it seemed like the end of the world as I knew it. A flyer propped up next to the sugar bowl informed me that today was 'The Third World Awareness Day'. Just my luck – I'd already missed the first two. As I pushed the plunger down on my cafetière, I half expected the Renault parked in the street outside to explode.

CHAPTER SEVENTEEN

Tales from the Riverbank

A wing must have fallen off a seagull as it was now lying on the path in front of Barney and me. It must have been a terrible shock for the bird when it happened, and I suppose it must have made him fly in infinite circles afterwards. We looked up, but he wasn't circling overhead anymore, and we couldn't seem to find the rest of his body anywhere. There was just the wing. I say, 'he' but, for all I know, it could have been a 'she'.

"No!" I barked at Barney as he went to pick it up, but he picked it up just the same. I had to resort to telling him to fetch it to me to get it off him and stop him from chewing it. We didn't know if the bird was going to come back for it, and it would have been very embarrassing for all concerned if Barney had been caught eating it.

We had passed a dead mole on the path the day before. His pale hands were splayed out either side of his furry face as if he had been doing an Al Jolson impression for his woodland chums, the second before he was mown down. "I'd walk a million miles for one of your smiles, my ma..." THWACK!

Barney is starting to be quite mischievous now and I often see him chewing away at something when we are sitting in the house. I'll ask him what he's got, but that normally brings no immediate response and he'll keep on chewing. I'll get up, go over to him and prise his mouth open and shake his little head so that whatever is in there will fall out. Most of the time, there's nothing. I think it's just a game he plays with me. After I let go, he will make that sort of grimace he does in wry amusement at the situation (aha Barney, think you can beat me in a game of wits do you? Well you've met your equal now!). I've told him that, if that's the funniest he can be, it's rubbish. Even the visiting priests were funnier, and that's saying something.

He is funniest really when he's not trying – the way he just potters about, tilting his head to one side if he is at all puzzled by anything; the way he spends ages staring at the other dog who seems to live at the bottom of his water bowl, or the fact that he likes to walk around in a little circle before he lies down. And why does he always think that, if there's a knock on the door, it's for him? I also like the way he runs in his sleep, or just lies there with his tongue poking out. Occasionally, he sometimes sleeps on his back with his legs in the air and I thought he was dead the first time he did that. When I mentioned this to one of the assistants at the dog school, she said that when her dog was lying like that, she did a health check on his bits but I believed that was probably a bit of a dodgy habit to fall into – and quite possibly illegal.

In fact it was the same woman who I confided in, telling her that one morning last week I had come down to find that Barney had done a little poop on the kitchen floor. I can scarcely believe what happened next. She had turned to me and quietly said, "Now Mr Donoghue, *you* are really responsible for that aren't you". What the fuck!! Have I got this right? She was accusing *me* of sneaking down in the middle of the night and laying one down just to frame my little pup? She must be bloody sick in the head! Sick I tell you!

For someone like me, who likes things in their place, Barney is a nightmare, as he leaves his toys everywhere. I for one will be quiet happy when Bethan eventually puts me in an old people's home (as long as it's not one of those you hear about that leave you lying in your own piss-drenched bed for days on end). I enjoyed the routine of living onboard ship and in barracks. I would be quite content to pass away my twilight years, just playing cards with my new old friends, and maybe once in a while sitting in front of the fire with a tartan rug on my knee; in fact, I could probably do without the rug – a tart on her own would be just fine. Maybe I would be a slightly grumpy old man by then, and spend my time making lists of what annoys me about the world. A list of technical flaws in the dog design department would be a good place to start. I've already covered the 'nose in bowl' fault and the 'showing off arsehole' too much issue. What is it with this 'opening doors with your head' thing too? And they never shut the door after themselves either. You would think they were born in a barn! (Well, I guess Barney has some sort of excuse in that he *was* actually born in a barn, but you get my drift). And for an animal that sleeps all night and kips most of the day, why, oh why, does he still potter about yawning all the time? And what about that couple of half-hearted kicks they do with the back legs after they've done a poop, as if they are trying to cover it up. Pathetic. Many a time have I shouted after Barney "You're not fooling anyone!" as he scampers off. If God ever wants to do a general recall to sort the problems, my list could prove invaluable.

I never realised dogs could snore so much either, and he has also taken to lying across doors like one of those stuffed snakes that are used to keep out the cold. I don't know if he is stupid for lying there, or if I am more stupid for not wanting to disturb him when I need to open the door. As he wakes, his one visible eye will move around in its socket as he follows my every move, and I will then hear a hollow banging sound. On investigation, I discover it's just his tail wagging onto the floor. It seems that a great deal of energy is expired when just another of those grins would suffice.

However, enough warmth – pointless nostalgia about Barney had to be a thing of the past as I had just received an important phone call from Kate and action was needed.

* * *

The quiet camping trip with Doctor Shit and his crew was

developing into a full-blown family exercise. Kate, her husband Woody (so named because he resembles Woody from Toy Story, or was it the other way round) and daughter Poppy were also coming down to camp for the weekend.

What is more, although he could afford for someone to come down in his place, Neil was also rumoured to be joining us with his clan. There would be fifteen of us altogether. This was going to be unique for me – a camping trip with the whole family, without being kicked in the back for three hundred miles first.

I had originally planned to arrive on the Saturday but, by then, everyone else would have already claimed the best pitches. I didn't mind who had the worst pitch as long as it wasn't me. If I did arrive last of course, everyone would be there to admire my twenty-second erection. It was a hard decision but, in the end, the pitch became paramount. I rang Deborah in Turkey and told her the change of plan, and then contacted the kennels to book Tess in a day early. Only Barney was going camping this time round.

On the last family camping holiday Neil had spent in Wales, his tent blew away in the middle of the night so I thought it best not to pitch next to him, if at all possible.

Paul and Neil had cycled along Offa's Dyke, or some such journey last year and, after a full day in the saddle, they had both spent the first night squeezed into Neil's tiny hiking tent. As the two of them emerged the next morning, Paul stretched out, commenting that his bum was really sore from the previous day's activities. As this drew strange looks from the surrounding campers, they decided that, rather than try and explain, it was far better to rapidly pack up their gear and make a speedy exit on their bikes.

Unfortunately, Bethan would still be in Jamaica but, saying that, if you can't make a camping trip, I guess Jamaica is as good a place as any to be. It would also have been an opportunity for her to see all her cousins again as she doesn't see them nearly often enough.

Meanwhile, I couldn't fail to see that this was an excellent opportunity for me to waste far too much time organising my emergency kit in preparation for the forthcoming expedition.

The laws of gravity are very, very strict – but even stricter are the laws governing male allegiance to torches, Swiss army knives, and pictures of ladies in the lingerie section of mail order catalogues.

My interest in torches had first proved useful when I was issued with my first military right angle flashlight. It did the job well enough, but not as good as the tiny AAA torch that I had doctored by colouring the lens red with a felt tip pen (to preserve night vision!) and tied with some parachute cord to my combats. Gradually it dawned on me that *all* of my equipment was actually provided by the lowest bidder. In fact it was even pretty hard to get *any* equipment from the quartermaster's stores as the store men seemed to live by the principle 'stores are for storing things' – and when they did actually issue any gear, it seemed to come in one of three sizes – too small, too big or tough shit. Sure, everything did the job more or less, so the MOD and politicians could say that they had issued all the relevant kit to 'our boys', but it wasn't the really good kit that you needed. It was the same when I was small and all my friends had Dunlop green flash, and I was still wearing 'Empire Made' daps (or plimsolls as the English people over the pipe bridge would call them). They did the job ...but...well you know ...it wasn't quite the same.

So I had initially produced my own small, but extensively stocked, hypochondriac kit filled with bandages, plasters, safety pins and more importantly the world's finest tablets, capable of curing 90% of the world's commonest ailments that I could possibly suffer from in the field. I also took the wise, if not anti-social, precaution of avoiding contact with anyone who could possibly have any cough or snuffle in the few weeks prior to deployment to prevent cross contamination. That is, contamination of me that would make me cross. During this phase I was also vulnerable to the power of negative suggestion. So if anyone even dared mention to me that I was perhaps looking a bit tired I would convince myself that I must be about to come down with man flu and immediately counter attack my mutinous eco system with a barrage of assorted pills. Whoever said laughter was the best medicine obviously hasn't tried industrial strength Ibuprofen!

My survival kit, even if I say so myself, was a beauty. All incredibly small so as to fit inside an old tobacco tin (complete with shiny inside lid for signalling), but every item a winner. A condom doubles as a great water carrier (I wasn't the only one pleased when Durex started making them in different flavours!), waterproof matches that I had made myself by dripping wax over the heads, small candle, garden wire and a tampon (kindling for fire-lighting). I could go on...so I will. Dark shoe polish that could be used as a fuel for a fire (and the smell it gives off when used this way is also good for warding off animals), hooks and line for catching fish, a snare for catching land based animals, knife, small compass, magnifying glass and so on. You can buy them ready made now but it's not the same!

All we needed now was some decent weather. In the meantime I decided to put my time to best use and hunted around for the Littlewoods catalogue.

CHAPTER EIGHTEEN

Kevin: Angel of the North

At the top of my stairs, underneath the photo of me with some other soldiers with their faces blanked out for effect, is a picture of me with the bloke from 'The Cure'. It's not really the bloke from 'The Cure' of course, but my friend Carol. It is one of those photographs where the flash was too powerful, and all you can see is a pale looking me and someone else with wild jet black hair and bright red lipstick. I know it doesn't sound very flattering, but she is actually very attractive. I went out with Carol for about five years on and off and I am pretty sure it was she who accompanied me to the last big fun family get together.

I haven't spoken to her for a couple of years now, but I'd love to come across her face again. I miss her company, but what I don't miss was the endless 'who is better' debate – Jesus or Father Christmas? I would tell her that it didn't really matter as most people thought they were one and the same anyway. He must be sick of people only praying to Him when they want something.

I never quite understood, as a child, the principle we had as Catholics of praying to Saints or even Mary. Surely, if you wanted something done, you went directly to the organ grinder. Maybe the thought process behind it was that if Jesus, or God for that matter, were stowed under with prayers, a quick one to Saint 'X' would probably get through and he would be delighted with some attention for a change. Furthermore, God would be far more likely to listen to one of the Saints coming to

Him with someone's request, rather than direct from a mere mortal down on Earth – a sort of cosmic queue jumping.

❖ ❖ ❖

I knew that the continuation of Project 'X', also known as the Christmas calendar, was dependent on Bethan's continued goodwill. Therefore, the trip to Snitter would have to be meticulously planned. Briefings could then take place as to what was required in the way of equipment, such as the model (Barney) and the precise dimensions of the black masking tape to be used. Questions needed to be answered, such as, "*Would the model need to be hoisted in the air to be displayed, grimacing alongside the sign, or had the occupants of the village central to this episode already prepared defence tactics as a result of previous sign sabotage attempts?*" We would have to be in and out in a slick, well-rehearsed operation.

A reconnaissance mission was needed and, with Bethan and Debs still absent from duty, I volunteered myself for the role. I accepted that the volunteer was fit for duty and briefed myself on what was required. It was a bit rushed but I think I understood most of what was said.

That night, I prayed to Santa for some good weather. Surely not even *he* could be busy in the height of summer.

❖ ❖ ❖

My journey took me past the Angel of the North, or 'Kevin' as the councillors of Durham would have probably called him. At over two hundred tonnes and twenty metres in height, with a wingspan the same as that of a Jumbo jet, it is hailed as the most viewed piece of art in Great Britain. I personally think that maybe this is just the tiniest bit misleading. From that build-up, you could be forgiven for thinking that thousands of people are flocking to some museum or other to catch a glimpse of its majesty.

In reality, it is the most viewed piece of art because you can't miss it! It's plonked at the side of the busiest road in the North East. You can't avoid seeing it unless you are blind, in which case you shouldn't be driving along the A1 anyway. If it were replaced with a big fibreglass penguin tomorrow, that in turn would then take over the mantle of 'most viewed piece of art in the UK'. That being said, I for one would probably flock to see such an enormous 'Pingu'.

Apparently, according to the official spiel, the Angel is trying to say, "Is that all we can be?" and as I passed him on my journey, I replied, "What the hell was all that about?"

That was also the only thing I could think to put on the 'comments' card when I visited the Baltic Arts Centre in Gateshead recently. The Baltic, along with many other contemporary Arts Centres seems to run along the lines of 'The Emperor's New Clothes'. If you can't understand the majesty, deep meaning and inherent aesthetic beauty of the rubbish peddled off as art on display, obviously you are not clever or artistically gifted enough!

Amongst other things, there was a sculpture made of hoover parts and upstairs there was a monopoly board with some rice krispies and cocoa beans stuck on it. It was supposed to be something to do with the plight of the Third World. I thought about taking along a bag full of Barney's poops and calling it, 'The Turd World Plight' just to see the reaction I would provoke. I would have probably won the Turner prize.

I had already notched up the 'No Place' photo for the calendar when I made a quick detour on my way back from the Sainsbury's, near Durham. I had actually felt a bit self-conscious, standing taking the photo as the cars rushed past.

They all seemed to be so blasé in a non barking dog way about the sign and it made me feel a bit 'touristy'; a bit like an outsider. I decided that I would put on my fluorescent security jacket for the next shoot and stand out so much that I would go completely full circle and fit in again. I would be Mr Council Official, viewed with suspicion, but obviously meant to be there.

Sadly, the 'Pity Me' shots were deemed unsuitable and would have to be taken again. We didn't look miserable enough and it really needed to be raining for full effect.

I wasn't looking forward to breaking the news to Bethan.

❖ ❖ ❖

Sometimes you don't have the luxury of a decent recce. When we used to dock in a foreign port, for instance, we had no idea where the best places to go were. Luckily enough, the Admiralty did and would tell us in coded form. Officially, they would promulgate a list of places that British sailors were barred from visiting and, naturally, we immediately knew these were the best ones.

Many years later, I was heading back from Poland with the two sergeants who had been looking after the border post with me.

We were told that, on no account, were we to visit Berlin on our journey back, so we duly headed straight there. We parked up our vehicle, disguising the fact that it was military and then 'demilitarised' ourselves. We only had our uniforms and the odds and sods we would wear when 'dossing' around the barracks during the limited time off between duties, so we duly mixed and matched.

Three ragamuffins then moseyed into the City. One of the sergeants had been a paratrooper when Berlin was a city adrift in East Germany during the Cold War and we were treated to a tour of sentry points and patrol routes. We went to Check Point Charlie and all bought bits of the old Berlin Wall. Apparently, enough 'genuine' Berlin Wall has been sold to build the wall again three times over, and mine even had a bit of graffiti on it to make it look more realistic. We saw part of the wall that was still standing and it seemed much thinner and lower than I had imagined.

We were all starting to get a bit hungry by then and looked for somewhere to eat. We saw a Mongolian Restaurant and were tempted but decided against it, primarily because a badly translated sign in the window promised 'Special cocktails for the ladies with nuts'.

The menu also invited us to discover "The Secret of the Mongols". It went on to suggest that it could be relevant for us in our over-urbanised and, in many ways, unnatural world. They stated that the Mongol has something to teach us with respect to our relationship to nature, as well as to the fruition and utilisation of our innate human potential. Maybe they did. They always seemed to look happy. However, just at that moment, it all seemed a bit deep for us. What we really wanted was cake.

The old eastern bloc seemed obsessed with cake, and very soon we also became hopeless cake junkies. We were barracked in an old Red Army camp in the former East Germany and drove daily to our post on the Polish border. Cakes would follow cold meats for breakfast; a stop off en route would be accompanied by cake and, at the morning meeting at the border itself, the Polish official would produce cakes for all the staff, us included. We liked cake. We duly stopped off at a beatnik style coffee house in Berlin and had our fix.

Still hungry, we decided on a Chinese. I have always been amazed that Chinese restaurants or takeaways can be found everywhere you go. I imagined the family sitting somewhere in rural China, pouring over a big map and wondering where to set up business next. Maybe it would be a pin in the map or perhaps they would decide to settle in the place name that sounded good. They could have no idea, as they sat cross-legged around the chart, what all these places were really like. Some would be delighted when they arrived in their new adopted home and found that Tenby, York or Winchester were such beautiful places, but others would be sick as pigs when their bus pulled up at the depot in Merthyr Tydfil. As the diesel fumes hung around inside the half lit, damp bus depot, avoiding the drizzle outside, the new arrivals would be gazing open-mouthed until one would eventually put into words what they all had been thinking. "It never looked like this in the film."

"Hey Dad, are you sure it was 'Dial M for Merthyr'?"

CHAPTER NINETEEN

The Happy Monkey

I had no idea how to solve a particular Barney-related issue I was experiencing, and all the dog books I had read seemed to avoid the subject. If you have a boy dog, as opposed to a girl dog, you will doubtless know what I am on about. If I tell you that my only solution is to sternly tell him, "Put your lipstick away!" you can probably make an educated guess as to what I am referring to. Something should be invented, and it's probably something very simple, that would end up doing the trick in the end.

Someone once told me that the Americans spent millions of dollars inventing a pen that could write in zero gravity, for the NASA space programme. It had to be able to perform upside down, not dry out in the sterile environment, and have ink that didn't freeze. The Russians saved all that money and took a pencil into space.

The other thing they don't seem to mention in all those dog manuals is why your pup finds it irresistible to eat other dog's poo. I mentioned it to the mad woman at the dog school once and she said she believed it was because the animal was lacking some nutrients in his food and, he then obtained these by eating other dog's droppings. She added "I don't know if there is any substance in this". I don't think substance was the right word to use to be honest.

This confirmed to me that the woman was deluded as well as sick in the head. I somehow find it hard to imagine Barney, who has a pea sized brain to rival Kate's, thinking "Hmmm, I seem to be lacking some basic vital nutrients in my diet. If I remember the lessons correctly from puppy school, I should gain these additional vitamins and antioxidants by feasting on the excreta of other canines."

I'd take him to the dog psychologist but it would be a waste of time – he knows he's not allowed up on the couch anyway. No, I've just come to the conclusion that he's just a dirty, greedy filth hound.

Sorry, I digress.

I was in a pub in Chichester with my friend Ruth a few years back when she spotted a guy drinking from a glass-bottomed tankard. She had asked me what the glass bottom was for and I had replied that it was so that, as he drank, he could see a life he had missed. I could be very morose sometimes. I don't know why I was then as I had met Ruth on the Investigations Course at Roussillon Barracks – a girl almost half my age and nearly twice my security clearance – and she was the most delightful company. Often I would pop to her room in the mess, where I would find her lounging on her bed sipping a chilled Chablis. In those situations I, on the other hand, found I just had a warm Semillon. She also helped me improve my vocabulary, as she was the one who taught me the meaning of unrequited. I knew then that I'd only ever get lip service from her.

Another explanation for the glass bottom is that, in the days when recruiting parties went out around the country, if you accepted the King's shilling, you could be conscripted into military service. It is said that sometimes a crafty recruiting sergeant would drop a shilling into someone's drink when they were unaware and, as the 'victim' drank the last of his ale, the coin would slide down the tankard and touch his lips. They had taken the King's shilling and were hauled off to serve King and Country. The glass bottom for the tankard was invented so that the drinker could check to see if there was a shilling loitering with intent in his ale. I'm not sure that's any more real than my version – I will have to check with Kate.

As far as simple inventions go, I am convinced that I invented 'Splat the rat' – that popular game at fetes, where a furry toy rat is dropped down a five-foot or so vertical length of tubing. The aim is for the player to 'splat' the rat with a baseball bat as he pops out of the end. The clue is in the title really. To avoid copyright, it may sometimes be called 'Twat the rat'. It is pretty hard to anticipate the right time to splat though and, if you are not careful, you can pay out a considerable sum in countless futile attempts to win a pathetic stuffed toy. A strange feeling of déjà vu has just come over me. (What do French people say when *they* have déjà vu?) I am not so convinced of my invention rights that I would take the next scout pack I see using my invention at some village summer fair, to every court in the land, but just convinced enough to tell Bethan, every time I see one, that it was *my* invention.

I woke up one morning convinced that I was French and had invented the periodic table. *(Bonne occasion pour une plaisanterie française. J'ai acheté un pantalon français mais il était Toulon et Toulouse).* I was wrong then and I may be wrong now.

I love weird inventions and quite look forward to the Bettaware and Kleeneze women calling with their catalogues. I can sit for literally minutes as I look through their curious pages. It is normally a good clue that, if something has a wacky spelling, it is probably quite an outlandish item. Take the Thylacine for example – that seems something straight out of a Bettaware catalogue. Often in these bizarre inventions, it's the left over letters in scrabble that are used aplenty, like the K and Z. They must be the same people who gave the names to the new republics created after the fall of the Soviet Union.

* * *

I know two people called Graham. The first is the Graham at work who used to be my trusted lieutenant. When I say, 'used to be,' it isn't that he ceased to be trusted; it's just that he's not my lieutenant anymore. I moved into Security Services and Graham remained in Operations. He is an ex-Warrant Officer in the Light Infantry and does everything very efficiently at Light Infantry pace which, for the uninitiated, is quick. If he were a record player, he would be spinning at 78 rpm.

He had recently returned from an outing to Edinburgh Zoo with Mrs Graham so I naturally enquired about Billy. It hadn't been a good trip, it transpired. They had plodded about the zoo in torrential rain and, to add insult to injury, most of the animals had wisely chosen to remain in their houses so there was very little to see. I think that is what is called a double whammy, although they had enjoyed the penguin parade.

The other Graham is Graham the builder. He is a serious sort of guy. Like 'work Graham', builder Graham does an excellent job but everything is performed in slow motion. If he were spinning at 33 rpm, he would still sound as if he was being speeded up. Having two Grahams is confusing, so builder Graham will hereafter be referred to as 'Laughing Boy'.

Laughing Boy was responsible for responding to the surge in renovation fervour in my house until, one day, Barney arrived and the money suddenly ran out. The Boy would estimate the number of days a particular task would take and then take twice as long, aided by Norman the (ex) foreman as his assistant. We had agreed costs up front so, apart from the occasional stomach-churning flash of builders' cleavage, I wasn't particularly worried about this over-run in the early days.

As the weeks drew on, however, I did start to dread returning home and finding the Boy pottering away, long into the night. He would chat for ages about how rushed off his feet he was and how he never had time to see his family and how he couldn't afford to take time off, all due to his heavy work schedule. I felt like telling him that, if he stopped chatting and just got on with the job, he might find he had all the time in the world. Even Bethan, who is very tolerant and tells me off if I make fun of the unfortunate, started to do impressions of Laughing Boy, speaking very slowly about all sorts of rubbish.

Things were so behind schedule at one point that I had to use the ultimate sanction and threaten them with Deborah, as they both seemed a bit scared of her.

Norman was a nice chap as, indeed, was Laughing Boy but he ruined a good prop for me. I had bought an exceedingly realistic latex mask from the magic shop. I tested it for realism when Tim, who I have known for almost twenty years, came up to visit. I had waited on the bridge for him to drive past and park up outside the house when I donned the mask and, for added effect, limped down the street. As Tim wandered up the path, I followed him. "What do you want mate?" Tim questioned. I said nothing and continued to limp towards him. Tim then started knocking furiously at the door, "John, John, let me in!" I thought he was playing along with me and took the mask off, chuckling. It was only when I could see that he was shaking like a butterfly and he requested a change of underwear that I realised just how effective the disguise was. We agreed never to mention the incident again.

The trouble was that now the mask also made me look just like Norman, the (ex) foreman. I couldn't feel scary in it anymore; I just felt like Laughing Boy's sidekick – affable Norm.

❖ ❖ ❖

In the kitchen that Laughing Boy and Norman the (ex) foreman had built, there is no cooker. Instead, I have a very large microwave which, if you have a pacemaker fitted, is best kept at a five-yard distance. I'm not much of a cook.

Barney does not suffer though and is properly fed twice a day. Both of these meals are 'dinner' to him. After being made to sit and patiently wait for a minute until the command to stuff his face, the concept of having to distinguish in his little mind between his 'breakfast' and 'evening meal' would just be too much. He doesn't mind what they are called as long as he gets his two square meals. Of course, in his bowl, they are actually round meals, but the term dates back from when sailors got their meals on square plates and it stuck.

I used to give lectures in the Navy about how Naval sayings and customs originated, travelling around in uniform or sometimes in 'mufti' (inspired by the practice of General Mufti, who found that sagging morale in the British Army was boosted by the policy of allowing the men to wear civilian clothing instead of uniforms on certain days of the year).

I'd usually start by telling the assembled gathering that I had just come back from the local RSPCA office and it was tiny. You couldn't swing a cat in there! As the room went quiet, apart from the regulation embarrassed cough from somewhere near the back, I'd quickly try to get the audience back on side by telling them what they had come to hear.

The 'cat' in Naval terms was the cat-of-nine-tails – a type of whip used to give lashings to sailors in the days of sail. Each of the nine strips of leather on the whip would be about three feet long. It would be too cramped to dispense a proper flogging below deck because, 'there wasn't room to swing a cat'. Floggings were always given up on deck where there was more space and, although the floggings have long ceased, we were left with the phrase.

Instead of a flogging, a sailor may have been made to 'Run the gauntlet'. This was a form of punishment that involved forcing a sailor to make his way between two rows of men, each armed with a rope cosh with which to hit the offender. The saying now refers to running the risk of being criticised or attacked from two or more sides.

After your punishment, you may have had salt rubbed into your wound. Salt was carried on board ship as a disinfectant and was applied to wounds to prevent gangrene. This process was also very painful and to 'Rub salt into wounds' has come to mean now to aggravate or to add insult to injury.

To balance things up we have 'Hunky Dory' meaning OK or satisfactory derived from Honki-Dori, a street in the port of Yokohama, Japan, where many a pleasure awaited visiting sailors. The crew might have imagined what adventures were 'in the offing' or about to happen. The area of sea visible from shore is known as the 'offing'. Therefore a ship visible from land was said to be 'in the offing' – about to enter port. They might need some extra cash – and what could be easier than selling lengths of old rope – 'Money for old rope'.

'Piping hot' and to 'pipe down' both come from the practice of the boatswain piping a signal on a whistle or pipe when meals were served and alternatively to signal the end of the day and time for lights out and silence.

'Clean sweep', meaning a complete change or nowadays also meaning an overwhelming victory, comes from the fact that in rough weather, waves washed (swept) over the decks of ships, shifting about anything that wasn't secured. It also refers to the few minutes after Barney in Che Sweep mode has had a bath and is relatively clean before getting up to his eyeballs in mud again. Barney of course has a bath in cold water, unlike Cleopatra who bathed in milk. I forget the film but still remember the bit where someone asks her 'Pasteurised?' to which she replied something along the lines of 'No, just up to my tits'.

Meanwhile, back at sea and at the Battle of Copenhagen in 1801, Nelson was signalled an order from the Admiral of the Fleet, but believing that if he followed the command his ships might have been in danger on nearby shallows, he famously put his telescope to his blind eye and didn't carry out the instruction. He might as well have held the telescope to his working brown eye – he wasn't going to act on it anyway. So if a person ignores something nowadays they are often said to 'Turn a blind eye'.

Everybody is on their best behaviour on a date but eventually we, 'show our true colours', or reveal our true intentions or personality. Early warships often carried flags from many nations on board in order to elude or deceive the enemy. The rules of civilised warfare called for all ships to hoist their true national ensigns before firing a shot.

Someone who finally shows his true colours is acting like a

warship, which would hail another ship, flying a friendly country's flag, but then hoist their own when they were in firing range.

Some say that the brass triangles that supported stacks of iron cannonballs on sailing ships were called monkeys. In cold weather, as brass contracts more than iron, the triangles contracted sufficiently for the balls to fall off. So, it's cold enough to 'Freeze the balls off a brass monkey', there you go – not rude after all. You can say it to your Granny now.

Back in the 'brass monkey' days, women occasionally came on board ship, to keep the poor lonely sailors company in port. What a nice thing to do. In the morning, the ratings had to get on with their duties whilst the women could lie in. The Officers would therefore go round below deck and shout, "Show a leg!" and, if a woman's leg poked out of the hammock, its owner was allowed to rest on, while a hairy bloke's leg had to get its owner's body off to work. The Army equivalent was, 'Rise and Shine!' which the sergeants would bellow every morning as all soldiers were expected to polish their boots at the start of each day. (The early morning wake up call 'Hands off cocks, on socks' is something totally different all together … I think it's a student thing).

'Sweet FA' was another naval term and actually stands for, 'Sweet Fanny Adams'. Fanny Adams was murdered in 1867 and her body dismembered. Her gravestone reads 'Here lies Sweet Fanny Adams'. At about the same time, canned corned beef was introduced to the Navy and, as the sailors thought the food looked like Fanny's mutilated corpse, they came to use the expression to refer to unpleasant meals. It subsequently came to mean nothing of value. The can, meanwhile, was used as a cup which was, in turn, referred to as a 'Fanny'. A sailor can always find a good use for a fanny.

As for the Air Force, when a Second World War fighter pilot loosed off all his ammunition – nine yards of it in one burst, he was going 'The full nine yards'.

Finally, dependant on audience reaction so far I might finish off by advising them never to stand behind Satan in a queue at the Post Office – 'because the devil takes many forms'.

Cue embarrassed cough.

Meanwhile, it was Barney's relatives who brought about the phrase, 'The dog's bollocks' to mean something excellent. Apparently, it arises from the fact that licking them seems to be a particularly favourite activity of theirs. Bizarrely enough though, 'Bollocks' on its own is just plain bad.

And I suppose Barney himself, after his turding activities on his long morning walk the other day, combined with the shortage of poop bags, made me into a real 'shit kicker'.

※ ※ ※

As much as Barney had made me into a real shit kicker, I think I was actually becoming a soft shit kicker, as messy as that may sound.

I didn't seem to be able to hold a grudge like I used to and was feeling all the better for it. Some people seem excellent at holding grudges, allowing their stomachs to knot up whenever they hear a particular person's name mentioned but I had concluded that life was too short for that. My mum, and my belly, would have been proud of me.

They say time flies like an arrow and fruit flies like a banana. Either way, Barney's metamorphosis into a grown up dog was continuing at a fair pace but was still only part way there. No longer did he lie on the floor like he had been dropped from a great height, with all four legs poking out, resembling a big letter 'H', but neither had he started to cock his leg when he had a pee. I wasn't sure if this was something instinctive or whether I would need to show him. Everyone also seemed to comment that he was growing larger all the time but, as I was always around him, I wasn't really aware of the daily differences. I spent ages once, just staring at him but, at the end of the exercise, I couldn't claim that I detected any noticeable increase in size during that test period. Other things *did* shrink however and I was sure that Bethan and Debs would notice a big change on their return.

CHAPTER TWENTY

See You Next Tuesday

We all used to play a game called 'Good dog; Bad dog' ever since we got the thumbs up at the 'Will we, or won't we have a 'Plan B' dog?' conference. The rules were very simple. When you saw a dog, you had to judge whether it was a good dog or a bad dog. The clue was in the title really. A good dog would be one that was neither pulling its owner's arm off nor walking on the lead in front of said owner. It was a dog that would bring the ball back during a game of fetch, or one that didn't wee all over the person it was greeting. Aha, that's where the skill in the game was involved. A dog could be both a good dog and a bad dog, depending on the circumstances. Well, the game kept *us* happy at least.

I was looking forward to playing this some more and I felt pretty confident in assuming that Bethan and Debs would feel the same. I had read somewhere that books concerning the Third Reich, cats and golf, all sold well. I also knew that fishing was the most popular hobby in the country. If I could somehow incorporate these into a board game version of 'Good dog; Bad dog' and it was marketed properly, I could make my fortune. (Perhaps 'Good golfing 'n fishing dog; bad cat hating Nazi dog' would do the trick with a picture of that naughty dog from Germany on the box).

When Susan and I went to Robin's wedding years ago, we had played an embryonic version of the same game called, 'Who is Tim?'

❖ ❖ ❖

By way of introduction, Robin had served in the Royal Anglians with Tim and me. He is a thoroughly decent chap and maybe it is unfair that he should be remembered in this way, but he is.

I couldn't be bothered to find out what we were fighting for but our story begins with Robin and me heading off to some grid reference in order to take up our position on the edge of the killing zone, or some such place. We were up against the clock, so we decided to commit the cardinal sin of cutting across an open expanse of land, instead of skirting around the boundary where there was cover. We crouched down and sprinted across the ploughed field, weighed down with weapons and webbing, half expecting to hear shots ring out at any moment. Hopefully if there was any shooting, it would be enemy fire. Friendly fire is not actually very friendly (in the same way that 'Intelligence Corps' might confuse people by suggesting intelligence), and also seems to be uncannily more accurate than enemy fire! At least there were two of us which meant I was only half as likely to get hit.

Robin was faster than me and had almost made it to the other side when he slowed down considerably and ran the last ten yards in an exaggerated John Wayne style, hopping from leg to leg. I was worried that he might have been caught by some type of booby trap, but instead it transpired that he had been caught by pure over-exertion. Too much straining and effort had caused a minor 'poop discharge' incident. He undid the elastics where his combats met his boots, shook his leg to eject the 'misfire' and we set off on our way again. Now that's what I call a soldier. I'd be proud to shake his hand anytime, but not just then you understand. We agreed never to mention the unfortunate incident again.

We hadn't seen Tim for a couple of years and I'm not sure what we expected him to have transformed into, but guesses were made at the big fat man with the beard, the short balding guy with three kids, the bemused looking Chinese chap holding the battered old film poster and Times New Roman – you know the type. In his effort to prolong the game for us, Tim turned up after the wedding looking exactly the same as he always did. Six foot something and pretty confident. Oh, except for the time he was banging on my door like a frightened girl, when I had the 'Norman' mask on. But we shall not mention that.

We had a fantastic time at the celebrations – so fantastic that I received a five-year ban from Robin's cottage in the Welsh countryside as punishment. Subsequent misdemeanours resulted in an extension to ten years and, eventually, I was banned from here to eternity. Tim seems to get off scot-free each time, by turning Queen's evidence.

* * *

Bethan was back from music school and came over early for Barney's morning walk. As we walked, we laughed at the bizarre names some dogs have been given. We once found one with a collar that said he was called '19 Sebastopol Terrace'. She pretended to beckon an imaginary dog with the long-winded name. She looked funny.

Bethan spotted what looked like a seal in the water and we watched, transfixed, as evolution happened before our very eyes and it emerged from the river as a dog.

We also passed two suppliers of Barney's favourite snack on the riverside path that morning and all he could do, as the horses trotted past, was to hide behind Bethan's legs and hope they made a delivery.

Swimming at the leisure centre followed and we sniggered at some woman who must have tried to sneakily pump in the water but was given away by the bubbles. (And to those people who say that 'ladies don't break wind' – I've been to a yoga class and I know you do!)

Bethan also made it two thirds of the way across the forty foot long inflatable, before falling off into the water, giggling. She even belly laughed at me relating the old joke about the

Native Americans, as we have to call them now.

Red Indian Number One: "Dad, how did we get our names?"

Red Indian Number Two: "All Indians are named after the first thing the mother sees when she looks out of the tepee after giving birth. Hence, your brother 'Sitting Bull' and your sister 'Rain Cloud'. Anyway, why do you ask 'Big brown dog having a poo?' "

It's got a sort of detachable ending so you can add an appropriate punch line to suit your audience.

On the journey back from the pool, she spotted a car with an 'NL' sticker on it. I explained that I thought it came from the Netherlands and Bethan howled at the thought of someone coming on holiday to Sunderland.

Durham was our next destination, for a trip to The Durham Light Infantry Museum. She went through the First World War tunnel system when she thought no one else was looking and we 'tee hee'd' as she wrote a postcard from the trenches to Deborah.

Bethan had held my hand as she balanced on the wooden fence on the journey up to the market place in the centre of Durham and even as we wandered around the town too. She said balancing on the fence was 'pympsey'. We weren't sure of the spelling but she told me it meant that it was easy. A white evening bag was required for some event she was going to attend on holiday and I enjoyed searching around the accessory shops until we found one. I was delighted when we discovered one that she really wanted. Naturally, as we had ventured within a hundred yards of a stationery store, Bethan also ended up taking home the requisite pencil case and folder.

As we walked into a near empty coffee shop, she bagged the leather armchairs as I bought her the biggest piece of chocolate cake to go with her coke. It had been a great day and, all in all, we had spent most of the time just playing and laughing.

"It looks like we are putting Café Nero back in business," said Bethan between mouthfuls. I certainly felt like *I* was back in business.

When Bethan was picked up, Susan dropped off the two goldfish to be looked after while they were on holiday in Jamaica. In front of Bethan, I was then made to solemnly swear to replace them if they died, with either new fish or at least a sliver of carrot.

* * *

I had received a postcard postmarked Turkey that morning. Deborah wrote that, one day, she wanted to take me to the library at Ephesus. I looked at the picture on the front – it didn't even look finished yet!

Debs had wanted me to go to Turkey with her on this holiday, but I was currently the casualty of a short to medium term financial downturn. Whoever said that life was like a shit sandwich was right. The more bread you have, the less shit you have to eat. Whilst Deborah was living it up in the sun abroad, I was working in the drizzle and damp that passed for a British summer, mending a split in my Wellington boots with my bicycle puncture repair kit. I had even resorted to sending a 'get well' card to my bank account as it was still suffering the ill effects of providing for Barney's well being.

Her card was very chatty but, reading between the lines, I could tell that she had not been impressed about my thoughts on cloning. Specifically, she seemed to take issue with the insinuation that she didn't laugh at all my jokes and implied that she did. I was ready to counter her response on her return when I would haul out all those times she had made comments like, "I was laughing, but just quietly," or "I was chuckling in my mind," or the one that was really hurtful, "I laughed the *first* time you told it." She would have to accept that, as much as she tried to convince herself that she thought I was funny, I was actually right. I wasn't funny to her at all. She wouldn't be laughing then! The postcard was so chatty that it was spread over three of them.

I find the hardest thing on holiday is choosing cards for people. For some strange reason, I spend ages at the card carousel, choosing various images when they are all going to different addresses anyway. It isn't as if they are all going to get together at some big party while I'm away (I hope) and, even if they did, I doubt they would worry if they had all received the same card. It would be more the case that they would compare card fronts and start to try and read some bizarre significance into why I chose a particular card for them. Or is that just me?

She said she was half board – I guess that's what happens if you don't take enough books with you. The food was great apparently and the meatballs were the dog's bollocks.

She said she was fine, which I was pleased about. I had read a story about an Australian soldier during the First World War. He had been wounded and captured by the Turks and taken to Istanbul. A doctor had started to amputate his leg but, half way through sawing, he became bored and just snapped the rest off. I thought it best not to tell her this.

She signed off in some type of text speak that I hoped actually meant 'See you next Tuesday'.

CHAPTER TWENTY-ONE

The Lights of Kilgetty

The goldfishes' vacation at my house was marred by an ugly incident on day two of their stay. On hearing an almighty crash, I had rushed into the kitchen. The floor was awash with water, mixed with miniature gravel and, in the middle of it all, next to an amusing sign proclaiming, 'No Fishing Allowed,' were Sparky and GoGo, apparently doing sit ups on the wood laminate surface. I quickly scooped them up and put them in a tumbler of water.

As I surveyed the scene, I could see a dog looking very sheepish in the corner, although I didn't want to jump to conclusions that it was Barney who had committed the crime, just because he was black. The previous day, an hour or so after the fish had been dropped off, I had received a mysterious phone call from someone who sounded suspiciously like Susan. I was told that, if the fish "happened to die," there was no need to make any great effort to replace them as the mystery caller had grown heartily sick of cleaning them out. I suspected Susan's hand might be afoot and, of course, Barney could have just been playing his part in a contract hit. Either way, I thought it best to move the fish to the top of the fridge.

This was not the first attempted murder that Barney had been involved in. Tess had once tried to kill Barney some time ago. I still believe it was a cleverly staged incident whereby Tess was seeking revenge on black dog for the original 'turd in bed' affair. Deborah denies this and, for the sake of harmony, I have officially agreed to let it lie. Unofficially, I still have my doubts.

Deborah's version of events is that she heard yelps and cries coming from the garden and, when she rushed out to investigate, she was met with the sight of Barney hanging from Tess' mouth. At first, she thought that Tess was trying to bite the 'Nazi's' head off (sounds like a confession to me!). However, on closer inspection (and this is where the vivid, storytelling school teacher imagination element comes in), it apparently turned out that Barney's collar was somehow caught in Tess' mouth and he was flopping to and fro as she tried to shake him free.

"He would have turned blue if he hadn't already been black," she had told me. Frantic shouts appealed for assistance from Kate, her quick thinking neighbour, who vaulted the fence and cut Barney free with a handy kitchen knife that was conveniently lying around, in the event of such an emergency. (As another Kate has now crept into the proceedings, neighbour Kate shall be known hereafter as 'Hello Kitty'). Frankly, it all seemed a bit far-fetched to me. I've had the odd gander over the fence at Hello Kitty's washing line since and there is a noticeable absence of 'Wonder Woman' type oversized blue knickers, liberally sprinkled with white stars (They are meant to represent the American flag – on a pair of big pants – charming). I digress again. I've seen the odd red thong, occasionally some lacy black things, but no blue belly warmers. As unpleasant and distasteful I find this task, I will continue my vigil though in the interest of maintaining truth and decency in all things Barney.

But I digress.

✳ ✳ ✳

One Christmas, when I was a child, I had been given a 'Plasticraft' set. If I remember correctly, it contained liquid plastic and you could make your own paperweights or jewellery by placing objects inside the liquid and waiting for it to set. My mother had been ill in hospital and I had wanted to do something special for her. One of my own goldfish, called

'Spitz', had died, which provided an excellent opportunity. Out of sadness would come joy. I took it into the lean-to shed thing next to the garage and my aim was to set the fish in clear plastic, as a gift for my mum. Unfortunately, the kitchen roll I used to dry the fish off also seemed to remove his orangey colour. He had been a fake all along! I pressed on regardless and was able to present my mum with a slightly mangy white 'goldfish', encased in his very own plastic tomb. You could even see down his little gulping mouth. I understand it proved to be a very popular exhibit in the hospital.

I wasn't sure if they still sold 'Plasticraft' so hopped into the car and set off into town. If anything unfortunate did happen to the fish, I could re-discover my skills by making a lovely and very low maintenance replacement.

✧ ✧ ✧

The next day dawned bright and clear. I set the alarm, locked the front door, drove to the end of the street, did a U-turn and went back to check that I had shut all the windows. I had. I set the alarm again, locked the front door, drove up to the end of the street, did a U-turn and went back to check I had turned all the taps off. I had. I set the alarm, locked the front door, drove to the end of the street, did a U-turn and went back to check if I had set the alarm and done the locking door thing. I had. I drove off again and reached the end of the street. Sparky and GoGo hadn't been fed. *"Sod 'em."*

I was off on the quiet camping trip that had been hijacked and turned into a family reunion. Deborah was back from Turkey and I was on my way to pick her up.

We had agreed that, due to the need to make space for Barney in the back, she wouldn't take her hairdryer, tongs and other assorted hair related products. We were in a field for goodness sake and, in the spirit of compromise, I agreed not to take my beloved emergency kit. Deborah had argued that taking the apparatus to trap and skin a rabbit was probably going a bit over the top when there was a campsite shop.

I did, of course, take my emergency kit, hidden in the bottom of my T-shirt bag, and Deborah took her hair stuff, hidden in one of hers.

By the time I had packed all her stuff too, the car boot resembled a giant version of those trick mustard jars – the ones where you open them and a springy snake jumps out. The difference with this 'mustard jar' was that it was eager to eject sleeping bags and airbeds. I had told her to deflate it first.

Naturally, as I had come to expect by now, lazy Barney stood by as I did all the hard work, just assuming that I had been good enough to pack his toys.

A heat wave was on its way and, if this was the result of global warming, I for one welcomed the Ozone hole. Those killjoy environmentalists would have us back, living in scratchy black and white, if they had their way.

We entertained ourselves en route, on our epic eight-hour journey, by quickly double flashing the headlights as the car in front of us passed a speed camera, sneezing on the windscreen and eating liquorice.

We were heading for the village of Amroth near Tenby, which is situated in the belt of the Pembrokeshire Coast National Park that hugs the West Wales Coast. After passing our original halfway point, then past Cardiff, then past places with names like Pantynylon and Aberbanana, we eventually entered the National Park. It was like entering a different world – pretty villages, breath taking scenery, rugged coastlines and beautiful sandy beaches.

The local newsletter seemed to sum up the difference between this paradise and where we had driven from. In Newcastle, the editorial bemoaned the continued increase in violent street crime, whilst the editor of the local publication, 'Notes on the East Williamston Scene' commented, "... am I the only one who finds the crossroads at Broadmoor rather frustrating as you approach from Kilgetty? You can see the light ahead is green – but you know that, if you slow down to observe the 40mph speed limit, it will change to red just as you get there. Life is full of these little aggravations ..."

Jim Codd, the County Councillor, had written in his article that he had spotted weeds that were growing, 'Between the pavements and the road'. Further in, under the 'Did You Know?' section, we were reminded that, 'Keiran Head, the Milkman, will still deliver to your doorstep – you don't have to go off to the supermarket for your pinta.'

I wondered if they had changed to decimal money yet. The only thing that spoilt the enchanting image I was building in my head was the inclusion of a rather tasteless joke about someone who had a wooden eye who went out with a girl who had a hare lip, and a rather suspect Easter quiz.

Question: What did Jesus say to his disciples when he was on the cross?

Answer (which I'm sure is not correct): Lay off my Easter eggs, I'll be back in a few days.

Even if it wasn't quite halfway between Cardiff and Newcastle, it was a pretty good choice.

❋ ❋ ❋

When we arrived on the campsite, the Simpsons, led by Doctor Shit, were already well established; large tent with separate accommodation pods, separate tent for food storage, well-organised kitchen/cooking area and a designated dining section. This was the tent of our Leader.

Twenty yards away, a limp, creased blue rag-like thing on sticks shivered in the light breeze. This was Kate's tent. I was momentarily impressed when she showed me the inflatable double divan that she and Woody had brought along although I was finding it hard to maintain this pretence as she introduced me to the other limited provisions she had brought on her holiday – a frying pan, two plastic plates in the shape of a flower, an antique kettle and two forty-year old fold up nylon chairs, originally bought for Paul and Neil as five year olds.

They had all been borrowed from Dad especially for the trip.

I am not sure what Kate expected to use the frying pan on, as there was no cooker to be seen. Believe it or not, Kate and Woody also part owned a trendy restaurant, serving trendy food in a trendy area of Cardiff. They always cease to amaze me.

I chatted to Paul and Woody while Barney got out of the car and relieved himself after the long journey, and Deborah busied herself putting the tent up.

I was then approached by someone who was beautiful, small and who talked about things I didn't understand. She wasn't speaking Welsh; she was just a baby. This was Poppy, Kate and Woody's daughter. I think I speak for all, including Kate and Woody, when I say that everyone was relieved that she had not inherited Woody's looks, nor Kate's pea sized brain.

That night, the 'Norman the (ex) foreman' mask was used to good effect, scaring the living daylights out of various family members as they made their way back from the toilet block in the dark, by jumping out of the shadows proclaiming, "I am the thing from Uranus!" The mask was later re-christened Barry. It sounded slightly scarier than Norman, but not very much.

❖ ❖ ❖

Great Britain was basking under the promised heat wave thanks, I believe, in no small part to my excessive use of deodorant spray in the late Eighties.

We had decided to go to the beach and Barafundul Bay was truly breathtaking, if the old guy wheezing at the top of the cliff path was anything to go by. A happy day was spent down on the beach, running in and out of the sea, throwing the ball for Barney to swim and fetch and, after getting that gritty noise when eating lunch, realising why they are called sandwiches. We arrived back at the campsite early evening, tired and slightly sunburnt after a full day in the sun.

Neil and his family had arrived on site by then and, after a quick shower, I emerged to greet them, pinky and perky – pinky from the sun and perky after being re-awakened in the shower. I just want to stress that I am not referring in derogatory terms to Neil and his wife Molly.

After games of cricket in the field, using the familiar 'backyard six' rule (hit a six into the boundary hedge and you are out), we were ready for a barbecue of various over cooked meat-related dishes, accompanied by beer and wine aplenty.

By late evening, a lantern took the place of the traditional fireplace and, as everyone, including Barry, sat round in the gentle electric glow, stories were swapped.

The stars had all come out to look down on us and, after more jokes about seeing Uranus, the conversation started to become more philosophical. Someone commented that, if there *was* a sophisticated life form somewhere out in the vast universe and, if they *had* mastered the dynamics of space travel and, if they *had* chosen to venture millions of light years to come to our Earth, why did they just make a few circles in a corn field somewhere in Kent and then fuck off? Oh yes, and pick up some pissed drunks from Kentucky on their way back? Ah, the mysteries of the Solar System.

As the chatter and banter ebbed and flowed around the lamp, Paul seemed troubled. Now that he was a policeman, he seemed to want to unburden himself of a matter that appeared to have been preying on his mind for a number of years.

It seems that, when he was twelve or thirteen, he had been told by Mum to do some odd jobs for eighty-odd year old Mrs Davies next door but one. Mrs Davies had asked Paul to pop down to the paper shop and buy her a copy of 'Woman and Home'. He had duly popped, only to be informed by Mrs Whitehead in the shop that they had sold out.

"Is there any other magazine that you were asked to get if we were sold out?"

"Errrr, I don't know," replied Paul.

"Well how old is the lady you were getting it for?" She was eighty-odd. It was eighty-odd year old Mrs Davies, the one next door but one.

"Errrr, I don't know," replied Paul, insipidly.

Mrs Whitehead duly packed Paul off with the latest issue of 'Cosmopolitan', which he then trotted back with, reading open-mouthed at the blatant tales of rumpy pumpy and female experimentation.

He posted it through Mrs Davies' letterbox and went home to play on his bike.

Mrs Davies was found dead the next day. 'Death by misadventure' was recorded.

Paul confessed to us that he somehow felt guilty. We all agreed that he probably was.

We looked to Neil, our legal expert, for advice. Neil thought for a bit in silence and then, addressing us all, regaled us with a limerick he had learnt.

There was a young man from Newcastle,
Who opened a brown paper parcel.
In it was shit,
And on it was writ,
'A present from somebody's arsehole'.

As if to balance out the loss of Mrs Davies, he also reminded everyone of the time I saved his life. It wasn't that big a deal really. It was after we had both been out drinking heavily in Cardiff and had then retired to a kebab shop in Caroline Street, to satisfy the inevitable beer-induced 'munchies'. I had shouted out to him in the shop, just in the nick of time, not to open his kebab in the light. When you actually see what you are about to eat, it can often be a very scary thing and could result in post traumatic shock from the ordeal. Outside in the dark, where you can't make out what you are munching on, is a far safer place to eat any badly packed kebab.

Everyone congratulated me but I just sat quietly, remembering the time I had sneaked downstairs in the middle of the night and laid a turd down on the kitchen floor just to frame

Barney because he was getting on so well at obedience school and I was jealous of him.

No! Of course I didn't do that really! I don't believe you could even consider I'd have done that for a second. I must admit though that the woman's allegation *was* playing on my mind. Do I really sound like that kind of person to you? (I'm expecting an emphatic 'No' answer from you at this point). I am seriously now worried about how I must come across to strangers.

The awkward silence was broken when Kate piped up to comment that there must be literally hundreds of stars in the universe. Thank goodness for pea brain.

* * *

I was right and Deborah was wrong. My emergency kit *was* needed. The next morning, I was called out of my tent to see if there was anything in my extensive hypochondriacs' kit to treat a sting. A bee had stung Rosie, Neil's daughter. A quick rummage around produced a tube of sting relief stuff. We also spared a quiet thought for the bee that had to fly off home, with his sting and half his bottom missing. How would he explain that away to the Queen?

A quick magic trick to take Rosie's mind off the sting and the job was done. Burn relief plasters were also needed later for 'a leg burnt on car exhaust incident' and my special tablets also cured a case of excessive farting for an anonymous sufferer. However, no rabbits were skinned in the completion of this chapter.

Deborah was also right, to be fair. Her hair care products were needed – desperately needed, looking at the state of her bonce.

We all went in convoy to Bosherton lily ponds for a final trip before Neil, Kate and their respective hangers-on departed for their weekday homes.

The next day, Paul and Co. also left and, as it wouldn't be

the same any more on our own at the site, Debs and I searched for a new campsite to spend the rest of our holiday.

It had been a fantastic holiday and the only element missing was Bethan who, by all accounts, was swimming in the crystal clear waters off Jamaica as we played our 'backyard six' cricket.

As we drove to pastures new, we cursed the lights at Broadmoor as we approached from the Kilgetty end. We could see the light ahead was green but knew that, if we slowed down to observe the 40 mph speed limit, it would change to red just as we got there. Someone should write in to the local newsletter about it!

CHAPTER TWENTY-TWO

Anywhere But Here

"Where shall we go?"

"You say if you want to go here, and we'll go there," came back the response from Deborah.

That sounded like dissension in the ranks to me. A quick glance over revealed that Debs was not challenging my position as top dog, but rather just pointing to different places on the map.

I still didn't like the sound of this though. This was holiday time and I didn't want to have to make decisions on holiday.

It had been easy when Paul was about as I had acknowledged his position as Leader and was happy to drift about, doing what I was told as long as it didn't involve the washing up. Debs was right to recognise my status as top dog in our pack, but this was my holiday from the daily grind of decision making which I was forced to face in everyday life. Every single day, I had to make important choices like when to have a cup of tea, when to play with Barney, when to stare aimlessly out of the window. I needed a break.

I toyed with the idea of sticking a pin in the map, but I remembered the poor downhearted Chinese takeaway owners who had ended up cursing their days away, running a shop in Scunthorpe or Staines.

I looked into the back seat of the car. Not for the first time during the holiday, Barney just sat there with a stupid, vacant expression on his face. Being the lowest of the low had its perks.

A quick glance at Deborah revealed her sporting a similar expression.

I was on my own. "Ross-on-Wye," I said to myself. I mulled it over for a bit and then reluctantly agreed. Ross–on-Wye it would be.

* * *

The borderland between Wales and England around Hereford and Ross-on-Wye, if you ignore the busy A40 and M50 Motorway, is a county of unspoilt countryside, market towns and ruined Marcher Castles, evidence of centuries of border battles and disputes. National Trust houses, historic cities and fascinating villages on the edge of the Forest of Dean complete the scene. Turning off the A40 felt like escaping into a different world where real life 'Postman Pats' and 'Windy Millers' might actually still exist.

Be warned though, as it is also a place of hidden evil. I was enticed by the enchanting siren call of the local cider but, if there is one lesson you can take away from this tale – remember, cider is bad.

After calling in at Tourist Information in Ross, we decided on a pleasant looking campsite at Symonds Yat. I remember visits as a child and what a fantastic place it was. I excitedly told Deborah and Barney how wonderful it would be, spending a few days camped there on the riverbank. The River Wye is one of the longest in England and, as it meanders through this beautiful county, it provides excellent salmon fishing, as well as being perfect for canoeing and swimming. There is a castle round every bend and twist in the river, with hawks soaring over the fields and forests, and secret places along every stream. Many artists, poets and writers have sought to capture its tranquil charm and elusive beauty. This was where we were heading for.

We arrived at our destination, which seemed to be at the back of a fun fair car park. The car park attendant, who resembled an overgrown special-needs kid, demanded to know what we were doing.

"None of your business old man – I am the top dog in search of tranquillity. I need not answer to the village monkey," I replied. Actually I didn't. I just said that I was looking for the campsite and he pointed a stubby finger to the corner of the car park.

We drove in and drove straight back out again. This was 'Craggy Island meets Alton Towers'. Not at all what I had expected. Surely some mistake?

A strange feeling of déjà vu came over me as I sheepishly looked over towards Deborah. She said nothing, but I knew she was thinking something along the lines of, "Symonds Yat? Symonds Yat? Symonds Shit more like!"

* * *

I was relieved when Deborah said she would choose the next site and, after a ponder over the map, we set off for a site on the banks of the Wye, closer to Hereford. I had been relegated to the passenger seat and, as I sat there in disgrace, I toyed with my mobile phone.

I had only recently learnt what LOL and LMAO meant in text language but the continual use of abbreviations was difficult for a Luddite like me to grasp. They made things much quicker though and I liked that. Despite the worry that my thumbs might be wearing out, I had embraced this new system of communication and I had even invented my own titanic text abbreviation language for the things that I would probably be saying most, during the summer with friends and family.

ORTI stands for, 'Oh really? That's interesting.'

ITIJSAT stands for, 'I think I've just seen a Thylacine.'

YIVVVH stands for, 'Yes, it's very very very hot.'

TWIWGTS stands for, 'That's what I was going to say!'

IDUYLSCYE means, 'I don't understand your last sentence, can you explain?'

O means 'Oh!'

SIYRSM means, 'Stop it, you are scaring me.'

LMAY*I means, 'Leave me alone you * Idiot.'

NIFIBGCOTL2DATGBRWYCIHHIWWWWIANT means, 'No, in fact it's been getting cooler over the last two days and that's good, because really, wow, you can't imagine how hot it was when we were in Amroth near Tenby.'

When we arrived at the site, Barney just looked on, not lifting a paw to erect the tent. I had come to the conclusion that he was taking advantage of my good nature.

* * *

The next day, I went round Goodrich Castle on my own, without Deborah, because a big sign outside the castle read, 'No Dogs Allowed'. Let me re-phrase that. I went round Goodrich Castle on my own without Deborah because a big sign outside the castle read, 'No Dogs Allowed' and Deborah volunteered to stay behind and look after the 'forbidden' one whilst I pottered round the ruins.

Superbly sited, high above the River Wye, Goodrich Castle was a fortified baronial palace and was first recorded in a document dated 1101, when it was probably just a timber palisade on top of an earth bank. It was likely that the stone tower was added during the reign of King Steven, around 1150, and subsequent generations added and modified the castle to suit their own particular requirements. Its medieval buildings are still largely intact, although they took a hammering during the English Civil War when both the Royalist and Parliamentarian forces occupied the castle at different times. Eventually, a massive mortar was cast, capable of throwing a 200-pound shot, which served to hasten the garrison inside to surrender.

In case you were wondering, I'm not a gifted historian, making snap judgements, or a computer based reconstruction of a Dark Age settlement based on someone finding a broken piece of napkin ring with a picture of Blackpool Tower on it, like they seem to do on those archaeology programmes. ("...and from this pile of old chicken bones in this Hessian sack, we can just imagine King Arthur riding out pillaging and killing people in his quest for the Holy Grail...or maybe just for fun.") No – this was all written in the guidebook I had bought. History to some may just be the thing that they hastily delete off their PC when they hear their girlfriend approaching, but not to me. Oh no, I had even invested some of my cider money in my quest for knowledge.

I had also hired a tape that talked me through the different areas within the stronghold, although for some strange reason it neglected to mention that probably the easiest way into any castle is through its weakest defended position – normally the gift shop. I had enjoyed a fantastic morning but I'm not sure how Deborah felt, having to sit in the car park because of the English Heritage prejudice towards Barney.

I remember telling her how I had read about 'the perfect crime'. The killer had stabbed the victim in the heart with an icicle and, once the icicle had melted, both the murder weapon and any fingerprints were lost in a pool of water next to the body. By the look of it, Deborah wasn't too angry, just a little bit pissed off, as I caught her on my return, poking my four-legged friend in the belly with the 'Fab' ice-lolly she was eating. I had come back in the nick of time!

I decided that she was in need of a treat and I told her as much. Her little face lit up but, as I informed her that I was taking her to Symonds Yat, her little face went out again.

There must have been some kind of terrible mistake earlier. The Symonds Yat I knew was a beautiful place. Surely the place couldn't have changed that much in my absence of twenty years?

Checking the map seemed to indicate a Symonds Yat East and a Symonds Yat West. My continued holiday harmony depended on East being the total opposite of West. It normally was. As we set off, I displayed a cheery confident exterior to my travelling companions but, beneath my boyish good looks, I was a seething mass of nerves and butterflies were fluttering about where my 'Fab' ice lolly should have been slowly digesting away.

The road we were following gave way to a steepish single track leading down to the river. The sign read 'Symonds Yat East'.

* * *

It was like listening to the audience at a firework display, hearing the, "Ooohs," and "Aaaahs," emanating from Deborah and these were good, "Ooohs," and "Aaaahs."

Arriving at the river's edge at Symonds Yat East was like entering a different world. Teashops and an ancient pub that could best be described as 'olde worlde' huddled together on the banks of the river. This was truly an area of outstanding natural beauty, with the Wye cutting a swathe through a wooded gorge on the edge of the spectacular Royal Forest of Dean. Further along the river's edge stood the old hunting lodge, built in the 1870s, which had now been converted into a hotel, where terraced gardens of magnolia trees and well established wisteria overlooked the river.

A hand-pulled ferry operated across to the other side and boats carried passengers along this lovely stretch of water. Rare wild Peregrine falcons could sometimes be glimpsed, flying overhead. The plaintive cry of buzzards could also be heard as they circled about the valley, along with a variety of kestrels, sparrow hawks, ospreys and red kites.

I had redeemed myself and felt confident once more to leave Barney alone in Deborah's care.

I felt happy and bought an ice cream from the booth on the quayside. I asked for a '99'. The vendor must have misinterpreted my smiling face as that of someone who was brimming with the milk of human kindness. "Would you like hundreds and thousands?" he asked me. I paused as I looked around me at the crowds of families milling about on the riverfront. I wasn't feeling *that* generous. "No, just two," I replied.

We chose a river cruise on which to enjoy our cones and, afterwards, walked the couple of miles to the 'Biblins'. The name alone was worth a trip and, on our arrival, we were delighted to find out that this was a lovely campsite, situated on a strip between the river and forest, complete with Indiana Jones-type suspension bridge.

We returned back to our own campsite, drunk too much cider and felt ill, but at least not as ill as my friend Gary had got on cider – although in his defence, at the same time he did also manage to solve the age old riddle – 'what's the difference between a dog and a fox?'.

Gary, purveyor of Gary the fish, had once gone to a 'real cider' pub when he was on holiday in Somerset – the type of establishment where the locals look like extras from 'Star Wars', and they serve that organic cloudy cider so you can't see the bits of apple core and occasional mouse's head floating about within. This local cider can be pretty strong stuff (I once bought a gallon of the stuff in a plastic jerry can and foolishly left it in a kitchen cupboard for a week or so. When I eventually remembered it was there, I found the container all mis-shapen and distorted as if the still living cider was trying to suck it's way out). However our Gary was fearless. Despite the pub having a notice recommending that you should drink no more than two pints of one particular cloudy concoction, our hero forgot that cider is a mischievous drink that lulls you into a false sense of security with its appley deliciousness, and downed several pints of the stuff.

Three pints in and the locals looked on in awe as Gary sported the kind of eyes that are normally reserved for an anti-vivisection leaflet. Four pints, and they cheered as Gary happily drank his own pee that he had cleverly decanted into a pint glass. (Well fair play, no one wants to lose a fiver in a bet – especially with their own Nan). Finally though, the gathered throng turned away in embarrassment as Gary finally solved the riddle as he tried to drunkenly chat up the old hag of a barmaid. For our intrepid hero at least, the difference between a dog and a fox seems to be five pints of cloudy cider. Hang your head in shame Gary. Hang your head in shame!

❖ ❖ ❖

As campsites go, it was a very well organised one – maybe a little too organised. A sign near the toilet block told of some unspecified 'horseplay' that certain children had got up to the previous season. If 'it', whatever 'it' was, was repeated, children would be banned from the site.

The showers were a 'twenty pence for three minutes' type affair. No 'thirty seconds to go' warning, just a clunk as the water cut out. Believe me, there is no feeling more vulnerable than being a naked bloke, covered in foamy shower gel when the water cuts out and you find you spent your last twenty pence on sweets an hour before. *Now* who was guilty of horse-play?

Deborah said it hardly gave her time to get her whole hair wet. I didn't check on the spelling but, either way, it was more information than I needed.

The next morning, we made the journey back up to the North East and reality.

As I pushed open the front door, a pile of letters on the floor greeted me. I looked through them. Bills mostly. I don't know why I had them as Bill lived next door, or at least his replacement did. Also in my absence, I appeared to have missed out on a special rate of five per cent on a ten-year loan, a miss-spelt personal invitation to a champagne reception at a local sofa showroom, and the chance to meet with some kitchen sales reps who just happened to be in my area. I was gutted.

Not as gutted as Barney was going to be in a couple of days time. He was booked in to be castrated so, in an effort to cheer both Barney and myself up, it was decided to press on with 'Project X'.

CHAPTER TWENTY-THREE

Party Town

The recce to Snitter had yielded some valuable information. The village appeared small, prosperous and humourless inasmuch as a village can look humourless. The signs leading into the place were written in block capitals to negate the possibility of a 'black masking tape' incident and an efficient local neighbourhood watch system provided a network of prying eyes against anybody trying to do anything funny. I had the feeling that any amusing alteration of their sign would be about as welcome as a fart in a spacesuit. Oh, how these sensible locals must have cursed their place name.

Their 'Achilles heel' was a crossroads about four hundred yards from the village. Here, a small lower case 'Snitter' indicated where cars should tootle off to, to reach 'Party Town'. In fact, even 'tootle' seemed too fun a word. No, cars driving to Snitter would proceed soberly to their destination. This crossroads road sign would be the site of our dastardly abomination.

Despite the fact that the place was in the middle of nowhere, there seemed an inordinately high volume of traffic passing our potential crime scene. The only explanation was that these were some kind of anti-masking tape patrols, funded by the local neighbourhood watch 'Czar'.

Once parked up, we would alert the residents to our wrongdoing so we had to act fast. Deborah would be camera operator, I would wield the masking tape and Barney would pose by the sign. We synchronised watches, wished each other good luck, rubbed the lucky rabbit's foot which had been very lucky for us, but less so for the rabbit, and we were off. With a screech of brakes, we pulled up alongside the sign. I was out, the sign was amended, Barney was hoisted into position and Deborah took aim with the camera.

Suddenly, out of nowhere a Snitter patrol came into view. Debs hid the gear, I leant on the sign to obscure our handiwork and we pretended to talk about the weather, while Barney clung on to me for dear life. The patrol passed and we waited in silence for a few seconds, listening for the peal of the village church bells that would signify that we had been detected. Nothing. We quickly posed again, the picture was taken, then we all bundled back into the vehicle and sped off in a cloud of dust and gravel. The 'Shitter' photo was in the bag!

Goodness knows how their nerve held out in the old days when such a jape would have involved the photographer crouching under a black cloak, the apparatus balancing on a tripod and the animal hoister standing next to the sign for a full minute while the 'Snitter' patrolman ambled ever closer on his patrol donkey.

❆ ❆ ❆

On a sugar high, due to our success at Snitter and, possibly due to the two bottles of Panda Pop we had just consumed in way of celebration, we decided to push our luck. We set course for Once Brewed and the mysterious Twice Brewed, which didn't actually exist on our map, but which I was confident did exist in reality. Why else would you say something was once brewed, unless you were going to follow it with 'Twice Brewed'? Otherwise you would just call something 'Brewed' wouldn't you?

Once Brewed lay close to Hadrian's Wall in Northumbria, about an hour's drive from Snitter, along winding country lanes.

Hadrian's Wall fascinated me. Here was a seventy-three mile long wall, built across the country from coast to coast, at the frontier of the Empire in Britain. Two thousand years ago,

Roman soldiers had built this fifteen-foot high wall, complete with turrets, forts and mile castles, to keep the civilised apart from the barbarians. In its heyday, the wall was even white-washed to make it seem more imposing and impressive to the heathen hordes on the other side. It even ended up on the Eastern side in a place called 'Wallsend' – how lucky is that! On the 'right' side of the wall, the soldiers of the Empire could enjoy Roman baths and worship at the temples they had constructed. Even so, a posting here, in this spectacular yet bleak, cold and windy countryside, would have seemed like a right bummer. Hmmm, a mandatory tour in Tunisia (complete with sparrows) or Hadrian's Wall? Which should I choose? If I had been here, I would have wanted something a little stronger than 'Once Brewed' to take my mind off things. I had total confidence in myself, which is more than my driving companions had in me.

※ ※ ※

Once Brewed was easily bagged for the calendar. The sign we photographed indicated the place a full fifteen miles away. The problem now was that everyone else wanted to turn back for home but I cleverly resolved the mutiny problem by pretending to be deaf as I drove on to our destination.

Even as we pulled into Once Brewed, there was no sign indicating the existence of a Twice Brewed anywhere. To say Once Brewed was a one-horse town would be a bit of an exaggeration. It consisted of a tourist information office and, in all my travels, I have often come across towns without tourist information offices, but never a tourist information office without a town.

I asked the old woman at the desk if she knew where Twice Brewed was.

"Why do you want to go there?"

"I just do."

"Who do you want to see there?"

I was beginning to think that I had stumbled onto

something that I wasn't meant to. I couldn't be sure, but I suspected she might be pressing some button under the desk as we spoke and I was now probably being projected onto some massive screen in an underground bunker, whilst simultaneously being x-rayed to see if I was packing a piece. A young woman at the other side of the room was now glancing over the top of her guidebook at me. I couldn't be sure, but she could have had a pair of .38s on her.

"I just want to pop there."

"Who told you about Twice Brewed?"

I was too embarrassed to tell her that I was doing a crappy little calendar project and I thought it would be fun to take a picture of odd place names and that this would probably be 'March' or 'April'.

"I know all about Twice Brewed. Just tell me where it is," I replied in a mock confident tone. It appeared to work and she crumbled. Clearly she now saw me as a senior official in whatever sinister organisation she worked for.

"Out of the car park, left and left again. You can't miss it Sir." She didn't say, "Sir" but I mentally added it onto the end of her apology. Oh, and I made it sound like an apology in my mind. Did I forget to mention that?

I couldn't miss Twice Brewed because it began before Once Brewed had ended. They overlapped and, for about ten yards, I was in the mystical realm of Thrice Brewed. Twice Brewed then took over proper and continued on for another hundred yards before it too ended. All that Twice Brewed consisted of was a pub. I took my photo of the sign and was off.

I don't know what the pub was a front for and I didn't stay to find out as I thought I had pushed my luck too much already that day. Snitter neighbourhood watch vehicles would be scouring the countryside for me and, sooner or later, the old woman would cotton on to the realisation that I was not 'one of them'. Besides, I had driven too many miles to have someone pulling the film out of my camera, especially since it was a digital one. Time to go home.

CHAPTER TWENTY-FOUR

Goodbye to All That

The term 'the dogs bollocks' would only be used in the past tense by Barney by the time the day was over.

I had thought long and hard about the subject of his apparel in a responsible owner-type way, as opposed to some kind of sick perverted type way. I had bought Barney to be my obedient companion, not for me to be the hapless bloke who would have to fund his canine playboy life of debauchery.

I had heard that, when dogs with the full equipment had got the whiff of some brazen hussy bitch in heat, all other thoughts would be ejected from their mind to the exclusion of having their dirty, filthy way with her. They could do all this too without having seven or eight pints first. They could run off, ignoring all the lessons they had ever learnt and camp outside the bitch's home for days until she came off heat. Fifteen minutes had been *my* limit, before I became bored and pottered home.

He was to be castrated, have his knackers chopped off, become a 'jaffa' or however else you wish to put it. I had tried to persuade Deborah to take him to the vet so that Barney would associate *her* with the deed and not me, but she was unavailable. I drove him to the surgery and stayed with him until the anaesthetic took effect. His tail kept on wagging, as he grew drowsier and drowsier. When the nurse led him off, his little legs wobbled as if he was pissed and she had to pick him up and carry him to his fate.

I received the call to pick him up about three in the afternoon. I had been warned that he might be a little sulky, which seemed like a bit of an understatement to me. I was also told that he would be very fragile for a day or so. The nurse suggested that I should make scrambled egg for tea, which seemed like a splendid idea. I love scrambled egg. Goodness knows what poor Barney would be eating.

She opened the door and Barney bounded in to greet me which wasn't what I had been led to expect. He bounced and leapt about, wearing a big 'buster collar' which, basically, resembled a large lampshade. The nurse said it was to stop him from licking himself. If she meant his balls, she was crediting him with more intelligence than he actually had. I don't think it had ever occurred to him to drive the ten miles back to the vet's, pick the lock on the surgery and rummage through the dustbins to find them. To be honest, as he bounded about as if nothing had happened, I began to wonder if the vet had charged me a hundred pounds just to tie the cone on his bonce.

What I like about Barney is that he seems to think everything is just meant to be. He didn't try to get the cone off because, in his little mind, it was meant to be. He just blundered away, bumping into chairs, doorways and legs because, like the departure of his knackers, it was just meant to be. He looked funny and I laughed as he crashed into everything with his oversized lampshade. Out of sadness would come joy. Sadness for him and joy for me admittedly, but sadness and joy all the same.

∗ ∗ ∗

That evening we were returning to Snitter territory. Mick Thomas, the acclaimed singer songwriter, was playing at a pub in Rothbury. The 'acclaimed' bit, and the, 'Well *I've* never heard of him,' thoughts occur in the same sentence because he is acclaimed in his native Australia but pretty much unknown in the UK.

He was a founding member of 'Weddings, Parties, Anything', who had a cult following in Oz before he split the band and re-formed as, 'Mick Thomas and the Sure Thing'. His single 'Father's Day', about a divorced dad seeing his kid each weekend, was voted 'Single of the Year' when it was released.

I was excited about seeing him live again and had a chat with him at the bar before the show. When I took my seat, I told Deborah that I had arranged for a dedication and her little face lit up. A couple of songs in, Mick told us about one of the new songs from his latest CD. At the time of the success of Father's Day, his record label had asked him to make another one like that. The result was a sort of joke song that he hadn't released until now.

He told us the story of how, in Australia, dog sharing is the latest thing between divorced couples. He then related how he had been approached by a guy before the show (me!), asking if he would dedicate the song to his dog. When Mick had asked why, the guy (still me) had explained how, on that morning, his dog had been castrated. "Poor Barney," said Mick as he started into his song, 'Half a Dog'. I was chuffed. I turned towards Deborah with a big smile on my face to see her reaction but a small black cloud hung over her. She obviously didn't like the song as much as I did.

She must have been tired too because she didn't chat much on the journey home.

Never mind, the next day was to be a cracker. As part of the calendar project, we would be heading for the small village that, according to the map, went by the name of Low Bell End.

* * *

There was no time for a full walk that morning so I just let Barney out into the back yard to do his business. A matter of minutes later, I went out to check on him and it was like shit central station. Turds abounded. I led him to the front garden, went back, cleared his mess, and then went to bring him back through. In the short space of time he was in the front garden, he had managed to uproot a lavender plant and upturn a tub of flowers. He either didn't appreciate the irony of going to Low Bell End, or Deborah had been stirring things with him. The realisation that I had put my pants on back to front completed the abysmal start to the day.

According to our map, we would be heading into the heart of the North Yorkshire National Park. As we journeyed through the picturesque villages that were dotted throughout the moorland, my spirits started to lift. The shit shovelling that had marred the morning was forgotten as the calendar took shape in my mind. The purples of the heather, the wandering sheep, the gurgling of the streams – maybe with the right angle, I could convey all this in the photo. We laughed as we drove on and then we turned the corner.

I couldn't believe my eyes at what I saw. More to the point, I couldn't believe my eyes at what I didn't see. It was there on the map and we were here on the ground, but there was no road sign. This was a big shock. On the plus side, it did cure my hiccups but, on the negative side, there was no photo opportunity. I felt conned. What was going on? Twice Brewed hadn't been on the map, but was there, whilst Low Bell End had been on the map, but wasn't there. I had the feeling that someone was toying with me.

There was a farm where the village should have been, with the sinister name of 'Bell End Farm'. All sorts of bizarre images were conjured up in my head – even more bizarre than the 'puppy farm' images. This was a bad place and I wanted to leave. If I was going to be toyed with anywhere, I certainly didn't want to be toyed with here.

It's surprising how fast you can travel on those moorland roads.

❖ ❖ ❖

Scotland seems to have more than its fair share of Twatt's. There is one on the Shetland Islands and another on the Orkney

Islands. There are also places called Muckle Flugga, Lamb Head, Chicken Head, Papa Little, Holm of Papa, Sound of Papa and following close behind, Butt of Lewis. My God, there is a calendar in the making just on the Scottish Islands themselves.

When I was a Midshipman, we had used the rugged West Coast of Scotland for our navigational training. The coastline, with its multitude of inlets, was ideal to take bearings on and every small fishing village seemed to have a church with a massive spire to line up on. We were all a long way from home, except for 'Worm'. Worm was one of our fellow Midshipman who came from this part of the world. He was called Worm because someone had discovered that he pronounced the word worm as, "Wurrrrrm". So, in the early days of our training, when everybody was trying to establish where they stood in the group, this hasty and clumsy moniker was given to our Scottish friend. Now with *him* telling the tale, the 'Lambton Wurrrrm' *does* sound scary!

Worm and I, along with the boys from the Mersey, Clyde and Tyne, were all given orders to attend elocution lessons at the Naval College to make us talk proper. Ballroom dancing lessons were also mandatory at Dartmouth. I considered myself pretty shrewd when I managed to move fast and 'nab' the College Librarian's teenage daughter as my dancing partner, as opposed to one of the gaggle of shrews that was wheeled in for such occasions. But I digress.

As much as I would have liked a 'Twatt' now, I was playing by the rules – that is, our self-imposed rules, which dictated that the place names for the calendar had to be local to the North East.

Hence, we were now headed for Swaledale to capture a couple of home-grown calendar girls. Both were clearly marked on the map – in as much as a tiny square can be clearly marked but, moreover, they were tiny squares with a name – funny names. Today we were off to Crackpot and Booze.

I'm not sure if we actually found Crackpot. We followed the map, turned off the main drag and onto a twisting single lane road, where we followed the sign for Crackpot and drove past a big house and onwards into a dead end in the courtyard of a hill farm. But that's not important. The important thing was that we had found somewhere, which *could* have been the place and, more importantly, the sign. We retraced our tracks back to the pointer. Barney and 'Barry the mask' were taken out of the vehicle, whilst Debs got the camera set up. Barney finished the apple core he was eating and, as he was propped up in 'Barry's' arms, he poked his tongue out for the camera in a dog-type, 'Say cheese' moment. 'Dog poking out tongue' antics in an oversized lampshade next to a scary looking Barry – Crackpot indeed. Perfect.

Booze was only a short drive away. This was turning into a very productive day.

Deborah followed our progress on the map as I drove. Turning off the B2670 at Reeth, we took an un-named road through Arkle Town and kept on driving until we got to Whaw. Too far. We must have missed it. The excitement in the car was mounting as we headed back down into Langthwaite. *"The excitement was mounting?"* What was I saying? What had we been reduced to, being excited about finding a sign for Booze? Still, we were excited all the same. Deborah told me to take a left turn. "This is it!" she exclaimed. She remained silent as I did an eight-point turn to try and extricate the car out of the small churchyard. After we had both examined the map, we agreed that it must be the *next* left. I turned down the lane and drove until the road petered out before parking up. We looked at what lay ahead of us, looked at each other, and then back at the map, then at what was ahead, then each other again, then back to the map once more. This was map-making at its laziest. No sign, no nothing. Just a pub.

I decided to cheer myself up with a 'Wetwang'.

* * *

Maybe I was pushing it slightly to get Wetwang in, as it was roughly a hundred miles to the South of me but, what the hell, it was *my* calendar idea. I relied on my assumption that, despite my repeated requests for visitation rights (for my family to visit me that is), not many would bother to make the journey in the end. It wasn't as if I was taking the piss by travelling way off area and visiting the brewery where they made 'Piddle Beer' not far from 'Wyre Piddle' (which sounds more like the symptoms of a rather unpleasant STD than a picturesque village). Neither would I be taking in 'Lord Hereford's Knob' or indeed 'Lickey End' (on the Welsh border and Worcestershire respectively). Likewise, I also respected the fact that 'Pratt's Bottom' and 'Brown Tongue' were out of bounds (the Deep South and the Lake District). 'Ham' and 'Sandwich' sounded appealing (Kent) but with my luck I'd get there and find it 'Peasedown' (Somerset). Anyway who would know of this deviation? My dark seedy secret would be safe.

I think they felt that travelling to fifty-five degrees North was something Shackleton or Scott could aspire to, but not them. Soon afterwards, I received a phone call from my sister Kate. Woody was going through his mid life crisis, she informed me, and they were moving to open a beach bar in Thailand. They too would need a servant, but would look for one who sounded a bit more oriental than Neil's maid. I suggested 'Minjeeeta'. *She* certainly wouldn't want to visit Wetwang (but could probably easily win me another goldfish with her extensive ping pong ball skills).

The people of Wetwang seem very proud of their village name and a large sign welcomes careful motorists. We stopped and had fish and chips at the Wetwang chippy. I reminded Debs of the great chip shortage, which had closely followed the great potato shortage. When I was a youngster, buying chips on their own was banned. It had to be chips and fish, or chips and sausage, or chips and something else, in a bid to deter reckless chip purchases. Chip prices had virtually doubled overnight – a perfect example of the supply and demand theory model at work. This precedent sort of stuck after that, as the prices never came down, even when the potatoes started flowing again. As she looked at me blankly, I began to doubt myself and wondered if it was a bizarre phenomenon that had only affected the Colchester Avenue 'chippy'.

Other events lost to history include the 'great baked bean war', where prices of beans tumbled to as low as a penny, as rival factions tried to corner the baked bean market. At the time, I had considered bulk buying penny tins of beans to hang onto and then sell on when the bean market stabilised – a rather tame version of playing the stock market. I literally shelved the idea when I discovered that the penny tins consisted of little more than a slack handful of beans, floating in a veritable sea of bean juice. The whole thing almost got out of hand and there had been a dreadful stink about it all.

Sufficiently sated, we photographed the 'Wetwang welcomes careful drivers' sign and continued on our journey to Scarborough, the seaside resort that had died.

Once majestic hotels had become shabby, once grand theatres now hosted shows by unfunny comedians and even the donkeys on the beach looked knackered. There was, however, a daily naval battle, held in the municipal park. The resident organist, who was located in a little gazebo on a small island, played on as the warships and planes fought their daily duel. Alas, we had missed it. Curse those Wetwang chips!

Deborah meanwhile still seemed to be harbouring some strange sort of bad feeling toward me following the Mick Thomas gig. She told me that her friend Jane was coming to her house that night to cheer her up – they were going to stay in, have a bottle of wine and enjoy a chick flick.

Is it me or are women just that much more brazen nowadays?

CHAPTER TWENTY-FIVE

I Alone Am Best

Is it just me, or does every other ex-squaddie I meet seem to have served in the Special Forces or shot some terrorist? It makes me feel that my time was just spent drinking brews in the NAAFI by comparison.

In hindsight, I tend to think that war stories and their tellers follow the same rule of thumb as pepper grinders and food. As you may know, the rule of thumb states that the quality of food in a restaurant is inversely proportional to the size of the pepper grinder. In the same way, the actual deeds of 'derring do' are inversely proportional to the number of tales told about 'derring dos'. In such cases, it normally turns out that the Walter Mitty plagiarising Andy McNab, or Ernest Hemingway, had probably served in the Pay Corps all his life and the full extent of his adventures involved a nasty incident with a rogue stapler.

I was normally too busy asking inane questions between brews, to pull up a sandbag and swing the lamp.

Where was it that the Navy bred those strange mutant chickens that had one hundred and ninety legs but no breast? (and how did they catch the distorted little fuckers? – they must run fast). What was the difference in the Army ration packs between a bacon burger and bacon grill? Why did they give us tracing paper style toilet paper that just served to spread stuff around?

I could never work out either how the human digestive system takes about twenty four hours to change food into shit, yet the Army Catering Corps could do it in just two!

I could no more find the answers to those questions than the reason why old women, who are invited for dancing practice at Dartmouth, pluck off their perfectly good eyebrows only to re-draw them back on (badly) with eyeliner.

Some of my questions were answered by experience. I found out what a monkey bath was when I lowered myself into an over hot bath, emitting, 'Ooh ooh ooh aah aah aah,' as I did so. 'Donkey Shite' was a mystery to me as well until I found out that was the soldier's version of, 'Thank you', in German. Meanwhile, a nine coiler was normally what was produced when you loosened up after a week on compo rations.

Other phrases peculiar to the forces seemed to get right to the point far more succinctly than the standard Queen's English ever could.

If a piece of machinery onboard ship 'failed under continuous testing', it was marked as 'FUCT' (much to the annoyance of the Engineering Officer).

The Devil dodger would be the Padre, just in the same way as a salad dodger is a fat person in civilian life.

The Turdis is, in my view, a much better name for a portaloo, whilst a Hitler Piss is the sort you have when you are drunk and you need to place one hand against the wall in front of you to retain balance as you stand over the urinal.

An ex wife was often referred to as a hurricane – starts with a gentle blow and ends up taking your house away.

A very ugly person would be called a baby eater with 'a face that would scare a police horse'.

And, if you were running around everywhere like a maniac, you were running around 'from arsehole to breakfast'.

But I digress.

The reason stress levels were running high was that my dad was due to visit at the weekend and, as a result, I was running around from arsehole to breakfast, trying to get things sorted.

Debs had lit the fuse under the 'powder keg' weekend by announcing that I was like my dad. It was a particularly hurtful thing to say that neither my dad nor I appreciated. Susan had then topped up the keg with more powder when she said that Bethan was just like me. I was initially delighted by this comparison until I realised from her expression that this only related to any negative traits my daughter might have.

Things could either go swimmingly or blow up big style. I could see myself now, staggering back under a hail of friendly fire, whilst someone else's heart fell off their sleeve because someone else was speaking off the cuff. Just a mess of chicken wire and fertiliser would remain. I shivered at the thought.

I had always tried to live by the 'six P's' – Prior Preparation Prevents Piss Poor Performance. As a result, over the next three days, the history of my life was effectively re-written in a frenzy of planning, cleaning, falling-outs, tidying, hiding things and ethnic cleansing.

My dad was only coming for slightly less than two days, but the explosives in the keg were unstable and could be set off just by a wrong word. I was taking no chances.

To mark the occasion of the visit, Barney's cone was officially removed. He pottered off into his kennel to continue with some private business and then emerged, seconds later, with a puzzled expression on his face. He then slowly and carefully retraced his steps, looking and sniffing everywhere as he went as if he was trying to find where he had left his balls. I swallowed hard and mentally retracted my previously optimistic claim that I would have nothing to worry about if dogs suddenly took over the world.

❖ ❖ ❖

My dad and Ann arrived earlier then expected, while I was still wearing my 'Jesus is coming, look busy' T-shirt. Barney ran around, excitedly jumping and wee-ing at the same time, while I hid my favourite stripper coffee mug and the video that had been confiscated as 'evidence' some time ago. The cavalry arrived moments later in the form of Deborah and Tess and, as my dad looked in disbelief at his photo, stuck onto the 'Iraq most wanted' poster, I scuttled away to change.

On the basis of the 'idle hands/devil' theory, I reasoned that we should be kept as busy as was practicable. Therefore, all of us were soon on our way to wonder at the structure that was Hadrian's Wall. Minor disagreements about whether Hadrian had a beard or not were quickly put to bed when I was proved right. (As well as the first Roman Emperor to have a beard, Hadrian was also considered by many to be a very wise and just leader.... and he had more time on his hands than other Emperors to do this. The average person spends about 3,350 hours shaving during their life. I only had a beard for a few months in the Arctic ...so that's my excuse – too much time shaving to be very wise...or just!). Four hours into the visit and no major arguments. Things were going well.

The evening's serial was a trip to the Italian restaurant opposite. Bethan joined us and her constant chit-chat contributed to an excellent evening, without incident. When my dad offered to pay, I remembered the warning I had received from Deborah about not being argumentative so, naturally, although against my better judgment, I agreed that he should indeed pay.

Sunday morning and the five of us squashed into the car. To avoid involuntarily igniting any of the powder keggers, Deborah sat in the back in the middle so that Bethan could have the window seat. Fair play to her, powder keg Bethan had already given up her seat in the front for her powder keg Grandpa. Ann had the audacity to suggest, mid-journey, that maybe it was a bit uncomfortable for Debs sitting there. She should try sitting curled up, wedged on the bump on the floor, being repeatedly kicked in the back for eight hours! I remained calm and pretended I hadn't heard. We were off to Alnwick Castle to see the new water gardens, the pride and joy of the Duchess of Northumberland.

As we drove on, I pondered on whether the undercurrent of tension, which prevailed during the weekend, was because it was perhaps one big challenge to see who could be top dog. No, that was ridiculous. Surely everyone knew *I* was top dog here.

The Castle itself has been in such films as 'Robin Hood, Prince of Thieves' and, more recently, was used in the 'Harry Potter' film as 'Hogwarts'.

Inside the castle, as in most stately homes, the rooms were furnished, fires were burning, 'Country Life' magazines lay open on tables and photos stood in their frames as if the family had just quickly abandoned the place in true Marie Celeste style.

In fact there were so many little photos in frames everywhere that I wondered if they were all real family members or had other visitors to the castle beaten me to it and already indulged in one of my favourite hobbies – mantlepiecing.

For the uninitiated, to quote from the Urban Dictionary:

Mantlepiecing: *verb: To bring a photo of yourself (preferably pre-framed) to a party at someone's house, then place the photo amongst other photos of host's family on such as mantle or dresser.*

Indeed, don't just limit it to party invites – I don't! Most people have photos on their mantelpieces that have been there forever and they never really look at them anymore – they are just things that they dust now and again. Your grinning photo may sit there for months before anyone notices and when they do, you can just imagine the confusion as they scramble through their minds wondering who the idiot is on their mantelpiece. I'm sure some of my photos of me grinning like a loon are still sitting next to grandparents and distinguished uncles in front rooms across the nation. For somewhere quite as grand as Alnwick Castle, I was to be wearing my full Royal Military Police mess uniform and sporting a rather fine Clark Gable moustache.

We perhaps lingered a little too long, walking the ramparts, admiring the wonderful water gardens, playing in the magnificent tree house and looking for a suitable spot to mantlepiece, as there was a real danger, on the return journey, of an outbreak of hostilities induced by tiredness. Deborah was ready to pour oil on the water if needed, but the whole episode passed off without event.

Two thirds into the trip and all's well.

That evening, the operational HQ for the visit was relocated twenty-five miles south, to Deborah's cottage. Things almost kicked off during the cheese course at dinner but order was restored and Debs silently re-pocketed the electric cattle prod she had covertly got out, ready to quell any disturbance.

Bedtime. Unless there was an unfortunate sleep-walking incident, only breakfast remained. How stressful could *that* be?

I hadn't bargained for my morning pee routine being disrupted by a queue for the bathroom and, as I hopped from foot to foot, making pleasant small talk, I released my secret weapon. Barney was brought in from the confines of the garden and, as he rampaged around the house, jumping up in his excitement almost knocking people over, I made best use of the confusion to queue jump. Aha, I alone am best.

My dad and Ann departed, thanking me for a good weekend. I had gone from the black sheep to the prodigal son in the space of a couple of days.

I don't think there was any real argument as to who was top dog and, against all the odds, the visit had been a success. Paul and Kate both rang, hoping to hear tales of pandemonium and were both obviously disappointed when I informed them that the whole thing had gone off without incident. I felt like Joseph – he of the amazing Technicolor Dream Coat. I had the feeling that, in future, people would look at me differently and maybe even come to me for advice or maybe to interpret the odd dream. The one with Miss Tucker in it had been very odd. She had been dressed immaculately in a kimono and wearing mad professor glasses ... but I digress.

Kate rang me, still deliberating whether she should go to Thailand. I contemplated long and hard about the pros and cons of this for a full three seconds – it would be good for cheap holidays. "Yes Grasshopper," I told her. "Fly ... fly like the wind."

CHAPTER TWENTY-SIX

Super Furry Animal

Somehow, Sparky and GoGo were still living with me. Susan always seemed to be in too much of a hurry to take them with her and I was seriously thinking of charging them board and rent. To be honest, I think she was just a bit fed up with them. After all, they didn't seem that exciting and had clearly outstayed their welcome at her house. I actually felt a bit sorry for them, just swimming endlessly around their little tank, past their ornamental sunken castle, until someone told me that goldfish only have a six-second memory. I felt sorry no more. What a fantastic life they must have! Every six seconds they were having a new adventure and what could be better than discovering a sunken castle?

"Look GoGo, a sunken castle!"

"Wow Sparky, that's amazing!"

"Look GoGo, a sunken castle!"

"Wow Sparky, that's amazing!"

"Look GoGo, a sunken castle!"

"Wow Sparky, that's amazing!"

Here I was, feeling bored with their apparent lack of amusing antics, whilst they were having the time of their lives. I thought about putting a little deep sea diver man next to the castle, but they would probably 'OD' with excitement and, by the time Sparky had finished telling GoGo about the castle and the diver, he would have forgotten what he had started talking about; it would be unfair.

"Look GoGo, a sunken castle ... and what's that ... Oh, my God ... a deep-sea diver! I wonder if he's dived... No, no, hang on, I've lost the thread ... what was I on about again?"

I had also been joined by Hammy the hamster. Hammy was no trouble really and spent most of the day driving about in his small toy car. He was meant to be the classroom pet at Deborah's school, but she had lent him to me in case I grew bored whilst Barney was away.

Oh, and in case I forgot to mention it, Barney was away.

If you suddenly become overwhelmed by a strong sense of déjà vu at this point, rest assured that you are not a fish. This is where the book started for some bizarre reason.

If you don't remember reading that part before, either the pages of the book are very wet or you'll start to do sit ups on the floor at any moment.

Anyway, Barney was *still* away.

With a heavy week of work commitments, which meant I could be popping all over the country at short notice, it had been agreed that Barney should be put into kennels during that time. I was missing him and going for walks without him just wasn't the same. Even with the benefit of his car, Hammy was too slow to keep up and so I was left to stroll around the circuit on my own.

The effect of the tidal flow on the river made for some strange sights. For a period of about three weeks, a fridge had floated back and forth downstream, then upstream until it became snagged in the moorings of a boat at Cox Green. Bethan and I had seen a duvet once, heading downstream with a water rat lying basking in the sun on top of it. Ratty must have alighted somewhere downstream because he was gone when the duvet made the return leg. And now, following the annual bath race down the river, an abandoned tub was making the daily trip up and down, outside my house. *"Barney would like to have seen that,"* I told myself. Deborah had even called the kennels to ask how he was getting on.

Then, the next morning a card arrived. It was from Barney!

When I had taken him to the kennels, I had mentioned about the jumping up and the guy in charge said he would see if he could teach Barney some things. I never once thought that he would teach him to write. I read it to Deborah.

> *"Hello Dad,*
> *Just a quickie to let you know how life is at Stalag 17.*
> *It's a bit 'ruff' really. Someone mentioned digging a tunnel but when a 'spayed' was mentioned we gave it a miss.*
> *I told everyone your Shih Tzu joke but they all thought it was crap.*
> *It's lights out so I'll have to go. I'll have a 'tail' or two to tell when I get home.*
> *Barney*
> *PS. It's great here, really."*

It was the, *"It's great here really,"* phrase that gave it away. Barney would never use language like that. He was a perennial ingrate and he would never let on that he enjoyed something I did for him. I concluded that the kennel owner must have had a hand in this.

We replied in a similar vein to the Kennel owner, marking it for the attention of Barney. We told him that we were sorry for having him castrated before he went away, but that Deborah loved her new earrings and we also hoped that the change of dog food hadn't had him shitting through the eye of a needle.

✳ ✳ ✳

If anyone is going to call Deborah a freak, it's going to be me. Not that I would, you understand. She is anything but a freak. Patient, kind, funny, attractive, with a heart as big as the moon – I'm a better man for having known her – and, even if her hair does go a little frizzy in the rain, she is still no freak.

If anyone dared call her a freak, it would cost them. At the electrical superstore that rhymes with 'Ruby Murray's', which apparently can't be beaten on price, it would cost them a tenner. Deborah had the audacity to ask a gaggle of five assistants, chatting together by the cookers, if anyone could help us with the vacuum cleaners. She was abruptly informed, in no uncertain terms, that they were 'cooker' assistants only and was called a freak for asking such an impertinent question. The management explained later that these staff were relatively new to 'Ruby Murray's'. I guess this meant that they hadn't yet attended the 'Don't call customers Freaks' induction course. She was subsequently offered a tenner off the Dyson cleaner that I wanted, by way of hush money. I tried to persuade her to go over to the girls again and ask which colours the cleaners came in and if could they be used on laminate floors, in the hope of inducing a frenzied outburst on their part and maybe halving the cost of the vacuum cleaner in the process, but she refused.

If only I had brought a real family of monkey-voting freaks down from Hartlepool. After the assistants had finished their pointing and jeering, 'Ruby Murray's' would be paying *me* to take a Dyson home.

Bethan had come over and witnessed Deborah's humiliation first hand. Still, out of sorrow came joy. Deborah's sorrow and my joy admittedly, but sorrow and joy all the same.

Bethan was quite excited that day as she had just learnt that she had been chosen to play Beauty in a forthcoming production of 'Beauty and the Beast'. I didn't like to say too much to Debs at this stage in case she thought I was implying that she should play the beast after the freak 'freak' incident. This was a dancing school production and followed on the success of the previous year's 'Snow White' show. Unfortunately, big business has its greedy paws everywhere and the dwarfs had to be called slightly different names to avoid a legal battle with the Corporation who has an oversized rodent as their mascot. Even *I* am having to run scared of the big mouse! It took the shine off it slightly for the children but at least the greedy shareholders were happy (or 'smiley' as the dwarf had to be re-named).

Bethan had also found out that a piece she had written about Hadrian's Wall had won first prize in a tourist competition about Northumbria. It was written on the theme of 'The spirit of Northumbria; Strength of the past and vision for the future'. (I have had to leave the actual piece by Bethan out of this book for two reasons. Copyright now lies with the Tourist Board and Bethan didn't want her masterpiece to be in any way associated with this drivel. And fair play to her, she's not a performing monkey...that's my sister Kate's job).

We tried the Dyson when we got back and then all stood round the clear Perspex cylinder, marvelling at the amount of dirt and Barney hair that was sucked off the apparently clean carpet. I then tried to put to the back of my mind the state of filth that I had unwittingly been living in, before Bethan and 'Freaky' had come with me to buy the miracle cleaner. Vacuuming was now a fun activity!

As Hammy drove around on the super clean carpet highway, I looked at the mass of Barney hair in the cylinder. I was surprised that he wasn't walking around naked! I must admit, the 'no fur coats' lobby had made me a little embarrassed about being seen out with him sometimes as he flaunted his furriness but, despite that, I was missing his little grimacing face. Still, he was due home soon.

※ ※ ※

If anyone *was* a freak around here, it was Hammy. And I wasn't about to stump up for saying so. He was as happy as Larry when he was driving round in his car but, if I picked him up, he would scream his little head off until I put him down again, when he would promptly clamber back into his vehicle and drive off at high speed.

Worst of all though was his fitness regime. He would sleep most of the day like the lazy layabout that he was until it was time for *my* bedtime. Then, as I lay in my bed, waiting to be taken into the land of nod, he would start his gym training and the house would reverberate to the sound of his treadmill spinning around and around and around and around and around. I think he knew very well what he was doing.

I hadn't meant to drop him on the kitchen floor when he had first arrived here, but clearly he took it personally. OK, I did snatch him back off the floor pretty quickly too, but that was only because I didn't want him disappearing behind the cupboards. I had a vision of him emerging several weeks later, with a scrawny body and bloated deformed head, after feasting on the various rotting flotsam and jetsam that had found their way behind the units over the years. I had been well intentioned in all my actions towards him, but obviously Hammy thought otherwise.

Our relationship just wasn't working out. I would tell him that it wasn't really him, it was me. I was still missing Barney and wasn't ready to move on. Yes, it had been fun in the early days and I still wanted to be friends with him, but that was all.

Little things that I would normally let go just started to really get on my nerves – the way he would climb into his food bowl to eat his dinner or the way he just left his little poops lying where they had fallen.

I toyed with the idea of annoying him so much that he would want to finish with me, so that, when we parted, I would still have a clear conscience and maybe even leave it open for me to return if I ever grew bored with Barney. Maybe I should tell him that we just needed some time apart. That way, I could play with Barney and *still* be able to play with Hammy later. Maybe we should just have a clean break. That would probably be the fairest way for both parties, but it had the disadvantage that it didn't really leave me with a safety net in case things went wrong elsewhere.

Sparky and GoGo had to go go too. I was sick of looking at their happy little faces as they kept on rediscovering the castle, while I was pining over Barney. I made the decision that, if Susan didn't pick them up at the weekend, I was going to get nasty and buy that deep-sea diver.

It was late and I was tired. As I set the alarm and turned the lights off, ready to go upstairs, I could just about make out a shadowy figure climbing into his wheel.

* * *

Meanwhile, I was struggling with my own fitness regime. In the few weeks that I had off from running, the machinery had seized up. As a result, the warming up times grew longer and longer, up to the point where they were almost exceeding the actual exercise period. It was taking a good ten to fifteen minutes of stretching, prior to each run, to guarantee that my calves wouldn't turn rock solid half way round, resulting in me making my way home doing a perfect, if not tasteless, impression of Douglas Bader.

I had once made the mistake of asking the Army PTI (Physical Training Instructor) the best way to warm up before my run. He asked me how flexible I was and I replied that I couldn't make Wednesdays. For some reason he then gave me a strange look and told me that a five-mile run should loosen me up sufficiently before my main event. I nodded wisely and told him that was what I had thought, keeping quiet about the fact that I was only planning three miles for the whole thing anyway.

It was all in stark contrast to my early sporting days and the ten-mile morning runs. I had been pretty good at athletics at school but I made the mistake of assuming that this meant I would be good at athletics out of school. When the Naval College wanted a team to compete against some Naval units from Portsmouth, I volunteered for a number of track and field events. The triple jump had been an event that the Donoghues had excelled at. During one school sports day, Paul had actually beaten the world record quite substantially for a period of about one minute, before they realised they had written it down wrong and he had jumped 'X feet' and not 'X yards'. He cut a sad figure as he sat despondently amongst the turds in the big cat litter tray, having risked a sprained ankle and cat poo blindness for nothing.

I was frankly shocked, when the first time I tried the event on Olympic sized stadium facilities, I didn't even *reach* the sand. I hurriedly staggered in a zig-zag fashion back to the events board and did some rapid crossing out. I'd stick to running.

I know my three-mile circuit wasn't that much, but at least I did that a few times a week. Most people I know who have exercise bikes only have three miles recorded on the mileometer per se. I have to concede that I haven't been able to check every one as, sometimes, there has been an unwillingness to move their drying clothes from their super expensive clothes horse for me to have a good look. These are normally purchased about the same time as the sandwich maker that had seen action about three times, before someone had suffered a furry tongue from an over hot filling and it was subsequently relegated to the back of a cupboard somewhere. It is probably next to the once used bread making machine, which in turn was probably bought around about the same time as the foot spa.

Customer: "I'd like to buy a foot spa please."

Salesman: "You mean you would like to pay out £45 for a foot spa that you will use once and then never use again, instead of putting your feet in a bowl of warm water which will do the trick just as well?"

Customer: "Yes."

Salesman: "Big twat."

CHAPTER TWENTY-SEVEN

Shakespeare My Butt!

It's just occurred to me that you may have bought this book because you thought it was actually a lively debate about who was the real author of the works attributed to Shakespeare – and instead you got the ramblings of a madman. In that case, and to avoid any further disappointment and more importantly to avoid any possible legal action under the Trade Description Act, here is a chapter devoted to who I believe is the real writer of all those plays and sonnets.

However if you sensibly read the back cover *before* you bought the book and knew the book was about all sorts of rubbish and are not interested in the bard, hop straight to the next chapter where normal service will be resumed as soon as possible. You won't be missing much!

Still here? This is your last chance. OK, I'll give you a few interesting facts, but then the boring stuff starts.

Even if you haven't read any of his work, I guess you can say that you speak Shakespeare as he literally invented 1,700 words in the English language. He was the first person to use words like *aerial, critic, submerge, majestic, hurry, lonely, road, assassination, laughable, reliance, exposure, shart, bump ......*

He's also responsible for many of the every day phrases we use without a thought to where they came from. *'Break the ice', 'all that glitters is not gold', 'hot-blooded', 'in the mind's eye', 'every dog will have his day', 'it's all Greek to me', 'the lady doth protest too much', 'method in his madness', 'like a wizard's sleeve'.....*

In Shakespeare's time copyright didn't exist either, so the actors only got their lines as the play was in progress. They also only generally got to know who else was playing what part on the day of the performance. Often they didn't even get their own lines. They did 'cue acting', which meant that there was a person backstage that whispered the lines to the person right before he was going to say them. This was because actors were not considered trustworthy people, and the market for good plays was large. The actors were all men in Shakespeare's day too. The parts of women being played by boys who still had high voices. Anyway, if you didn't like the play, you could always hang around until later when there was something else more to your liking as The Globe Theatre also doubled up as a bear pit, brothel and gambling house.

As for me, I only know about Shakespeare because the Battle of Agincourt was also the subject of one of my obsessive projects for a while. (It was somewhere between other time sapping and girlfriend alienating obsessions that have included the likes of the Indian Mutiny, the Zulu wars, Mutiny on the Bounty, the French Foreign Legion, Waterloo and the Greek myths and legends). As a result, 'Henry V' became required reading for longer than is socially acceptable and I even journeyed to Stratford-Upon-Avon to see the play a couple of times as well as watching the various films showing how no more than 6,000 soldiers under the English king took on a French force of over 30,000.

Of Henry's force, about 5,000 were archers, each with stock of about 80 arrows. Each archer could shoot about ten arrows a minute, so the army only had enough ammunition for about eight minutes of shooting at maximum fire power. However, this fire power would have been devastating. Fifty thousand arrows a minute – over 800 a second – would have hissed down on the French cavalry, killing, wounding and maiming. The sky would have been black with arrows. The function of a company of medieval archers seems to have been equivalent to that of a machine-gunner, so in modern terms we can imagine Agincourt as a battle between old-fashioned cavalry, supported by a few snipers (crossbow-men) on the French side, against a much smaller army equipped with machine guns ...and we won! Hooray!

OK that's your lot, skip to the next chapter unless you really want to find out about Shakespeare and pretend you are an expert down the pub.

✻ ✻ ✻

Prior to the publication of *this* book, the great British playwright and poet William Shakespeare is/was generally acknowledged as the greatest writer who ever lived. Whilst there is no argument about the talents and achievement of the author (at least 36 plays and over 150 sonnets) there is a good deal of dispute over his identity. The orthodox view is that he is the same person as William Shakspere who was born in Stratford-Upon-Avon in 1564 and died there in 1616. (No that's not a typo, he used different spellings and even spelt his name Shagspere on his wedding banns ...wishful thinking maybe?) So, let's look at the facts:-

During his lifetime, Shakspere was not considered to be the author of the plays, nor did he ever claim to be. The whole notion that Shakspere may have been the great playwright William Shakespeare did not arise until 1623, seven years after Shakspere had died.

It was then only *hinted* in the first folio of Shakespeare's plays that appeared in 1623 that the man from Stratford-Upon-Avon was the author. Hinted – but never said directly.

The biographers claim that our man attended Stratford Grammar School, although there are no records of him being a student there at all. Indeed for such a famous old boy, doesn't it seem strange that no one has ever claimed to be his classmate or teacher?

He is said to have become an actor but even that is unclear.

OK, you might say that he lived 400 years ago so most of

the documents about him must be lost by now. Hang on though, this was the reign of Queen Elizabeth and a well documented era where printing presses and writing material were commonplace and many people knew how to read and write. An army of scholars have trawled through the several million original documents that still exist from that time, and whilst they have uncovered reams of information about every other major poet, they only discovered about three dozen references to Shakspere. And guess what? None of them describe him as a playwright or poet.

Galileo was born in the same year as Shakspere and we know loads about him. Isaac Newton was born just 78 years later and we have thousands and thousands of documents about him. Alas, references to our Stratford hero are thin on the ground.

He was supposed to have spent twenty years in London but there is not a single record of anyone ever meeting the great man in the flesh. When people saw a famous actor like Richard Burbage or the playwright Ben Jonson, it was a notable event. Yet nobody ever bothered to note the fact that they had met our man at a party, seen him on stage, written to him or discussed poetry with him?

During his lifetime not one of his friends, family or neighbours ever referred to him as a poet, playwright or literary figure of any sort.

He left no notes, writings, letters or diaries in his own writing either. Just six signatures on legal documents – and even then he couldn't decide on the way to spell his name. Maybe our Shakspere was barely literate? Indeed his parents, wife and children were all illiterate.

Would such a prominent writer and wordsmith really allow his children to grow up unable to read or write?

Even in his will, where specific bequests are made, there is no mention of poems, plays or literary rights.

And in an age when those in the artistic world would make a big event out of the passing of one of their circle, the death of

Shakspere went un-noticed. Clearly the poets of the day saw no link between the Stratford man and the great playwright.

So if Shakspere wasn't the author, who was?

Step forward Edward de Vere, the 17th Earl of Oxford. Born in 1550, the son and heir of the 16th Earl of Oxford, de Vere had the rounded education that befits a young Lord. He earned a bachelors degree in Cambridge, a masters in Oxford and studied law in London as well as being schooled in the military skills, riding, hunting, music and dancing.

At twelve, when his father died, he went to live with his appointed guardian, William Cecil, Lord Treasurer and one of the most powerful men in England. He was later introduced to Court and became one of the Queen's favourites.

It is said that playwrights often take inspiration from actual events in their lives.

At twenty one, de Vere married his guardian's daughter (just like the hero in Cymberline).

At twenty four, he embarked on a lengthy European tour, only for his ship to be attacked by pirates on the return journey. The pirates wanted to hold their captives for ransom, but when de Vere informed them of his friendship with Queen Elizabeth, they thought it prudent to let him go (a similar incident happens to our hero in Hamlet).

Meanwhile eight months after he had departed on his tour, his wife gave birth to a daughter. De Vere insisted it was not his and refused to live with her, only perhaps realising the error of his ways five years later. She forgave him and they were reconciled. (False charges of adultery are common themes in Shakespeare's plays such as All's Well That Ends Well, The Winters Tale, Othello and Cymberline). After an affair, he also had a dispute with another family and street brawls between the two families were common, until the Queen threatened to gaol them unless they stopped fighting (Romeo and Juliet?).

Monarchs often patronise talented artists in the hope that they will glorify their reign. De Vere was one such man, interested in poetry and the theatre, even writing a number of plays in his own name. In 1586, the notoriously tight fisted Queen granted de Vere a lifetime pension equivalent to around £70,000 per year. After that date, not another word was written in de Vere's name, but a few years later, poems and plays started appearing from the invisible William Shakespeare. De Vere then disappeared from Court life presumably to concentrate on writing.

So de Vere seems to fit. A well educated aristocrat with an insider's knowledge of Court life and Court intrigue. Repeatedly described in his own right as brilliant and talented, he not only had a huge amount of time to devote to his writing, but also had a wealth of experiences that seem to be mirrored in the plays.

So why did he keep his identity a secret?

Firstly, there was a strong taboo regarding noblemen writing poems or plays for publication.

Secondly, a lot of people would recognise themselves from his writing – recognise the insulting parodies too! In those days it could not only result in a lawsuit, but a duel too. A pretty good reason for remaining anonymous!

Finally, many of the sonnets were addressed to lovers and this could prove very embarrassing for his wife and children.

So it looks like de Vere is our man! So how did Shakspere get considered?

Most likely is that de Vere's family perpetrated the hoax in about 1620 to keep the real author's identity a secret.

Shakspere fitted the bill with a similar surname ...and he was already dead so he wasn't going to speak up and blow the arrangement.

Ben Jonson (not the sprinter!) was brought on board to write a few lines hinting that the author came from Stratford-Upon-Avon, a monument was erected near Shakspere's grave with some faint words of praise and the deception was complete.

By the time the first biography of Shakespeare came out in 1708, myth had taken over reality. There ...happy now?

A whole chapter about Shakespeare and no corny jokes ...can't be bard!

CHAPTER TWENTY-EIGHT

Salesmen, Cheats and Liars!

Red sky at night, shepherd's house on fire. The summer had been persuaded to stay on for a few more days and it was on a lovely warm balmy evening that the chilling discovery was made. It was Bethan who noticed first. Something wasn't quite right. Something was missing. The hand of a thief was afoot.

I would have suspected a cat burglar except that it was a theft from a dog. While Barney had been away in kennels, someone, or something, had crept into my back yard and stolen his toys. How low can someone get? Stealing the toys from a dog. I'll tell you what's lower, stealing toys from a six-month-old puppy!

Just to clarify, I feel quite happy switching from dog years to actual time where Barney is concerned. Whichever gives best dramatic effect will be wheeled out and blatantly exploited. It's no different to the tactic that old people employ – the one where, in one breath they elicit sympathy when they tell you that, in their day, they only earned ten shillings a week and then, in the next breath, they tell you how stupid you are, paying so much for things and how cheap things were when they were young. "Aye lad, in them days you could go to the pub with tuppence, drink until your kidneys failed, get a fish supper from the girl in the chippy, wear an oversized flat cap, buy a tortoise from the market and still have thruppence change." Ah, old people, you can't beat them. Shame.

Barney's 'denty bone' for healthy teeth, two hard plastic bones, a food ball that he would push along with his nose to make the treats fall out, a three pointed rubber thingy that wouldn't look out of place in an Ann Summers shop, a rubber kong that you could stuff with food and he would spend all day getting it out again, cuddly toy ... the list goes on. They were all missing, but no 'Brucie bonus' for Barney. He didn't do well; he did very badly. I wasn't looking forward to telling him and seeing his little face drop. Even the 'lowest of the low' sign that Bethan had made for his kennel had been stolen. I guess the crook knew that this accolade rightly belonged to them now.

They clearly needed help and obviously had psychological problems. I pondered on what I would do if I caught them. Would I talk the issue through with them? Would I invite them to a self-help workshop? Maybe I could persuade the government to give them an all-expenses paid trip to Alton Towers? Would I employ them in various menial tasks so they could earn some money to buy an iPod, which would clearly help them out of their desperate state and allow them get some much needed self-respect back? No. I wouldn't even bother to beat them senseless with a large stick, bind their feet and stuff them into a Hessian sack. Instead, I decided if I ever caught them, I would just get Barney to piss on their troubled head.

* * *

When Barney returned from the Kennels, he was a different dog – literally. A mistake had been made somewhere along the line and they brought a Dalmatian out. Confusion was resolved and, soon after, Barney was waving goodbye out of the rear window to his new found chums as we drove homewards.

It wasn't only Barney though that had undergone a change. I was regularly being told that I was changing and what is more, changing for the better. I wasn't aware that I was *that* bad before, but I am sure there will be a steady stream of women ready to testify that they knew my evil twin. I'm not sure how much I buy into this 'adult changeling' theory as it means acceptance of 'bad John', but even *I* felt much more relaxed and easy going than I had done for a long while. Much more than I had been for the last decade (a.k.a. 'the wilderness years') if truth be known. Deborah had started to tell me how I was different until I interrupted with, "Don't," and then, "Stop." I had actually meant to say, "Don't stop," but in between getting the two words out, I did one of those little burps where a bit of sick comes up too, which had put me off my stroke slightly. By the time I had re-composed myself, she had wandered back into the kitchen. I would therefore have to try and interpret how and why these changes were taking place. I know it's not very British to accept praise and even less so to tell everyone about it, but may I remind you of the old maxim,

> *"If you don't blow your own trumpet, someone else will use it as a pisspot."*

Certainly having a daughter had made me a shadow of my former selfishness and, more recently, the arrival of Barney had given me a renewed sense of responsibility.

He certainly had a lot to do with it and, if I was the great dictator, I'd have all the shorthand typists in the land typing out compulsory orders for everyone to own a pet. Apart from fish, which just make me jealous, a good majority of the other pets love you unreservedly, just for being there. Now, that has to have a positive effect on anyone. And, since I had long stopped believing that cats were Catholic and dogs were Protestant, either variety would do. I mean, how good do you feel in those few brief seconds when your Bonzo or Puss comes over to greet you, wanting you to stroke them because they love you so much and they want to see that you love them too. As secretaries across the UK turned all those seconds into minutes, we would be reading about thousands upon thousands of feel good factors.

I realised how my idea, during the Foot and Mouth epidemic, of using all the sick cows and sheep to clear landmines in former war zones was bad too. I had become more humane.

It was cruel as well to threaten Bethan, telling her that when she was older, if she didn't come out of the nightclub at the agreed time, that I'd go in and start dancing myself. 'Dad dancing' – that would clear the whole place out in no time.

I also realised it was wrong to say that talk of famines made me feel peckish.

I also spent far too much time worrying about small trivial things instead of appreciating that there are people with a lot more to worry about than me. On the eve of the new millennium, with all the talk about the potential havoc caused by the millennium bug, there was me worrying that my toaster might not work or that I might have to reset the central heating timer, when poor old Stephen Hawking must have been shitting himself.

The other thing is that I've never been much of a diplomat and office politics has always been beyond me. I'd much rather sit at the back of a meeting and play 'bullshit bingo'. (If you have never played before, all you need to do is write in a grid all the pseudo-intellectual business-speak words these highly paid consultant gurus spout. Things like 'think out of the box', 'wow factor', 'etched in stone', 'walk the talk', 'playing hardball', 'mind share', 'strategic fit', 'touch base', 'synergy', 'win-win' etc. As your boss or some highly paid consultant, sits with his legs apart as if he's got two prickly pears for testicles, and regurgitates these magic words of wisdom as part of his spiel, you cross them off your grid. When you have crossed them all off, you jump up waving your piece of paper and shout "Bullshit!").

I've also never been one for sucking up to the big nobs in the company either. It just leaves a bad taste in your mouth and, anyway I wasn't very good at disguising the fact that I only respected those people who I felt deserved it. Therefore, I've never had to sell my soul to any company in order to get on because nobody has ever wanted me that much. The great and good in business were gradually being replaced by the greedy and mean anyway. Too many hands in pockets and not enough hands on hearts. There are too many people who would be quite willing to betray you with a Judas kiss if they thought they could get some benefit out of it. I didn't really want to be a part of that.

At our last annual conference in some swanky hotel my boss boasted "I'm a country member". I remember alright. In fact he was such an irritating one that I gave him the nickname 'Thrush'.

Later on, after she eventually finished with the important people in the company, informing them all no doubt that she loved the consultants talk but personally preferred to avoid clichés like the plague, the HR (Human Resources) manager wandered over in my direction. She took a moment to look me up and down and then greeted me with the same sort of kiss that had brought Him down at Gethsemane. I guessed that this could only mean one thing – she had got the course report back.

Six months ago, I had obviously been identified as someone who was in need of 'warm fuzziness' training as I had been selected to go on an external training course. According to Human Resources this was to – 'make me a more balanced individual'. I suspect they were implying after my time in the military I might be lacking in tact and finesse. I'd show them they were wrong!

The course was at a conference centre in the Cotswolds. To show I was keen I had arrived early, placed my pad and pencil on the desk next to a particularly attractive young lady and joined her and the others for coffee at the back of the room. She looked full of warm fuzziness. Maybe her warm fuzziness might rub off on me if I was lucky.

We were then told to move our chairs into a circle. Shit! – I found myself next to a geeky looking librarian type and a bloke who looked like a geography teacher. Still I could see my potential new friend (or Lindsey, as deduced from her name-badge) sitting almost opposite in her pale coloured dress (Virgin Mary blue I do believe).

This clearly wasn't going to be the usual type of presentation that I was used to in the military – where you sit through a slide show of enemy tanks, battleships and fighter planes, and just when you are getting bored, the instructor slips in a slide of a naked woman pretending that he had left it in by mistake. That always got a good laugh.

I wondered if Hugh Hefner did the same when he was trying to decide the Playboy Bunny of the year. Halfway through a show of all the bunnies, would he suddenly slip in a slide of the Russian T-90 battle tank, complete with the 1A4GT integrated fire control system. I'm sure after the initial shock, the sweeties would be laughing their little ears off!

Sorry I digress. Anyway, PowerPoint had spoilt that bit of fun for a whole new generation. Sorry again, that was a digression of a digression. Half of you reading this book are probably wondering what the hell I'm on about. I know how you feel. It's ok for you though, you've just got to read it ...I've got to live it!

Back to the course.

We were sat in a circle and our 'mentor' explained that we would start with an ice breaker. "List the two worst sounds known to mankind". I sat back smugly whilst the others chewed on their pencils and looked deeply engrossed in some internal dilemma.

This was easy! I knew my hours spent making lists of things hadn't gone to waste!

My favourite CD (*Donkey Serenade* – Weddings, Parties, Anything), favourite song (*Subversives* – The Lowest of the Low – and probably the rare, faster version of it), book (*A Mouthful of Rocks* – Christian Jennings), film (*Dogma* or maybe *School of Rock*) and so on. I could go on, so I will. Ten places to keep a torch, ways to tell if everyone else is an alien except for you, three ways to humiliate ants, where I would visit if I was invisible, signals I would make if I came back as a dog to let people know it was me, which one would I go out with if they both asked me out at the same time – Cameron Diaz or Miss Tucker (I'd probably come down on the side of Miss Diaz) – and a late entry, but an obviously inspired choice – sounds that I don't like.

When our mentor asked for a volunteer to start the session, I was the first on my feet. I looked over at Lindsey and then formally addressed the group.

"The two worst sounds known to mankind are:
The sound of coat-hangers clanking together and
The sound of the washing machine sloshing away"

I sat back down waiting for the nods of acknowledgement and murmurs of approval from my colleagues – particularly Lindsey. Except everyone just started at me. Someone coughed, but other than that, just silent stares. I don't know if you can have good silent stares, but even if you can, these weren't. I wondered what had happened. Had they thought I had farted when I sat down? Those chairs sometimes make it sound like that. I hadn't though. I was on my best behaviour.

The mentor spoke. "Lindsey, maybe you would like to tell us what you think are the two worst sounds known to mankind?"

The Virgin Lindsey then told us she believed the first was the sound of a baby crying whilst the rest of the world ignored the plight of poverty in the third world. There was clapping, some stood up, I could hear people scribbling on their pads. The place was buzzing with "So true" and "Oh yes" comments of appreciation.

I just sat there looking down at my pad, felt very red and warm and thought "Fuck". I don't know what they thought the second worst sound was – probably the sound of me spontaneously combusting. And I had another two days of this to go!

OK, I admit I wasn't totally 'a new man' but I was improving and was beginning to see what was important in life.

I believe it's all about being able to retain your own self-respect. This was becoming more important to me, and I didn't need a list of all those I was apparently superior to, just to feel good about myself. My dog thinks I'm the best, why should I need a second opinion?

The other payback was the time I now had for the hobbies and interests I had cultivated outside work (magic, 'Project X' and '*Shakespeare My Butt!*' amongst other things), which made me feel that I *had* achieved something. This was now serving to make me a much more relaxed and contented individual. Indeed, just writing about the things that have happened in my life was a very cathartic experience, even if it did result in two books in parallel, one being named *Here be monsters* which was ritually consigned to 'file thirteen'.

I know that growing old is unhealthy, but I guess that worldly wisdom had also contributed to why I was much more tolerant. I used to be pretty bitter about some things when I was young, to the extent that, if I bit a lemon, the lemon would make a face, but now I know that all the pent up grievances in the world won't change anything. What's the point? Don't get me wrong, I'm not saying that I'm going around committing random acts of kindness or senseless acts of beauty, ('Pissing on their troubled head,' being a case in point) but I am more open minded. You could never make good wine out of grapes of wrath and, anyway, I was finding out that it was exciting and fun to run back across burning bridges. Who knows what you might find on the other side? Generally I only get bitter now when I go down the pub.

I was also being told that I was more approachable and listened more. It probably just seemed that way because it takes me a bit longer nowadays to think of a witty one liner to come back with. I normally think of a fantastic one after the other person has just left the room. Still, if people thought I was a nicer guy because of my slow reactions, so be it.

The milkman of human kindness must have visited one morning and left an extra pinta. I had developed 'communism of the soul'.

"Hello reader, you are looking good today. Have you done your hair differently? Of course, I love everyone who has bought my book. But you ...you're my favourite! I'd never do that thing to your toothbrush where you've got to throw it away as soon as you find out about it. Read on you splendid thing."

I was learning how to enjoy life more stupidly, and it felt good. T'ai Chi, self-discovery workshops, hugging trees, colonic irrigation? You can shove them up your arse. Just get a daughter, a dog, and some hobbies; get older and get over it.

I looked at my horoscope and, apparently the moon was in my seventh house. What the hell was that supposed to mean?

* * *

Barney was in his third house so far that week – the kennels, a sleepover at Deborah's and now back to his own home, sweet home.

The work that John, the kennel owner, had put into Barney seemed to have tipped the balance. As he explained, any dog only understands two things: pleasant and unpleasant experiences. If the owner can cause the dog to experience these two totally opposite sensations, then dog training is easy.

When the dog understands you are top dog, the leader of the pack, the worst punishment that a trained dog should suffer is the word, "No," uttered from his master's lips. Praise was at the other end of the spectrum.

We chatted some more about how to assert yourself as the top dog, before John showed me how theory had become reality. As Barney pottered away to sniff at something or other, John delivered a sharp, "No!" The black one looked up from his sniffery with a devastated, "What have I done wrong now?" face. He genuinely meant it too. It wasn't the sarcastic, "What have I done wrong now?" that Deborah gives me if I am brave enough to tell her off – the one with the long emphasis on the word, "now". No, this was genuine concern that he was doing something that he shouldn't be. It was an, "Oh My God, what can I do to please the Boss to make up for my wrong doing?"

John gave him the opportunity with a "Good Boy" and Barney came running to his side, delighted with the fact that he could make up for his misdemeanour. It was like the final piece of the jigsaw, the one that always seems to be missing. It's never the first part of the jigsaw that's missing, never the middle piece; no, always the last part. How is that?

His first evening's walk round the circuit, after returning home, was a delight and, even with the lead off, Barney never left my side. It was like walking with an invisible lead, as opposed to the old days when I would be walking with an invisible dog. I was keen to apply the lesson to his jumping up too and was slightly disappointed that he wasn't doing anything wrong for me to correct!

The one thing that hadn't changed though was his chewing capacity and, by the end of his first day back, the front door 'map' had changed from the outline of Australia to resemble one of Tasmania. And, as my Australian friend Digger will tell you, that is one place Barney would have no desire to visit, following his op.

CHAPTER TWENTY-NINE

How Long Will Breakfast Be?

Doctor Shit was on the phone. He had gone camping.

It was a weekend trip, and the six of them – his wife Linda, Ceri, Gethin, Rebecca and Joseph – had set out on the Friday night, pitching the tent on the Friday evening, looking forward to a lovely weekend in the Welsh hills.

Linda had gone out on the Saturday morning and come back with bacon, sausages, beans and eggs that were arranged carefully around the frying pans. The children sat round expectantly with a knife and fork in each hand.

When Paul starts a story like that, you know it's not going to have the happy ending it should. It's not going to be a funny "How long will breakfast be?" – "Four inches – it's a sausage" type tale. No, this was going to be something else altogether. But I digress.

Meanwhile back at the campsite, Paul turned on the gas bottle. 'PSSSsssst' – the gas had run out.

No worries, Paul then hopped in the car to get a refill from any of the seven local garages. Paul returned half an hour later reporting that none of the seven garages have any gas.

All six then get in the car to make the seventeen mile trip to Brecon where there *must* be somewhere that has gas.

Sixteen miles into the trip, BRRRrrrrrrrr, the car conks out.

The RAC are called; the RAC arrive and look at the car; the

RAC go away and come back with a low loader to put the car on, because the car is totally dead. The RAC then take Paul to the campsite; RAC man waits patiently whilst Paul takes the tent down, empties the portable toilet and chucks the uncooked breakfast away, and hooks trailer onto back of low loader. The RAC then take Paul and family home – hungry.

Not a good weekend so far. The car was taken to the local garage and they rang him on the Monday to say it would cost £1,100 to repair. I asked if he'd have to pay for that out of his savings. After a few minutes of maniacal laughter, Paul reminded me that he had four children and that the term 'savings' had left his vocabulary many years earlier. Fair point.

It hadn't been a good start to the week for him. As for me, it was the start of what should be an excellent week.

It was an important day. After the bad course incident, I had been in the doghouse. Here was an opportunity to show that I could be a team player and make up for the course debacle.

I had arranged to meet my Boss, the Security Services Director, to discuss an imminent operation. So, after the sticky up haired morning walk, I planned to clear the car of 'Barney' debris (as I was going to be driving the Boss), before getting ready for our meeting. With Barney ensconced in the house, I ethnically cleansed the vehicle and was going back into the house to get ready. This is the point at which I started to doubt Barney's new found angelic status. He had locked me out!

He hadn't yet mastered the mortice key operation but his little paws had managed to push the bolt across. I stood and pondered on my predicament. As a good security professional, all the windows were closed, of course, so climbing through one was not an option, and calling a locksmith would be no good as the locks were fine; it was an internal bolt that was the problem. Barney obviously hadn't thought this through properly as I hadn't prepared his breakfast yet and his little pea like brain wasn't able to link the, *"Unlock bolt"* and *"Have breakfast,"* thoughts that were pottering around aimlessly somewhere within. I fetched Bethan's folding hairbrush with a mirror on the handle from the car and, going down on my knees, pushed it through the letterbox. I could see the bolt and the big knob that Barney had pushed across while, all the time, an excited dog was leaping up to lick my fingers and grab the new toy I was clearly pushing through just for him.

They say a good way to catch a monkey is to put a monkey nut in a bottle. The monkey can fit his hand in but, when his fist is clenched around the nut, he can't get his hand back out and, being a stupid greedy fellow, he gets stuck. So it was that I was stuck. I couldn't get my hand back out with the brush held tight and, if I loosened my grip, Barney would grab it and run off. Worse still if the mirror dropped and broke, it would be seven years bad luck for me and forty nine years back luck for Barney. The musical sit competition that Barney had won a month earlier suddenly inspired me, so I sung a little song and then, just as suddenly, stopped.

> *"The bushes dance and the world outside just makes you tense*
> *So once a year you stick you head out to see if the coast is clear*
> *Thylacine, the way they treated you was a tragedy*
> *And I don't know the things you must have seen*
> *You're a 10,000 year old has been*
>
> *In another place, on a school excursion I first saw your face*
> *Through a glass case*
> *And I had a million questions and the least of which was ...*
> *Why?*
> *But I knelt down and saw no answer in your marble for an eye*
>
> *You're famous...*
> *The Marsupial Elvis*

You've been seen in places I know you've never been
SIT!"

As he sat, the brush was quickly withdrawn. After a rummage through the shed, I returned with a bungee rope. I couldn't fit the brush/mirror in as well, so the bungee was left to go it alone. I fed it through the letterbox in the direction of the knob but, as I imagined the hook to be in about the right place, the rope went limp and floppy. This was an experience that I was unfamiliar with and, if any girl tells you otherwise, she's a bloody liar. This was a job for a wire coat hanger!

I don't know if you have any wire coat hangers in your house, but it seems they are now an object of derision and their plastic moulded counterparts have all but driven them into extinction. The traditional old hangers that left a nice line across the place where your trousers were folded over, are not welcome anymore in polite society it seems. I tried next door but 'Bill's replacement' didn't have any either and things were starting to look bleak.

Then, into the breach, strode Jack. Jack lives two doors down and is the type of guy you would want as an uncle. He always seems to know the right thing to do and, in the case of the door-locking dog, he was not going to disappoint. He too had succumbed to the lure of the moulded hanger but, being Jack, he had a wire one squirreled away in his own shed for just such a 'dog locking door' occasion. Equipped with the hanger, converted into a knob-hooking device, we returned to my house. I must admit, as I knelt there, peering through the letter box at the brush/mirror and then poking my hook device through and scraping it about, I felt more like a back street abortionist than a dog rescuer but, within seconds, the dirty deed was done and breakfast and dog were once again reunited.

Meanwhile, I quickly hurried upstairs and got ready to leave. As I drove down, I rang my Boss to let him know I was running late. As I explained, I felt like a schoolboy, saying that the dog had eaten his homework, and I sensed that my Boss felt the same way. When I eventually arrived, Karen, his secretary, asked what else the 'dog' had done. Had he deleted the week's itinerary I was supposed to have sent the previous Friday, or maybe he had persuaded me not to action the things I should have done after the last meeting. Call me intuitive, but I suspect she was not being altogether straight with me. In fact I'm sure that if I listened really carefully I could just about hear the sound of my contract being torn up.

CHAPTER THIRTY

Project X – A Place Oddity

The sky was filled with birds flying south and the windscreen wipers on the cars seemed to be waving them goodbye. It was as if the weather had realised that it was being too nice for that time of year and felt it had to make an extra effort to be cold and wet, just to make up for it. The rain was torrential and I was expecting to see two of every animal wandering down the road at any moment. Perfect!

I rang Deborah and arranged a rendezvous at Pity Me. The original shoot hadn't quite captured the 'pitiful' element but now, with the rain and cold, a snap of me shivering beneath the sign would be ideal. If we weren't miserable enough in the first picture, we had certainly made up for it now. Things were definitely a bit strained between us and I'm sure the 'half a dog' dedication had kicked off this whole episode.

As the rain came down, with the cold wind biting into me, I stood below the sign as if it were some type of strange, old fashioned advisory caption to explain away the situation to anyone who was in any doubt about how I was feeling. I tried to think what the opposite was of 'saying cheese'. I guess it must be chalk. I decided against saying it out loud as it might look as if I was pouting at the camera. Instead, I just thought it. I thought about the scary man we had seen the first time round too and I was scared, thinking of chalk, cold, wet and miserable. This is what they must mean by suffering for your art. Excellent!

Deborah had brought her teddy bear along to the shoot and that could only mean one thing – a trip to 'Bearpark' was on the cards. As we drove on through the rainy streets to 'Beau Repaire', it looked anything but a beautiful retreat. I'm sure, if the Normans had seen it like this, we would be converting 'Merde' into an unusual, Anglicised place name now, but they didn't, so we're not.

We found an old rusty sign, the type with a hand on the end pointing the way, for Bearpark colliery. Barney stayed behind to guard the car as we hurried over to the sign. The area looked a bit dodgy but, even though he wasn't much of a barker, I'm sure he would put up a decent fight if anyone tried to break in. I'm not sure what he would be like at putting fires out though. As Debs poked Teddy's head over the top of our pointing signpost, I took the photo. I suppose, as a model for the calendar, Teddy should have been covered in body oil so he would glisten in the light of the flickering orange street lamp, but it would only have become matted in his fur.

It would have slowed us down too. We wanted to be in, get the job done and out, before any locals saw us. That's the thing about these places with funny or strange names. The locals seem to be overly protective and take any mockery of the name of their hometown personally. Goodness knows what the Twats, (or whatever you call the locals from Twatt) would do if they caught you sniggering as you photographed their sign. They seem exceedingly proud of their home town and even have a Twatt web site which lists, amongst other things, Twatt Celebrities and Twatt eating places. My kinda place.

❖ ❖ ❖

We were on a roll. Well, I was anyway. Deborah didn't seem to share my enthusiasm and I spent the rest of the evening persuading her that, the sooner we could get the calendar finished, the sooner life could go back to normal although, as she pointed out, I would probably just embark on another stupid quest as soon as life became *too* normal. I think she liked it best when it was just an idea. I told her of my new name for Project 'X' – 'A Place Oddity' in an effort to cheer her up but that didn't work. In the end, I agreed that we would do one more sign tomorrow and that would be it for the rest of the weekend.

❖ ❖ ❖

The next day was bright, dry and fresh as we set off – destination Cockfield. The name literally means a field full of cocks. It was a lovely looking village, with a well-tended war memorial, a couple of nice looking pubs and wide clean streets. There were a number of wriggly tin buildings on the outskirts of the place that looked as if they could have been garages once upon a time. They were covered in black pitch and some had small windows, obscured with cobwebs. In contrast to the orderliness of the Cockfield streets, the garages seemed to have been plonked, in a haphazard fashion, on the outskirts. What I would have given to have one of my very own – my own big shed. Surely, that's every man's dream. I would have an old desk in there, with a vice attached to the end of it. There would be a pile of old papers on the floor, tied up with string, along with some old copies of *National Geographic*. There would probably be some copies of *Look and Learn* too and an old Encyclopaedia. I'd have lots of jam jars on a shelf, containing bits of screws and nails and a couple of bottles of fortified wine on the end. An old piece of carpet would do for the floor and an oil heater, with one leg missing, would warm the place up. I would have all the gear as well, in case anyone wanted any wood planing or the chain putting back on their bike.

The seating would be an old armchair and an old wooden school chair, in case I wanted to do a bit of writing in there. There would be lots of other stuff too. It would be cluttered, but not messy, and have the pleasant smell of an empty tin of biscuits. An old clear glass bulb, without a shade, would hang from the roof, with that sort of woven material covering the wires. Barney would just curl up on the piece of carpet while a stray cat, that seemed to have come with the big shed, would sleep in an old cardboard box, lined with a blanket, next to some useful bits of spare wood. Barney and the un-named cat would just ignore each other and an old, half-used tin of pitch would sit by the door.

The sign welcoming us to Cockfield was yellow and blue, on a stone plinth. To make it more amusing, I decided to get my cock out and have it photographed next to the sign. Technically, it wasn't a cockerel but a rubber chicken, but I doubt whether anyone would look that closely. Again, like the teddy, it was decided not to oil it up. It was a prop for one of my magic tricks and I didn't fancy cleaning the slippery thing afterwards. Shots were then taken from several angles, with the chicken in various poses.

Once the shooting was over, I bid goodbye to the big sheds, and we drove over the cattle grid and away. I liked Cockfield and, although she wasn't saying much, I think Deborah did too.

CHAPTER THIRTY-ONE

The Secret of My Excess

Concurrent Activity. That was what was always drilled into me in the Forces. While you are at your orders briefing, the soldiers can be getting their weapons prepared or kit organised. A lot of Forces life is spent waiting about, so there was lots of concurrent activity opportunity. Getting a brew on was a particular favourite of mine.

I had a problem and it needed sorting fast. Deborah was not in the happiest or indeed erudite frames of mind I've ever found her in. Apparently I was becoming (expletives deleted) obsessed by this project and, as is normally the case, I think she was probably right – it was taking a toll on our friendship. The word 'autistic' had been used. I am not sure if that particular word can be used in a complimentary way but, even if it can be, it was not being used as such in this instance. Even Bethan agreed, and told me I was fixated. They were right too. If I'm involved in a project I usually focus on that and everything else goes out the window. With me, things that start as hobbies usually become obsessions and eventually end up as grounds for divorce. This was the secret of my excess. I needed to complete the 'place oddity' and try and get things back to normal as soon as possible.

As a consequence, morning walks were no longer mindless meanderings and had, instead, transformed into brainstorming sessions as I racked my brain for other place names that could grace the calendar. We were only three months short, but those three months were proving elusive, although Deborah hadn't helped things by (rather selfishly in my opinion) putting the veto on my photo suggestion for 'Wide Open'. To be quite honest the maps were not being at all helpful either.

As a sailor, when navigating across the Atlantic, by day we took sun sightings and, by night, we established our position by moon and star observation. Global Positioning was in its infancy and, anyway, in case of war, the Russians would probably target the satellites. I would use a sextant that hadn't changed that much from the one developed back in 1757. If it *was* a celestial sighting, first I would establish where particular stars in the sky were, using complex astronomical tables. Then, after using the sextant to calculate the angle of the star from the horizon, another series of calculations would allow me to draw a line of position on the chart. After a few more sightings of specific stars, the chart would have a number of lines of position, criss-crossing. Where these lines intercepted represented the position of the ship which, in this case, was HMS Fearless. In mitigation, it is a complex and lengthy process, compounded by the fact that the ship was constantly steaming towards the Americas, as well as being buffeted by the Atlantic swell as the sightings were taken.

My lines of position would normally criss-cross to resemble a cocked hat type of affair and, I could reasonably assume that we were within five to ten miles of the middle of the hat. It can also be reasonably assumed that celestial navigation was not my forte. However, compared to the people who drew up my road atlas, I felt like a new age Vasco da Gama.

After a study of our map, we had set off into North Yorkshire to capture such beauties as Blubberhouses, Kettlesing Bottom and an even smaller New York than its Tyneside namesake. It was a fresh, bright autumn morning and the light at the end of the tunnel seemed very bright too. Three months to go, and three places to visit.

My mind was full of thoughts and questions as we drove into the low September sun. Blubberhouses was a sort of

'Octobery' month or it may even be given the coveted 'December' spot. I could understand a Blubberhouses near the coast too, but in the middle of land locked Yorkshire? My investigations hadn't even managed to find an origin for this strange name and what would the hamlet or village look like? Wobbly?

After passing the massive golf balls that formed the American Menwith Hill Listening Station, we saw the sign for Blubberhouses seven miles ahead. We drove on excitedly and I asked Deborah to keep an eye out for signs, as we grew closer. But that was the problem; there were no more signs. There were signs for Dacre, West End and Pately Bridge, but nothing for Blubberhouses. We scoured the area, leaving no dodgy 'B road' or lane unscathed in our search – it had just vanished. We drove up past fields with sheep in, past fields *without* sheep in, past what looked like a graveyard for trees, with their little wooden posts as headstones, past tumbledown barns, but not once past Blubberhouses.

Deborah finally piped up saying that, when she had lived in Doncaster, she went to the Lake District via 'Blubberhouses Way'. And I think that's all Blubberhouses was – an 'over there, somewhere' type place; a 'Blubberhouses Way' type direction, only to be taken seriously by non-Yorkshire folk like me. I'm sure it was their little 'in joke' that even the council had bought into by erecting signs – not a 'Blubberhouses Way' sign but a specific, 'Blubberhouses – 7 miles' sign. I couldn't just have the sign in the calendar without having set foot in the village. It would be a betrayal of everything that the 'Place Oddity' stood for. I wasn't quite sure *what* it stood for actually, but a sign to nowhere just didn't seem right (although a sign to No Place, of course, was fine).

Anyway, I knew my target audience. If I told them there were three billion stars in the sky, they would believe me but, if I told them the bench had just been painted and the paint was still wet, they would have to touch it, just to make sure. Also, if they ever did make the journey North, visiting Blubberhouses would definitely be on their list of things to do. It wasn't a good start to the day. Disaster number one. I refused to let it get to me; we still had another two to knock off.

❖ ❖ ❖

I wasn't convinced that New York was all that funny. After all, there was York itself just down the road but I suppose, if I could get the photograph to include a rural sleepy village instead of a city metropolis, it might raise a wry smile. It looked tiny on the map and that was ideal.

There is a mill in New York. I knew that because, as we entered the place, a big sign told us that we couldn't turn down that way to it. There is an industrial estate in New York too and I know that because I saw a big sign for it as I left the place. In between the mill and the industrial estate, which is a distance of about a hundred yards, there is a fire station. It has the sort of neon sign outside that you would normally see outside a dodgy gambling bar (The type where the girls would wear T-shirts saying things like 'Liquor in the front and poker in the rear'). It also has a bus stop with a rather impressive bus shelter made of stone, with 'New York' chiselled into the side so the bus drivers know where they are. I guess they need it because, search as I might, (and I know I search pretty well as, on more than one occasion, Deborah has told me that I have eyes like a shithouse rat), I could find no conventional sign for the spot. No sign, no photo, no month, no smiles all round. Disaster number two.

Still, we had Kettlesing Bottom to finish the day with. The 'Kettlesing' bit was alright I suppose but, being puerile, I thought the 'Bottom' bit might crack a smile. We found Kettlesing easily enough (and a lovely village it is too), by following the well-posted signs for the village. At last, some order seemed to have been restored. The 'Bottom' must be close and we even found a sign for Kettlesing Head, which was strange because there wasn't a 'Head' on the map. In my experience though, the 'Bottom' was never that far from the 'Head' so the search continued. More signs instead of less appeared, which was a novelty. We smiled and we searched and searched and searched. All to no avail – here was disaster number three.

The audacity to have a 'Kettlesing Head' sign, but no 'Kettlesing Bottom'. It's on the map! Have the sign people never thought to look at the map? What did they think they were playing at?

And why oh why did the bastards invariably put the places we wanted to find in the crack between two pages!

Great Cock Up is rumoured to be in Cumbria. The 'Up' means valley and this valley was apparently occupied by a cock; a woodcock probably. But can I find it? The place I mean, not the woodcock, although I can't find that either.

It's becoming an epidemic. I live near Shiney Row where we have the Shiney Row Cobbler, Shiney Row College and we even have 'Shiney New Appliances' – a shop that sells shiny new appliances, as luck would have it, but there is no 'Shiney Row – You are here' sign. I know because we looked for one that night.

How those Frenchies, with their 'In' and 'Out' signs to their towns must be laughing their berets off, as they weave all over the road, trying to control their onion-laden bikes, shrugging and making a, "Haw he haw he haw," sound. Two can play at this game. That's the last time I buy any of *their* letters.

❖ ❖ ❖

My mood didn't improve at all the next day. It was a leaving do for someone from work. Sadly not mine, but some lucky fucker who had managed to tunnel out of the organisation. I was standing at the bar with the others, coiled like a spring waiting for the drift towards the dining table. It always ended up the same. If I wasn't quick enough I'd end up sitting on the boring end of the table with people talking about year end results, margins and strategic business plans. At the other end of the table, people would be laughing and misbehaving, talking about all kinds of dirty, depraved stuff ...that was where I should be!

Worst case scenario would be a whole evening sitting next to a guy they called 'Shit Crack' because his banter was so rubbish.

Then the age old dilemma. Have I got time to pop for a piss before it all starts? No, no, hang on John, as soon as you go they'll all meander over to the table and you'll be left with the reject seats next to the blokes with the humour by-pass. Good thinking John ...I'll wait.

So I wait, and wait ...and everyone is still milling about and chatting at the bar. Damn ...I've wasted the opportunity ...I could have gone and dropped the kids off while they were all chatting. Fuck it, lets go for it John, if you walk out the door, and then run down the corridor to the toilets, you can still get a quick piss, run back and wander nonchalantly back in through the door, exchange some pleasantries and still be in pole position for the move to the dining table.

GO! Big steps to door smiling and nodding at colleagues, out of door into corridor, sprint down corridor, concurrent activity ... unzip as push bog door open, ignore shocked look from bloke coming out of bog, urinals busy, quick think ...push into trap, Hitler piss (You're a genius John ...this is working like clockwork! ...even time to make little joke to fellow pissers) "This waters cold!", finish, unexplained little shudder, shake, zip, wash hands, no time to dry, run up corridor, walk into room triumphantly. SHIT!

Curse you Donoghue – you and your stupid plans!

Everyone was seated happily, breaking their bread rolls and discovering that the hardness of the butter is inversely proportional to the softness of the bread. Above it all, a big finger, invisible to everyone else but sadly only too visible to me was pointing at the only seat left. To the left of the big finger was seated Shit Crack, to the right was the Thrush. I slowly did the walk of shame and took my seat and did a feeble and unconvincing grin.

Gradually as the evening wore on I began to lose the will to live. As the Thrush talked to me I could see his lips move but all I could hear was a 'blah blah blah' as I strained to catch the fun at the other end of the table. I could just about overhear someone describing how they had taken a laxative and a sleeping tablet on the same night and woken to find he was covered in paste. Through the raucous laughter I could just about make out someone else telling the tale of when his girlfriend went to the ... then suddenly, oh shit! The Thrush's lips stopped moving. I've got to say something now. Was it a sad tale or happy tale? Will a laugh and a nod suffice? Is he expecting a response?

The Thrush looked at me expectantly. I glanced over at Shit Crack. He had his eyebrows raised in a sort of 'What do you think about that then?' type gesture. Why-o-why didn't I take up smoking a pipe? This would have been the ideal time to look pensive and buy some time by puffing away for a minute or so. Instead, I sat like a teabag for a few seconds before I decided to resort to my tactic of choice – change the subject entirely.

"Do you know what the two worst sounds known to mankind are? ..."

By the end of the evening I had convinced myself that it would be perfectly acceptable to use violence to get a decent seat next time.

CHAPTER THIRTY-TWO

Blubberhouses Revisited

I had calmed down sufficiently by the following Wednesday to reconsider my rashness in writing off the 'Blubbery' one. I was due at Leeds Bradford Airport and I thought a quick detour wouldn't do any harm.

I approached the area from a different direction to last time and eventually picked up a sign for Blubberhouses. 'Blubberhouses 7', it read. I drove in the direction indicated for half a mile until I reached the next sign. For some bizarre reason, it read, 'Blubberhouses 5.5'. I drove on until I reached the next one, which indicated, 'Blubberhouses 6'. Clearly the 'blubbery' nature of the place meant that even the council couldn't pinpoint where it was. I continued along the road until I came to, 'Blubberhouses 3' but then, at the next junction, ten yards further down the road, we had apparently gone backwards as the sign indicated, 'Blubberhouses 3.5'. As I proceeded, I found 'Blubberhouses 3' again. This was the last time the council were prepared to commit themselves because, after that, it was just general, 'Blubberhouses – This Way', type signs. I set the mileometer to measure the distance from the last specific indicator and duly stopped three miles on. There was no Blubberhouses village, not even a single 'Blubbery' house. I had gone 'Blubberhouses Way'. At least, if you are sent to Coventry, there is somewhere you can call home.

As sad a confession as it may be, I considered myself something of an expert on signing. In wartime, one of the prime functions of the Military Police is to get the troops and supplies to and from the front line (not to be confused with the Regimental Police whose main duty is to beat you up) and we spend a lot of time practising signing routes. You may have noticed them as you drive around. The signs are normally attached to posts about headlight height by the side of the road, or attached to existing road signs. Basically, an arrow indicates the direction of the front, whilst an arrow with a line at the end indicates the way back. There is also a name on each sign, like 'Dog' or 'Crab', so soldiers know they are following 'dog route' instead of various road numbers. The point I'm making is that all the routes lead somewhere and, when you get there, you have a sign informing you that you have arrived. So far, 'Project X' had been plagued by either roads to nowhere or places that existed on maps, but with no signs to them at all.

I might be a confused man, but I was also a man without pride when it came to finishing 'A Place Oddity'. I needed to fill in three more months on the calendar, with a depleting supply of odd place names. I quickly got out of the car, photographed the sign and drove off before security at Menwith Hill reported me to the police.

❖ ❖ ❖

I like to know the history of the places I visit and how the village acquired its name, especially if it is an unusual one.

That morning, we were off to Quaking Houses, a small mining village near Stanley in County Durham but, as much as I tried, I couldn't discover why it was called that. Maybe one of the houses has fallen down because the ground became unstable with the mining works. Perhaps it was on the Durham equivalent of the San Andreas Fault, except there was no Mexican to blame over here. Maybe it was something religious to do with Quakers. Perhaps, once upon a time, a Mr Quaking had lived there. There were a number of villages called '*Something* Houses' in the vicinity. Obviously, we have the 'Scarlet

Pimpernel' that is Blubberhouses but, not too far away, there is also a Halfpenny Houses, with Burnthouses only a few miles away from that. They are starting to sound like places the three little piggies would build!

Quaking Houses is on top of a hill, and seemed to consist of a number of busy back-to-back streets, with beautifully tended fronts. The backs all had low walls, where a blackboard would have been hung out when the mine was still going. The miners living in the houses would write down what time they wanted to be up for their shift, and the Colliery would send a man to wake them up at the designated hour – a sort of human alarm clock. It was a logical sort of place, with street names like First, Second, Third and Fourth Street. There was a colliery wheel embedded in the village green, along with two coal carts, to commemorate the mining heritage. At the bottom of the hill was a park, dedicated in memory of the dead from both World Wars, along with a couple of churches, one of which had the shiniest Jesus I have ever seen on a large wooden cross. It came over as the sort of place that would have a strong sense of community.

We took the photograph to get in both the road sign and the coal carts. This would be 'November'.

I looked around to see if there was anything that would give an indication of how the place got its name, but drew a blank. I guess it just evolved over the decades.

Evolution amazes me, although it generally happens too slowly to be a true spectator sport.

All dogs started as wolves I guess, from pretty amiable ones like Barney, through to real nutcases who would tear your head off as soon as look at you. You have big sturdy beasts through to ones that look like a long sausage. You can clearly see the proud looking dogs with a strong work ethic who have been bred to assist man, while others must frankly be ashamed of themselves, being raised just to travel around in a handbag. Mind you, if evolution was all it was cracked up to be, they would have grown an extra pair of arms. A dog that can run really fast, open his own tins of food and, more importantly, shovel up his own poop – now that's what I'd call proper evolution! And instead of all that woofing, they should learn to speak. Haven't they noticed how useful it is for us humans? And what's this about dogs only seeing in black and white? Even if they did ever learn to drive, it would be chaos at the traffic lights. "Do I stop when the light goes grey, or do I go when it goes grey?"

Despite all this though, you can see how humans have had a controlling interest in the way the species has developed.

Plant evolution is another thing altogether. It seems to me that plants had a free hand to evolve as they wished, for pretty much all of their time on earth. In my garden alone, there are a variety of species, all with different characteristics. It's almost like they had a list of qualities to choose from when they were setting out. If they chose some particular characteristic, there were pros and cons.

Plant: "I want to be a quick grower so I can spread quickly."

God: "OK, but you'll have to have shallow roots, which means that you can be cleared easily."

Plant: "Oh, how about me being really pretty then, with flowers and things so people want to cultivate me?"

God: "OK, but that means people will want to pick you too, you realise?"

Plant: "How about me being poisonous or thorny so that people won't want to pick me?"

God: "OK, but they won't want to cultivate you in their gardens will they? Fair's fair now plant – you can't have it all ways."

Plant: "What about the Rose?"

God: "D'oh! That happened on my day off. It's the last time I let one of those bloody Seraphims stand in for me! Last week he let through a bendy yellow fruit and the week before that it was a platypus. Jesus Christ, no wonder people think I move in mysterious ways!"

CHAPTER THIRTY-THREE

Victim of Geography

For some reason, Barney had turned on the ones he loved most. His blanket bed, which he seemed to love to the extent that he would try to hump it, had big chunks bitten out of it. I also came down to find that my walking shoes and trainers had been strategically chewed to render them useless. Perhaps he had seen the state I was in when I returned from my run and wanted none of it.

He must have had some dark secret to hide as well because the bank statement in that morning's post had been shredded. Was he ordering stuff on the phone or on-line that he didn't want me to know about? Maybe it was a surprise for me for Christmas? Actually, that thought only came to me later. At the time, I was convinced that he must be up to no good. In fact, it's a good bet that he *was* up to no good.

I pondered on what might have caused this. The previous evening, I had given him some left over vegetables with his dinner, which must have been the four vegetables of the apocalypse as far as he was concerned. If Bethan drinks cheap fizzy pop, she gets hyperactive on some kind of sugar high. Barney must have had the vegetable equivalent as it had driven his existing chewing habit into overdrive.

He clearly knew that what he had done was wrong, as he made a special effort to be my friend on that morning's walk. Even when I threw the ball and it bounced off his head by accident (yes, it was an accident), before landing in the stingy nettles, he made three valiant attempts to retrieve it. He eventually emerged, with the ball and so many 'stingies' in his mouth that I was stung when I took it off him but I gave him the benefit of the doubt on this. Ball bouncing on head and hidden 'stingies' were both accidents. No specialist personal injury solicitors were summoned.

Maybe he was becoming frustrated with 'Project X' too, but there was only one remaining month to fill.

We had both been amused by the legendary newspaper headline, 'East Fife 4, Forfar 5', but we had now discovered our very own place name headline, 'Nasty man weds Ugley woman'. Apparently, there is a village called Nasty down in Essex, with Ugley not that far away. They even have an Ugley Woman's Institute. Just to balance the issue, in the village of Idle in Yorkshire they have the splendidly named Idle Working Men's Club. It's had thousands of requests for affiliate membership and even the club logo – a man leaning on a shovel – helps to give the impression that the Idle Working Men's Club is just that.

It's a shame, of course, that this isn't a sports book as sporting quotes are ten a penny. Take, 'The bowler's Holding, the batsman's Willey,' or my own particular favourite. 'Kournikova has given us a semi to remember.' She always does.

Crime can also generate some decent headlines. A budding tabloid writer more than a century ahead of his time penned the headline 'Bastard stole my horse' in an 1866 copy of the Shields Daily News. The report actually referred to John Bastard, a notorious horse thief who was up to his shenanigans again.

Still, place names do have their own potential. In Devon, there is Pennycomequick with Brown Willy in Cornwall – that's two places by the way. Westward Ho! is the only place I could find that is named after a book and has an exclamation mark as part of the place name. Deborah noted that some places we had been looking for were difficult to find and that most men find it hard to locate Clitheroe. Oh, I see what she's made me write. I feel dirty, telling you that now.

Llanfairpwllgwyngyllgogerychwyrndrobwllllantysilio-
gogogoch is in Anglesey but couldn't be included on two
counts. Firstly, it was out of our area and, secondly, I didn't
have a wide-angle lens. Muff would be easier to fit in but, again,
that was in Ireland and so beyond our catchment area.

Apart from the obvious strange names, the scary thing
about living in Great Britain is that a lot of names don't seem
strange until an outsider points them out. It's that non barking
dog thing.

Crook in County Durham is just another ex-mining town,
with nothing strange about it until you apply for a job with the
Police and tell them that you attended Crook School. Try to be
taken seriously when you live in Derbyshire and tell people that
you went to Clowne School.

"Did you have to wear big shoes and an orange wig?"

Maybe though, we have got it easy. How do people react in
America when you say that you come from Wanker's Corner in
Oregon; Horneytown in North Carolina or Monkey's Eyebrow
in Kentucky?

They might laugh at us for needing a licence to be able
watch the telly, but I think they drew the short straw (yes,
foreign readers, unbelievable as it may sound, just as you may
need a licence to own a shotgun or to drive a car, you also need a
licence just to watch the telly in this country!).

Then again, there are short straws and there are shorter
straws. I would guess that, if you come from the tranquil
isolated retreat for outdoor enthusiasts in the foothills of Ohio,
you may be used to people being a bit tongue in cheek, when
they talk about where you come from. What did you really
think they would say when they know you come from
Gobbler's Knob?

❖ ❖ ❖

Somewhere in rural America, two Jehovah's Witness women call
on an unsuspecting household.

"Knock, knock."

"Hello, can I help you?"

"Howdy, there should have been three of us gals calling on you but Rubella from Horneytown is laid up. Let me introduce ourselves. I'm Latrine from Wanker's Corner and I've got Chlamydia from Gobbler's Knob. If we pray together, we can save our souls."

"It's OK thanks. You can save some other arseholes; I'm already signed up for the Catholic Deathbed Repentance Scheme."

CHAPTER THIRTY-FOUR

We Should Have Gone Swimming

Me: "I'd like the Welsh Rabbit please."

Waitress: "One Welsh Rarebit?"

Me: "No, I want the Welsh Rabbit, not the bloody Welsh Rarebit!"

It's a touchy subject for me. I haven't been a big fan of political correctness, but haven't made too much of a fuss about it either, as I've always wanted to keep my job. However, the process of 'PC'ing' cheese on toast was too much for me.

Welsh Rabbit is cheese on toast, just as Bombay Duck is a type of curried fish; a Yarmouth capon is a herring and a Scotch woodcock is egg on toast. When poor Welsh folk couldn't afford meat, some English wag ridiculed them by calling their meagre toasty snack 'Welsh Rabbit'. It's no good trying to make amends now.

Actually, I'd probably just mutter, "Yes please," and that would be the end of it. I have always made it a practice to stay in with the cooks and serving staff, wherever I've been. You never know what they might be doing to your food before it reaches your table. My sister Kate confirmed this with some horror stories. I suppose it was best summed up for me by the cartoon where the nasty food critic who, for ease, we shall call 'Mr W', is eating in a fictional establishment.

Waiter: "Mr W would like another bowl of your lovely tart tasting soup?"

Chef: "Duz ze think zat I am *made* of piss?"

Note: the consistency of soup and bodily function involved can be mixed and matched to suit the appropriate audience. Oh, and it's a French chef.

As for the 'cheese on toast' thing, I guess the thing to do would be to run back into the restaurant, after you've finished your meal and shout your objection to the use of the 'rarebit' word and then rush out again, but I've never really felt *that* passionate about the whole rabbit thing, especially when I've got a full belly.

There are more important things in the world to become irate about, like asking someone if they want a bag of chips too because you're getting one and they reply that it's OK, as they'll just have some of yours. There are other things too, of course, besides food-related topics that get me going.

Tim: "Did you get my last e-mail?"

Me: "For fek's sake. How am I supposed to know?"

Another touchy one. How am I supposed to know if the last one I received was the last one he sent?

"Don't forget to remind me to take the holiday photos to work tomorrow."

Why? Why me? Why should I remind you?

You have just the one thing to remember – the photos. I, on the other hand, have two things. To remember something that I have absolutely no interest in *and* I then need to remember to tell you about it! *Plus* by agreeing to remind you, I have then taken on the mantle of blame for when *you* forget. And you *will* forget!

No. I will not remember for you. Get a reminding bear or something. (For those blue chip retailers reading, a reminding bear is *my* idea, so no stealing it and making loads of money out of it while I sit here with my puncture repair kit mending my Wellingtons. After years of 'Don't forget to remind me' episodes, I invented the 'John Donoghue Patent Pending Reminding Bear'. Ok, so it's just a teddy bear I gave to Deborah to prop on the door knob on the inside of the front door, but the idea is, as you go to leave the house you will see the reminding bear sitting there. 'Aha' you will think 'What did I leave the reminding bear there for?' You will then think ...and think ...and think ...and eventually remember what you needed to remember before you left the house.

So you remember what you wanted to remember. No blame for Johnny. Bear feels as if he has done a good job. Everyone happy! (Well except for the poor hapless workmates who then have to sit through someone else's holiday snaps, which are only ever fun if someone has left in some photos that should have been taken out. Are you listening Mr Hefner?)

Oh, and how about when your expectations are raised and then crushed in the cruellest way? Like when a girl rings and tells you she is bringing over a DVD to watch – and tells you to have a box of tissues ready. Then when she arrives you find out she has actually brought over a girly weepie movie!

And what about those annoying know it alls who pipe up in the middle of some amusing anecdote to inform everyone that "actually you'll find that Frankenstein was the name of the man who created the monster and *not* the monster itself". Was he? Was he really? Thank you very much Professor killjoy clever dick. Tell me, are you able to suck the enjoyment out of *every* situation or did you just want me to look a twat specifically today?

Or what about those bloody lights at Kilgetty?

The 'Barney eating my running trainers incident', it turns out, was just his way of showing me he loves me. I would have been happy with a box of Milk Tray, but he had to go just that bit too far. It's the sort of love gesture that kind of backfired.

"I'm Spartacus."

"No, I'm Spartacus."

"No, I'm Spartacus."

"No, I'm Spartacus," and so on.

That was a joke that backfired if ever one did!

"2004: A Place Oddity" was in danger of disintegrating from a joyous romp through the summer countryside into an onerous trawl along the 'B roads' of Britain, in the wet and windy cold winter evenings, unless we got a wiggle on. It was all so tantalisingly within our grasp too, with just one month to fill.

I decided that New York was the, 'I'm Spartacus,' of place names. After my disappointment in the Yorkshire New York, the whole appeal of small big apples had gone. There was one in Newcastle, one in Lancashire and, hell, we even had the original York. Another place name had to be sourced.

❖ ❖ ❖

During my life my travels have taken me from the Gulf of Mexico to the Arabian Sea and from the Arctic Circle, down to North Africa. For the most part, the British Government paid me to go there.

I have been on patrol with the French Foreign Legion in Djibouti, and waded through swamps with American Marines in Puerto Rico. The Russians caused me to split my head open in the Barents Sea, and I have played football with our former enemies in an old Red Army camp in Poland. I have swapped various items from the ship's supplies to buy some presents in India, and got embarrassingly drunk on Sangria on every visit to Spain. In New Orleans, I tried to sell my blood for beer money and have ferried gold back to Britain from Qatar. Our ship was almost wrecked on rocks near the Eddystone lighthouse, and sailors were washed overboard on manoeuvres in the Bay of Biscay. I could go on, so I will. I almost went mad through lack of sleep in Germany, and have climbed through the internal passages of a pyramid in Egypt. I've seen a desert night sky fall and roll the whole day over, and I've experienced the majesty of the Northern lights. I've felt the sun beating down so hard on me and felt the bitter Artic chill. Hell, in Oman I had even eaten sweets after I had brushed my teeth one night.

The point is that all these experiences were special to me. I have enjoyed all the places I visited and love the thrill of discovering new ones, with their unique experiences. But I didn't want to go to Quebec.

Quebec is a small village in the County Durham countryside. It is a lovely village and no doubt full of lovely people too and its only failing was that this would be the place that would complete the calendar. Once Quebec was in the bag, 'A Place Oddity' would be complete. My personal project would be complete. Finished. Over.

Deborah and Bethan would be over the moon that life could revert back to normal but, for me, the chase is always better than the kill. I wanted to keep them happy but I also wanted to continue my quest. I didn't want it to be over. I was in a quandary.

Between the deep blue sea and the devil, that was me.

❖ ❖ ❖

There was Barney, the sign and John; there was just the sign and John and, sometimes, there was just the sign. Since the 'happy Pity Me' had been replaced by the 'sad Pity Me' photo, something was missing.

The calendar had started with the idea of making sure people remembered Bethan's birthday. Subsequently, it had also developed into a romp through the outlandish place names of the North East, with the intention of persuading the family to come and see what they were missing out on. All those places that we had taken photos of for sure but, more importantly, I was trying to encourage them to visit my daughter.

What was missing from 'A Place Oddity' was Bethan!

So it was that, on a cold and windy October afternoon, Bethan accompanied Deborah and me to Quebec.

Quebec was a mining village and apparently named as such because the fields in the area were enclosed in 1759, the year General Wolfe captured Quebec from the French in Canada. It was not unusual for fields to be named after foreign towns and places and, often occurred where they were situated at a considerable distance from their home farm. Fields might be given names like Botany Bay or Nova Scotia, playing on their remoteness from the farm. As settlements grew up around the fields, they often adopted the field's name.

You could go on a virtual world tour, without leaving the North East, as you travelled from New York near Whitley Bay; onto Toronto near Bishop Auckland; Philadelphia and Columbia in Washington and finally Canada, which is part of Chester le Street. Battles in foreign lands also provided a plethora of places, such as Bloemfontein near Stanley; Portobello near Birtley, from a Battle of 1739, and Inkerman near Tow Law, named after the battle of the same name during the Crimean war.

Bethan and I adopted a shivery pose next to the sign as if we were freezing in the middle of a cold, unforgiving Canadian winter. Once the photograph was taken, Deborah and Bethan resisted the temptation to do a little victory jig, but it was over all the same, and I knew then that we should have gone swimming instead.

CHAPTER THIRTY-FIVE

The Thirteenth Month

Sometimes I don't believe that women *can't* read maps; I think it's that they don't *want* to read maps.

Maybe Deborah knows that, like any man, I hate to ask directions and, if she pretends that she can't follow the route on the page, she will witness a demonstration of how men are different from women. It's not just me. Moses, it is said, wandered in the desert for forty years because he refused to ask for directions.

She watches me turn the music off so that I can concentrate better as we reach a series of complex junctions. She also hears me request that both Bethan and Deborah stop chatting and look out for the signs which, apparently, confuses them as they feel that, as women, they can both talk and look for signs simultaneously.

When we arrive at wherever we are going to, the two girls may then disappear to the rest room together. Why? I don't know. I've never shouted over to Tim that I was off to the toilet and asked if he wanted join me.

And what is it with women and sharp knives? I've seen Deborah digging stuck toast out of a plugged in toaster with one, using another as a screwdriver and generally using a knife for any task that a normal person might use an adjustable spanner for. As a result I've felt compelled to doctor the knives in my house to the extent that they are now so blunt that I could ride bare arsed to London on them, just in case Deborah arrives and decides she fancies loosening a jar lid or opening a tin with one.

Mind you, I admit that when I go shopping with Bethan, and go to the cash point, as the money emerges, I have an overwhelming urge to punch the air and shout "I've won! I've won!" Poor Bethan then glances around hoping that no one she knows is within hearing distance and drastically tries to pretend that she's not with me. Also as we get to the counter to pay for her new top or shoes, I have a overwhelming compulsion to say to the young girl serving "I'm not sure if it'll fit me though!" As Bethan hangs her head in embarrassment, their response is to either shoot Bethan a "Don't worry, my dad does the same" sort of look, or else they will think I'm serious and give me a "Hey, it's a free world, I'm not judging you" look, to which *I* then hang my head in embarrassment. I tell Bethan, I don't mean to embarrass her, I just can't help it, it's an illness!

Mind you, I confess as a man that if someone tells me something is really hot I've got to touch it to make sure – and in the process lose the skin off whatever part of my body I decide to poke it with.

Sniffing – that's another male thing. If I find a bottle in a garage marked 'Do not inhale' and marked with a skull and crossbones, I, along with 80% of the male population, feel compelled to have a sniff just to 'check' before reeling back croaking 'Jesus Christ!' and waiting to black out.

Deborah knows that, like a lot of men, I also suffer from a strange form of butter blindness. As much as I search, I can swear that the butter is nowhere in the fridge, only for her to come over and find it instantly.

It was probably a fair deal. We were different. I couldn't find the butter and Deborah couldn't find Kirkby Overblow.

What can be more frustrating than reaching December and wanting to plan some dates in January? You don't want to bin last year's calendar because you're still using it, but you haven't got the space for two calendars on the wall.

Solution? The thirteen-month calendar. Patents pending, that was where Kirkby Overblow came in.

It might not have the funniest name, and it might not boast the most exciting history ('Kirkby' means church village, whilst 'Overblow' is a reference to smelters who presumably worked there), but it was a good reason to go and do another shoot.

I had become a place name junkie and needed one more fix.

✲ ✲ ✲

Barney was bundled into the car and the journey was made to Kirkby Overblow. We drove at a sedate pace – I say 'we' but mean 'me'. I drove and Barney just laid in the back and slept, his snoring punctuated by the occasional fart.

I thought about turning the radio on to try and drown him out. *"...and now a request for his daughter who is 111 today. My goodness, that's a wonderful age. Oh ... no, sorry, she's ill"*. Or maybe not. I'd stick with the snoring for now.

We drove down an autumnal tree-lined lane with the low sun behind, accentuating the russets and browns of the leaves. We eventually pulled over onto the grass verge, next to the sign alongside the Kirkby Overblow cemetery. *"This must be the dead centre of the village,"* I thought. It was a delightful place and one that I took an instant liking to, and the fact that it had two pubs helped immensely. I fetched the camera out of the back and, a few minutes later, the dirty deed was done. The thirteenth month now joined Bearpark, Once Brewed, Twice Brewed, Crackpot, Wetwang, No Place, Shitter, Cockfield, Pity Me, Quaking Houses, Quebec and Blubberhouses.

The project was over. I allowed myself a moment to stand in quiet contemplation.

About thirty seconds was enough. I was glad when it was finished. To be honest, I'm not really sure what you are supposed to be thinking of when you do meditate. I usually find my mind wandering and thinking things like, *"What if the Hokey Cokey is REALLY what it's all about?"*

Mind you it's the same when, after some romantic interlude (delicately put – even if I say so myself), your girlfriend rolls over to you and says those words every man dreads – "What are you thinking about?" You know what you *should* answer – what she *wants* to hear. Tales about chasing a dream, skipping barefoot hand in hand through poppy fields, the both of you having a picnic in the park, feeding each other strawberries, laughing together on sunny days ...maybe a puppy is in there somewhere as well. The trouble is what I'm normally thinking (and I think speak for most men here) is something like *'How do flies land on the ceiling upside-down?', 'What's on telly?'* or *'Where did all the change go to that dropped out of my pocket when I took my trousers off? I'm sure I saw a couple of one pound coins rolling under the bed.'* I know though what the reaction will be if I share my true innermost thoughts at that point in time. After years of bitter experience I have finally learnt my lesson. I find it best to lie.

Anyway, Project X – a place oddity was over. It was time to think of something else to do. I'm not sure what Deborah and Bethan's reactions might be but, hell, if they have a blacklist, put me on it.

"My name is John...and I'm in love with my addiction."

I need to have my own hobby, stupid boy project, pointless quest – call it what you will. If Deborah and Bethan think that this is a crime, then I'm a self confessed recidivist.

A penguin, swan, goose, emu, scorpion, baby crocodile, dog, cat, sheep have all bitten me and I almost had my finger taken off by a piglet. Maybe I could get bitten by the A-Z of animals?

I've eaten Pontefract cakes, Eccles cakes and Cheddar cheese. Perhaps I could eat all the foods named after places, in the actual place that bears their name.

Maybe I could start talking in the third person. Could John manage a whole twelve months? What would John do when he actually *needed* to talk in the third person but he was already doing it because of his stupid project?

It might even be fun to watch every episode of Sgt Bilko in succession, with only a cup of tea and a packet of chocolate Hobnobs for company.

Then again, I was almost forty and Bethan's first decade was almost over. Maybe I should do something to mark the occasion. Maybe I could write a book.

CHAPTER THIRTY-SIX

Here Come the Fuzz

So, yesterday afternoon, that's what I did. Certain subjects were considered 'a bridge too far' and I was encouraged to leave them out. They were either deemed too bizarre or just too plain boring.

I met up with a girl once, after I had come back off military exercise, and was suffering from sleep deprivation. She said I talked a load of rubbish. I met her a week later, after I had a decent night's sleep, and she said I spoke a load of rubbish then too.

Anyway, you will not find out about the women I've kissed in places I'd better not mention, nor will you find my list of things that should be invented anywhere in print. You will hear nothing of 'The Cobbler who knew too much', nor will you find out what would be banned or made law if I was king of my own island. You will not read about how I was abducted by aliens and neither will you know how I survived the 'Wilderness' years. How annoyed I become by students in coffee shops in Durham, hogging the tables as they nurse a single cup of 'Mocha Latte' for three hours, as they work on their dissertations, will not be fully explored either. If you are going to sit there for hours, do something useful. How about designing the perfect pet? I've already started on it and it's coming along pretty well. Obviously it would have to have dog-like features and instincts but also include some cat elements to balance the Catholic/Protestant angle. I had solved the arsehole showing off problem relatively simply. (This was both a multi-denominational issue, facing cats as well as dogs. They say that the chap who invented 'cats-eyes' did so because he saw the reflection of the eyes of a cat caught in his headlights as he was driving slowly down a fog bound road. He patented his invention and as well as saving countless lives, also went on to become a millionaire. If fate had played a cruel trick that night and a happy cat had been walking the other way, he would have probably just invented the humble pencil sharpener instead).

However, I digress. My solution? A stiff tail.

Finally, my pet needed some sort of carrying device to bring the paper back or carry around a few tins of beer. A pouch maybe? In fact, my perfect pet was starting to look something along the lines of a Thylacine. I think I'll put in a call to the Kleeneze people tomorrow. Maybe I could even start a rumour that I had spotted one to drum up a bit of publicity. Where better for a phantom sighting of my elusive marsupial Elvis than No Place? I could send out a text 'ITISATINP'. On second thoughts, I think that girl was right – I do talk a load of rubbish.

I also digress far too much it seems (but not as much as the taxi driver in London who made me realise that from the train station to Neil's house isn't the mere three miles that it shows on the map, but rather a whole hefty twelve miles).

I know it's good to be there on the bad days as well as the good days. It is supposed to be character building, and I am probably in need of some. I haven't forgotten the bad things – it's just that it's more fun to remember the good times. So the bad stuff is not here either.

To keep you totally up to date – Barney and I have moved to a little cottage in the country where he looks longingly at the fields where the sheep potter and munch the grass all day. He doesn't want to chase them but I think instead he remembers that we lost a tennis ball somewhere in there. Indeed, ever since the horny toad episode, Barney has had a 'live and let live' attitude to life. So much so that he now only chooses to recognise other dogs and humans. Other dogs so he can play chase with them or bark hello as they go past, and humans because they might have a biscuit for him. As for any other four legged creature – he just refuses point blank to acknowledge them. I tried to point out a hedgehog on the path to him the other day but he just pretended that he couldn't see it, looking everywhere except directly in front of him where our spiky friend was waiting expectantly. It's the same with the farmyard cats who wander by – to Barney they just don't exist.

Barney has also developed an intricate pooping ritual which he seems to put into practice mainly when he knows I'm running late for work. I'll take him up the lane to do his dirty sinful business before I can rush back and get ready to leave. However Barney's sixth sense clicks in at this stage and he'll try and wind me up. In the middle of our walk his little brake light will come on to show poop time is imminent (well that's what it looks like!) but then he'll potter around and around his desired patch of grass looking for the ideal place to lay to rest his doings. He'll just continue to potter away, back and forth, back and forth, back and forth over the same little patch of ground until he knows I'm ready to shout in desperation "JUST POOP YOU FOOL!".

We live at the very end of the village, and on one side I have a cow for a neighbour and a very pleasant lady on the other side.

I have also taken my own advice and changed jobs. There is no point staying in a job if you don't enjoy it, even if the money is good – life is too short for that. Anyway, I missed the days when I got up and didn't have to think what to wear. Choosing what tie went best with which jacket was taking its toll on me. Tying the knot so the tie ends up at belt level is no easy task believe me. First attempt gets it ending up mid belly – second attempt, and it's down at crotch level. The solution – get a job with a clip on tie! So I did.

I joined the Police. After being an Officer in the Royal Navy, leaving the Army as a Captain, being something senior in security, I was now a Police Constable – and loving it. I've made my own year zero, restarted on a new Monday in my life and I am happier than I've been for ages. Sometimes in life, instead of travelling down the same old road – the same endless grey ribbon – it can be good to reach a crossroads and re-evaluate life. Do I carry on doing the same old thing – following the same old routine – or do I try a new path and see where that leads. Actually that's more like a T junction than a crossroads isn't it? Possibly even just a right turn.

Anyway, I feel like I'm making a difference to people's lives and love the variety and excitement of the job as well as building up a wealth of new stories. Most of all, there are some great laughs to be had.

On being called to a domestic incident and finding that the signs of a struggle were actually a failure to tidy up, being told by the householder, "The TV doesn't watch itself you know." Classic.

The detective who went to a house that had recently been broken into, in an area where the MO (Modus Operandi; the way particular villains do their villainy) was for the burglars to disable the alarm system with quick setting spray, and asked the young woman who answered the door "Have you got foam around your box?"

In custody, trying to establish what job the prisoner did in the transport industry.

Me: "Haulier?"

Prisoner: "Thirty Seven."

The least comforting thing said to a depressed man who had just found his wife in bed with his best friend, "At least it wasn't a stranger."

Observing an interview where we were trying to find out why a wife had assaulted her husband.

Question: "What was the first thing your husband said to you when you woke up that morning?"

Answer: "Where am I Rebecca?"

Question: "And why did that upset you?"

Answer: "My name is Louise."

There are other times though when you wonder if people have got the hang of the 999 system. For example, after a hectic blue light drive to a house, the woman of the house explained to my friend that she called the Police because she had been making Sunday dinner and had found her husband making a sandwich for himself. A bit naughty maybe – but hardly 999 emergency material!

And talking of material, I recently attended a frantic call from a householder, only to discover that she wanted me to put her curtains up for her.

Still out of sadness comes joy – sadness for me shaking my head in disbelief, sadness for the sandwich eating man who won't eat his dinner now, sadness for the lady who cooked the dinner only to throw half her husband's dinner in the bin, sadness for the lady who had to put up her own curtains without Police assistance – and joy for ... well I'm not sure exactly who has the joy bit, but I'm sure someone does somewhere. It usually works that way. With me and Barney it normally does anyway.

Actually I love dealing with different people each day as you never know what they will say or do next.

Last week I went to a house with a colleague to investigate a case of criminal damage. I sat on the sofa with a cup of tea whilst my colleague took down some details from the husband and wife.

Police Officer: "Can I take your name please?"

Wife: "Lesley."

Police Officer: "Do you spell that with an 'ey' or 'ie' at the end?"

Wife: "It's a different spelling for men and women."

Police Officer: "I can never remember which is which."

Husband: "Women are the ones with boobs."

There you go – that gave me joy!

Barney seems pretty joyful most of the time actually too as he sits there scratching his head with his leg with that funny little grimace that he does – then does that little surprised look as he startles himself with a fart. Maybe I don't need a Thylacine. Maybe I've got the perfect pet after all.

Deborah is smiling and keeping her fingers crossed as there are rumours circulating that asbestos cladding might be found in the school hall roof.

Bethan is growing up fast and turning into a clever and very attractive young lady. She has even promised me that she will eventually get around to marking that piece of work that I had prepared for her prior to the Donoghue house school closing down.

I even cheered Kate up when she rang the other day. She told me she was depressed as the company she works for were moving the call centre where she worked to India. I told her not to be so glum. "You'll love it over there, the sun, the exotic food, you'll live like a queen with the ..." The phone went dead before I finished the sentence. She must have been so happy she'd gone off to start celebrating already.

Epilogue

I toyed with the idea of calling these scribblings 'I get a dog, call him Barney, then ramble on about all sorts of things and nothing at the same time, hopefully raising a smile / forced grin (*delete as applicable) along the way' but that seemed a bit long winded. I read recently that to drum up a bit more interest when they launched their memoirs, the author was going to call it 'Harry Potter and the Da Vinci book of Sudoku' to cover all bases. That sounded like a good idea – but in my case I think something a little bit snappier was needed. Something to show that I didn't consider this as an epic of classic literature, but just a bit of fun.

I'd have to put my thinking cap on. In the meantime, if you want to see some photos of the places in the book or even drop me a line, just pop to www.marsupialelvis.com. I'd love to hear from you – unless you're going to tell me something disappointing that is – like telling me I've won a year's supply of Marmite, and then letting me find out that it really means it's just one small jar.

Everything in this work is true and I believe that I have only made up three words in the entire book – 'scamperee', 'doggery' and 'sniffery' are, to the best of my knowledge, not listed in the Oxford English Dictionary. But they sound funny and, in my view, they should be listed, so I kept them in. Shakespeare made up stacks of words in his works.

Shakespeare? Shakespeare, my butt!